9/30/79

PRESENTED TO THE
WOODBURY MENNONITE FELLOWSHIP
IN APPRECIATION FOR
ALLOWING US TO SHARE
THE WYCLIFFE "MOUNTAIN
OF LIGHT" PROGRAM.

SEPTEMBER 30, 1979

EDWIN SELL
ROY HETRICK

JAARS AREA REPRESENTATIVES

INTO THE GLORY

INTO THE GLORY

by

Jamie Buckingham

Logos International
Plainfield, New Jersey

*to those who mount up
with wings as eagles—
the men and women
of the Jungle Aviation and Radio Service.*

Contents

Two sections of pertinent maps and photographs
are located after pages 60 and 202.

Foreword

Two years ago I was having lunch at Chicago's O'Hare Airport with United Air Lines Captain Bob Burdick and Dan Piatt, both members of the JAARS Board. After hearing one of my stories of God's miracles in JAARS, Dan put his fork down and looked me straight in the eye.

"Bernie, for twenty-five years I've been hearing stories like that — miraculous things. But I'm disgusted with you and JAARS for keeping them hidden under a bushel. Why don't you have a book written so the world can know?"

A few days later, JAARS pilot Tom Smoak, home on furlough from Colombia, South America, was leading our Day of Prayer at the Wycliffe-JAARS Center in Waxhaw, North Carolina. His testimony of God's unusual direction in his life led me to ask him why he didn't write a book. Tom said he couldn't write a book because the last chapter wasn't completed yet.

"Why don't you contact my friend Jamie Buckingham?" he said. "He may be interested."

Jamie Buckingham was just a name when I flew down to Melbourne, Florida, to talk to him about the book. Writer Jim Hefley had told me Jamie was the best Christian writer in the USA for our kind of stuff — whatever that meant. I took it to mean human interest and adventure material. My wife had read his book *Run Baby Run* and some of the fellows in the hangar said maybe he would call the JAARS book *Fly Baby Fly*.

The moment I met Jamie, I liked him. A pilot, he was quick, enthusiastic, and obviously knew and loved God. It was instant friendship. After thirty minutes, I felt I had known him all my life. He asked questions and scribbled constantly on a note pad as I answered. His final question, though, threw me for a loop.

"Why do you want this book written?"

I stumbled around and told him about Wycliffe's goal to get the Word translated into every language in this generation. "Besides hundreds of translators, we need right now twenty more airplanes and thirty more pilots. I believe we can develop interest, funds, and personnel through a good book."

Jamie hesitated, then said, "Well, at least you're honest. But that's not why I write books. I write to bring glory to God, to point people to Jesus — not to promote things."

I realized I had ground-looped. Back-pedaling, I tried to appear less mercenary. I felt the same as I did that day when I asked a Brethren missionary in Peru where in the town his church was located. He said he didn't have a church, God did, and it was located in the hearts of His people all over that town.

Jamie was different from the missionary. He wasn't trying to straighten me out theologically as much as he was making sure he was where God wanted him to be. But I carried the message back to Waxhaw with me. What was the real purpose of JAARS?

Two years have passed, and the book is finally ready. In the meantime, God has supplied not twenty, but twenty-six aircraft— and the personnel needed to keep them flying. And He didn't need a book or a super-duper promotion scheme to accomplish His purpose.

This book is all the flap copy says it is — an aviation classic. But it's more; it brings glory to God. And we at JAARS—we're more than just pilots, mechanics, and radio technicians. First of all, we're men and women of God. And we've learned to just praise God and trust Him to supply all our needs. After all, it's *His* program, not ours.

—Bernie May
Executive Director
Jungle Aviation and Radio Service

Preface

Our single-engine plane was over the broad expanse of the blue Caribbean Sea. Behind us was Kingston, Jamaica, our last fuel stop until we touched down on the South American continent —far over the southern horizon.

We climbed to eleven thousand feet in order to ride the tops of the white, fluffy clouds that hung suspended between us and the blue-green water two miles below.

Orville Rogers, an off-duty jet pilot for Braniff Air Lines, was in the left-hand seat of our small plane. I was beside him, uncomfortable in my life jacket, making my third trip to the Amazon jungle. We were delivering the plane to a small group of jungle pilots—the Jungle Aviation and Radio Service (JAARS). Backed up by mechanics and radio personnel, they were flying Bible translators into the most remote sections of the earth.

Orville nodded out the window.

"Look below."

There, skimming along on the tops of the clouds, was the shadow of our tiny plane. It was surrounded by a bright, almost golden halo.

"In the jungle," Orville said, "that halo often becomes a circular rainbow. It's called 'the pilots' halo.' "

I stared down, fascinated by the little shadow speeding along on the tops of the fleecy clouds.

"Airline pilots refer to that ring of light as 'the glory,' " Orville said softly, his voice barely distinguishable over the roaring engine in front of us. "Sometimes as we start our descent toward the clouds, that circle of light grows intensely brighter, and the moment the plane and shadow converge in the cloud, there's a brilliant burst of light. We call it 'flying into the glory.' "

I sat for a long time, looking down at the shadow, clouds, and water far below. I remembered, from my childhood days in Sunday school, the angels who appeared after Jesus was caught up into a cloud. "So shall He return again in all His glory," they said.

My mind raced ahead to where I would be tomorrow — in the Amazon jungle. There my pilot friends were risking — even giving — their lives, that the Bibleless tribes of the world might read that wonderful promise in their own language. These pilots, too, were flying into the glory. Only they weren't descending, they were climbing on course . . .

—Jamie Buckingham
Melbourne, Fla.

Chapter 1

Certain Flight

There is a Power whose care
  Teaches thy way along that pathless coast—
  The desert and illimitable air—
Lone wandering, but not lost.

. . . .

He who, from zone to zone,
  Guides through the boundless sky thy certain flight,
  In the long way that I must tread alone,
Will lead my steps aright

            —William Cullen Bryant
            "To a Waterfowl"

Ralph Borthwick, lean, prematurely gray for his forty-two years, eased his lumbering old single-engine amphibian down through the thin deck of broken clouds. Below him, stretching as far as the eye could see, was the green hell of the Amazon jungle. Strapped tightly in their cramped seats behind and below him, in the innards of the vintage plane, were four passengers from the jungle base of the Summer Institute of Linguistics (SIL) at Yarinacocha, Peru. Far down in the hold of the vibrating old plane, almost sitting astraddle the giant pontoon that stuck out in front like a huge yellow banana, was Ralph's wingman and mechanic friend, Ernie Rich. Both men were members of an elite group of pilots, mechanics, and radiomen who were dedicated to flying linguists and missionaries in and out of the most savage, remote sections of the earth. They were the men of JAARS — the Jungle Aviation and Radio Service, the flying arm of the Wycliffe Bible Translators.

The vintage Grumman Duck, a prewar biplane, was the backbone of a small fleet of planes based at Yarinacocha on the huge Ucayali River east of the Andes. The four translators, half-deafened by the roar of the plane and the vibrating metal side panels, had given up comfortable lives in the States to live among the savage Indians of the Amazon. There, with great patience and faith in God, they would master the tribal language, devise an alphabet and rules of grammar and syntax. Finally, after these endless knots had been painstakingly unraveled, they would begin the mammoth work of preparing a literature in the language. The book they translated and left behind for the Indians to read after sometimes twenty years of danger and work: the Bible.

Leveling off at ten thousand feet, Ralph reached up and slid back the scratched Plexiglas canopy and peered over the side. Forward vision over the barrel-shaped cowling of the engine was obscured by a big, open air scoop that sucked in the tepid jungle air and fed it to the engine.

Ralph was one of the few pilots at the Yarinacocha base who

2

enjoyed flying the Duck. He loved it almost as much as he loved his wife Vera — and that was a lot. Besides being a pilot, Ralph was a licensed mechanic, and he loved to work on the Duck's big engine. With its short stacks, the huge Wright 1820 made more noise than the other three airplanes at Yarina put together — and they included a lumbering old Catalina PBY with two twelve-hundred-horsepower engines.

Ralph grinned to himself, remembering the first time he saw the Duck. Ernie had crawled up into the cockpit and started the engine, deliberately failing to warn Ralph, who was standing near the tail. Ralph had been sprayed from head to foot with a bath of black engine oil. Ernie got a good laugh out of that; he loved to tease Ralph's quiet Canadian dignity.

Oil was one of the Duck's weaknesses. It drank oil like an alcoholic guzzles wine, never seeming to get enough. When Ralph first came to Peru, arriving on the same banana boat that brought Ernie Rich back in 1952, the old Duck was burning more oil than gasoline. Once it was airborne off the lake, the Duck looked like it had a mile of angry bees flying behind — smoke, fumes, and droplets of oil that spewed from the engine. But it would carry anything you could get in it, and once in the air, it would climb like a homesick angel.

Once, Ralph and Ernie had loaded the Duck with more than a ton of dry cement to carry to a mission base up the Ucayali River. The cement, plus a full load of gas, plus fifteen gallons of extra oil, plus Ralph and Ernie made quite a load. Taxiing off the ramp into the water, the big old plane sank all the way down to the edge of the bottom wing — completely immersing the big pontoon and the little outrigger pontoons on the wingtips. Ernie, sitting in his seat in the hold and peering out his little side window, thought the plane was going under. But it floated, and Ralph gave it full throttle, heading down the long river on a takeoff attempt. Thirty seconds later, the engine "bellerin' and blattin'," as Ernie described it, the plane began to come up out of the water like a big porpoise. After three minutes of mad roaring down the placid river, water spewing in all directions, and oil and smoke streaming behind, it came up on "the step," ready for takeoff. Ralph pulled back on the stick, and the Duck was airborne. They flattened the rear wheel when they made a ground landing on the dirt strip at the mission base, but they had proved the Duck could haul anything that could be stuffed into its ancient interior.

Now over the jungle of northern Peru, Ralph adjusted his goggles and looked down. Far below him was the mighty Marañón River, a magnificent Peruvian tributary laden with Andean silt which gave it a light chocolate color. Collecting runoff from a spectacular array of snow peaks, the broad Marañón was born in the cloud-piercing Andes which were just miles behind the lonely plane as it droned through the empty skies. The river plummeted and churned down the mountainsides until it thundered through a narrow gorge just one hundred feet wide which the Spanish and Indians called *Pongo de Manseriche* (Gateway of Fear). Then, moving sluggishly into the dense tropical jungle that stretched away from the lower regions of the mountains, it snaked eastward to join the Ucayali, taking on the fabled name of Amazon.

The Duck had been in the air for almost an hour and a half, rumbling through the lonely Peruvian sky on a routine flight from the Indian village of Angamos on the Marañón to Iquitos. Situated just below the point where the Ucayali and Marañón join, Iquitos was, a century before, a garrison village — literally hewed from the jungle. Now a metropolis of more than 70,000, it was able to accommodate huge ocean liners that steamed upward from the sea.

Ralph slid the canopy back into place, readjusted his earphones, and checked his instrument panel. Everything was going smoothly, and in front of him, the one thousand horses of the huge Wright 1820 roared comfortably along. The old Duck wasn't much to look at, but she was as sturdy as they come. Her pontoon, which

4

produced the drag that slowed her through the air so she sometimes resembled anything but the sleek duck for which she was
named, was her greatest safety feature. In case of bad weather or
engine failure, the pilot could always sit her down on one of the
countless jungle rivers. Ralph stretched his legs and breathed a
prayer of thanksgiving for the mile-wide Marañón below. Although filled with swiftly moving logs and debris, and sometimes
broken with rapids and twisting turns, it was nevertheless a beautiful twelve-hundred-mile runway that was always there in case
of an emergency.

The thin cloud cover had dissipated, and the heavy plane,
pulled along by its three-bladed prop, was only thirty minutes out
of Iquitos. JAARS pilots always stayed within gliding distance
of the river they were following. At ten thousand feet, it was not
necessary to stay directly over the meandering course of the jungle
waterway. Ralph could fly straight ahead and pick up the river
at its next turn. The only exception to the glide-rule was when
a plane needed to cross over from one river to another, the most
treacherous type of jungle flying.

Ralph shouted into his ancient intercom system to Ernie, hoping he could hear him over the roar of the engine. Strapped into
a seat and virtually surrounded by luggage in front and back,
Ernie had access to a small window just above the big pontoon
where he could make a visual check of the landing gear and any
obstructions in the river that might hinder a takeoff or landing.
Ralph let Ernie know he was starting his crossover from the
Marañón to pick up the Nanay River and follow it directly into
Iquitos.

The rivers of the Amazon basin make up a strange mixture of
color. From the north, the streams tend to flow black, darkened
by the stain of rain-forest vegetation where swamp leaves soaked
in the 90° Fahrenheit waters cause the river to look like tea that
has steeped too long. From the south, the rivers gain clarity from
the filtering of white sandy country and pick up the sky's deep

blue. From the west, they churn with the brown silt of the Andean highlands. The rise and fall of the waters — the clock and calendar of riverine life — produces constantly changing hues. The Nanay, recognizable by its black color, was approximately ten minutes away.

Ralph had radioed his home base at Yarinacocha before he took off from Angamos. They had given him a good weather report to Iquitos, but that had been almost two hours before. Afternoon thunderstorms in the Amazon could build with amazing rapidity, and to the east — at right angles now to his direction of flight since he had started his northerly crossover — Ralph noticed a buildup of clouds. He was not concerned, however, for in a very few minutes he would reach the Nanay, and he could follow the river, through the occasional clouds, if necessary, into Iquitos. He never dreamed he was only minutes away from the most terrifying experience of his long flying career.

Minutes later, over the black waters of the river that churned through the lush green jungle on its way to blend with the muddy Amazon, Ralph made a 90° turn to the right. Banking gently, he pointed the Duck's nose to Iquitos, now only twenty minutes away.

But ahead of him, from horizon to horizon, the sky seemed to be supported by a series of castles, battlements, and walls. Through the various indentations, a few jagged gashes of the green jungle could be seen as the river disappeared into what seemed to be a wall of clouds that stretched from as high as one could see to the tops of the trees below. Ralph was not afraid of bad weather and knew the combination of terrain, jungle heat, and humidity often served to produce spectacular monuments of clouds. He also knew the cautious pilot would much prefer admiring this grandeur from afar rather than from the inside.

Ralph switched his radio to the Yarinacocha frequency and tried to call the base. The only answer was the sharp crackling of electrical static in his earphones. He tried to contact Iquitos, without success. A final switch of the radio put him on the CORPAC channel, the official Peruvian government organization that controlled all flying in the nation. Again, no answer.

Still unconcerned, since below him was the Nanay, Ralph decided to fly through the storm. Since Iquitos had earlier reported clear weather, he assumed this was simply a thin squall line stretching across the jungle, and at ten thousand feet, he should be through it, or over it, in a few minutes. It was a horrible, almost fatal mistake.

His big prop bit into the front edges of the white fleecy clouds, and suddenly it was raining. Hard. Curtains of water were cascading over the plane, leaking in around the canopy and the side panels of the fuselage. The jungle and river below disappeared, leaving only the churning gray clouds and the sound of the big engine keeping pace with the noise of the rain hammering against the canopy. It seemed to be, in the terms of an old Indian adage, "raining from the sky and the earth."

Picking up his microphone, Ralph pressed the button with his thumb.

"Yarinacocha, Yarinacocha, this is Lima Alpha Omega. Do you read me? Do you read me?" Again the only answer was the ear-splitting crackling of electrical interference.

Ten minutes passed, and the turbulence was shaking the plane almost hard enough to make the rivets pop out. Then Ralph heard a Spanish voice, barely intelligible through the barrage of static in the headphones. From the words he could pick up, he realized it was the radio operator in Iquitos talking to the base at Yarinacocha. Ralph cut in and asked for the weather in Iquitos.

The static was deafening, and he could grasp only fragments as the message gurgled through. "Thunderstorms over . . . heavy rain . . . ceiling treetops . . . lightning . . . high winds . . . " and then the voice faded from the earphones to be replaced with constant, ear-shattering static.

Great fists of dirty white churned against each other off his wingtips. Inside the darker areas, the frequent explosions of light were marked simultaneously by savage crashings in his earphones. The pelting rain slashed against the plane, and Ralph wondered what his four passengers, and what poor Ernie down in the belly of the plane, were thinking. But he was on his own, separated from passengers, mechanic, and home base. Relying on his pilot's instinct, he moved the control stick, which extended upward in a curve between his knees, to his right. At the same time, he exerted right pressure on the rudder pedal. He was going into a maneuver which had saved his life many times before — a 180° turn. At this particular instant, Ralph wished very much he was home in his little house on the big lake at Yarinacocha. Vera would fix him something to eat, and he'd take a cold shower.

But he wasn't home. He was riding out a storm at the controls of a bulky airplane — with five souls behind him depending on his skill to keep them alive.

Suddenly, it was as though someone had turned a firehose full on the windshield. He was not in an airplane, but a submarine — one that leaked very badly. Water spewed through the windshield, seeped in around the cracks, and dribbled down the instrument panel, soaking his pants. It came through the overhead canopy, finding holes and cracks he never knew existed. He couldn't even see the ends of his wings. But it wasn't the amount of water that startled him, it was the sound. A roaring, angry, sense-shattering cascade that completely obliterated even the noise of the big engine.

Holding onto the stick with both hands, Ralph tried to keep the plane on course, to get out of the clouds as quickly as possible. Even though he would not meet another airplane in the swirling darkness, he could confront something terrifying and completely invisible — the force of the thunderhead. It was inconceivable, he thought fleetingly, how that huge engine up front could swallow so much water and continue to function. It was like flying through the depths of an ocean.

Ralph had a new and strangely sour taste in his mouth. He

8

was wondering about it when the bottom fell out of everything — as if he had smashed against a solid obstruction. Instantly weightless, he felt the top of his thighs jerk hard against his seat belt, and his pencil, clipped tightly in his shirt pocket, followed his glasses upward, smashing against the overhead canopy. The instrument panel shivered so beneath the shock that for a moment not a dial was readable.

When the instruments settled, Ralph saw that in spite of all his efforts, he was going down at the rate of two thousand feet a minute. The altimeter was unwinding like a clock with a broken spring. His brain seemed to be pressing down on his eyes.

He moved the propeller to full low pitch. There was no familiar howl from the engine. Nothing could be heard above the roar of water, but the instruments showed the prop had responded. Rolling the stabilizer wheel back to ease the ship into a climbing attitude, Ralph pulled the stick back until it dug into the pit of his stomach. He should be gaining at least six hundred feet per minute. Instead, his descent continued as if the ship were actually in a dive. He realized he was within the grasp of a power far more formidable than any the Wright Engine Company ever produced.

The altimeter read eight thousand feet when a second collision occurred. Once more the instrument panel danced on its rubber mountings. The dials blurred, then shook themselves back into readability. Now the rate of climb indicated they were going *up* at two thousand feet per minute. Reversing itself, the altimeter wound back up and passed the eleven thousand mark. In spite of the fact that Ralph was shoving the nose down with all the strength in his arms and shoulders, the plane continued to rise.

Suddenly, there was an explosion of white fire which seemed to occur directly within the cockpit. The lightning continued in a series of flashings, each accompanied by a blasting cannon. Every salvo pierced to the marrow of his bones.

The lateral gyrations of the plane had become extremely violent as it was swung back and forth. Tossed beyond its limits, the artificial-horizon instrument "tumbled" and became useless. Now Ralph was forced to fly on only the ancient military "ball and bank" instrument and the airspeed, an arduous commitment in such rough air. He preferred not to look out at the two wings on each side. Even if he could have seen them, some things are better unknown.

All at once, the sound changed, making all the noise prior to that time of no consequence. He was in hail. A thousand machine guns were trained upon the canopy and metal fuselage as the plane bounced through the turbulent air. Mercifully, the hail was of short duration, perhaps only a minute at the most.

Suddenly the plane ceased its wild bucking and leveled off again at ten thousand feet, its original altitude. The only sound was the driving rain beating against the canopy, and the steady roar of the big engine up front. The old oil guzzler was still there, keeping them alive and heading on course.

Minute rivulets of perspiration glistened along Ralph's forehead, converging where the earphones pressed against his flesh, running along the line of his chin, and sliding downward to his collar. He could feel his shirt sticking to his back and the back of his high bucket seat. Leaning forward, he peered down over the side of the plane. He was still in solid clouds, although he had obviously flown out of the thunderhead. The rain was still hammering at the plane, but according to the compass, that blessed little instrument that sat on the top of his instrument panel like a proud bantam rooster on a barnyard fence, he was at least headed in the direction he had come from. He started to take a deep breath, but didn't finish it.

Abruptly, everything was silent. The familiar vibration of the plane, the slight shaking of the stick in his hand, gone. The engine had quit. Stopped. Not a warning cough, not even a clearing of its throat. It was dead. The only noise was the sound of the torrential rain still pelting the plane and the frightened sound of his own escaping breath. Nothing, absolutely nothing, could terrify a pilot more than to be caught in the staggering silence of an engine failure in the clouds.

A seasoned jungle pilot, Ralph reacted automatically, pushing the stick forward, tipping the nose of the plane over into a glide. He remembered a pithy line attributed to Amelia Earhart, "Think with your nose down." At least it wouldn't stall. But the heavy Duck was not made for long glides. Its two wings, flat nose, huge pontoon, outrigger pontoons, all produced so much drag that without the throbbing of the one thousand horses to pull it through the air, the plane began to drop like a rock. Building up airspeed as it went down.

The rate-of-climb indicator went wild. Ralph frantically opened and closed the throttle. He switched the fuel selector. Mixture control. Gauges showed plenty of gas. He switched the magnetos. Again the throttle, in and out. Nothing. It must be the ignition harness, he thought. The altimeter was unwinding madly again, only this time there was no big engine to pull him out of his dive. His only hope, as far as he could see, was to glide out of the storm before he went down in the jungle.

Then a new and equally terrifying thought elbowed its way brutally into Ralph's mind and stomped its foot on what was left of his fading confidence as a pilot. What if the river wasn't there when he broke out of the clouds? Or even more terrifying, what if he never broke out of the clouds and the next thing he saw was the trunk of a two-hundred-foot tree rushing at him through the swirling mist?

The airspeed had built up until the needle was over into the yellow. Even the sturdy Duck could stand only so much before it came apart in the air. At fifteen hundred feet, it burst out of the overcast, as though the cloud had spat out some unwanted substance. Below was the endless stretch of gray green jungle, shrouded in mist and sopping up the still-falling rain. The river was nowhere in sight.

Fear and fright are two different things. Fear is a state in which people live, a quality of being — perhaps the result of some evil spirit that lurks in the inner recesses of a man. Fear requires time for culture, usually building up in intensity during a period of helpless inactivity. Fear breeds on itself and is capable of limitless reproduction. It is a contagious disease, spreading from its first victim to others around until it takes charge of an entire group, at which point it becomes mass panic.

Fright, on the other hand, is only the impingement of fear. It barks rather than growls, bites rather than chews. Its explosion is instantaneous. Being more of an instinctive physical reaction to danger, it can be self-destructive. However, since fright strikes with lightning swiftness and then withdraws, it does not have time to ignite the fires of fear and thus often clears the mind of everything but that which has top priority. In fright, clear thinking is often possible, and the surging of adrenalin through the system many times accelerates the muscles to a superhuman degree of strength. Through fright, people are sometimes able to survive situations that would, in normal conditions, spell their end. This afternoon, belched forth from an angry cloud and hurtled toward the impenetrable jungle below, Ralph Borthwick was frightened — but his body was vibrant and his thinking electric. The muscles about his jaw were hard. Only his breathing, which was quick, betrayed the depth of the crisis he was going through.

The old adage that jungle flying is two hundred hours of boredom and two minutes of sheer terror was more right than funny.

Where was the river? Probably somewhere to the north. No time to think about that now. Through the mist, he could see the trees rushing up to meet him. The terrain was gumdrop. Rugged. Below those dripping trees was the foliage of the smaller trees, perhaps only one hundred feet high, straining to reach sunlight. Below them were the giant ferns and strangling underbrush reaching heights of twelve feet. Finally, at the base of the steaming mass was the swamp, seething with reptiles and stinging insects.

Never for an instant did Ralph believe they could live through the pending crash.

"Call upon me in the day of trouble: I will deliver thee, and thou shalt glorify me." The words rang through his head. He had read them just the day before from the fiftieth Psalm as he and Vera sat at breakfast in their house overlooking the serene lake at Yarinacocha. He could feel his wife's warm hand on the back of his clammy knuckles where he gripped the stick.

"We do our best, God does the rest." It was the motto of the men of JAARS. During all the time of emergency, he had not called upon God. Why had he waited? Why had he not cried out at ten thousand feet? Now, with death only seconds away, he gulped the words.

"Father, if You still have work for me and for my passengers, please bring on the engine . . . "

It was a sensible prayer. He could have prayed for a giant hand to rise up out of the jungle and cushion his fall. He could have asked for ten thousand angels to bear him up on wings of down. But like Moses at the Red Sea, he was content for God to work in natural ways — not by sending a strong east wind to blow back the sea — but by bringing the engine back to life.

The carburetor heat! He hadn't pulled the little handle that would shut off the outside air to the engine. It was a silly thought, one that did not come in the normal checklist of things to do in case of an engine failure. The carburetor heat was used primarly to prevent ice from forming in the carburetor. Cutting off the outside air, which was sucked in through the big air scoop on the top of the cowling, allowed the warm air in the engine to circulate and thaw any ice that might form and block the intake. But there were no known instances of icing at this altitude.

The carburetor heat! Again he tried to dismiss the thought, to spit it out of his mind. But it pounded against the inside of his temples. It rang in his head. And his hand was obedient. He reached down and jerked the carburetor heat handle and at the same time pulled back on the stick. The jungle had arrived. The only thing to do was flatten his glide just at treetops, lose as much speed as possible, and settle into the foliage. Certainly forever.

Suddenly there was a mighty roar up front. The big prop, which had been slowly windmilling in the streaming air, roared to life. As if they had never quit, the thousand horses were up and running again, straining at the traces, trying with all their might to pull the sinking old Duck out of the jaws of death.

Ralph's C · ·dian dignity, shaken all the way to the soles of his soggy socks, finally broke. It came forth like the sound of a shipwrecked sailor thrown at last upon a sandy beach. From the very inner part of his soul, there came forth an utterance of thanksgiving.

"Praise the Lord!" he said with deep reverence. And then repeated it. "Praise the Lord!"

But they were still not out of danger. The quivering needle of the airspeed was hovering at the stall point. Hot, sticky, hearing the rain pelting down, Ralph had the sensation the plane was still sinking. Despite all those thousand horses could do, he was only mushing through the soggy air, the treetops swishing against the big banana of a pontoon.

"Climb, baby, climb," he coaxed.

The engine was now howling at full emergency takeoff power. The giant prop blades were biting at the thick, muggy air like the fingers of a man slowly slipping off a precipice, striving, straining to pull them out of the grasping death below.

For a fleeting second, Ralph wondered what was going on in the mind of Ernie Rich down in the hold — and in the minds of the passengers who had ridden this thing out behind him. If the plunge out of the clouds had frightened Ralph, it must have meant unspeakable terror down there in the inner bowels of the old plane.

But he could not think about his passengers. He was astraddle a lumbering locomotive, buffeting and shivering with ague, which at any moment could drop out from under him into the dense vegetation below.

Ralph had the throttle pushed all the way forward. If he released the carburetor heat, he could gain perhaps another 150 RPMs on the motor. But he didn't dare. It was the carburetor heat which had closed off the big air scoop on the nose of the plane, the scoop which had sucked in so much water it had simply drowned out the engine. With the warm alternate air now swirling from around the cylinder heads, the engine had dried out enough to come back to life. No, Ralph would not release the carburetor heat — at least not just at this minute.

Hardly daring to believe the instrument, he watched the airspeed needle gradually creep past seventy-five.

He saw it at seventy-six.

He saw it at seventy-seven.

The big engine out in front continued to roar, and the airspeed held, finally slipping over the eighty mark. Ahead was a giant tree, extending perhaps fifty feet above the other two-hundred-footers in the jungle, its branches spreading up and out like a huge net waiting to ensnare them. The old Duck was still on the threshold of stalling. The quickest way to finalize a semi-stall and turn it into a spin is to bank the airplane. But pressure on one rudder, a trifling bank of the wings, would subtract those few critical miles of speed which kept it flying. The down wing would simply stop flying, and the plane would spin into the jungle. To pull back on the stick would risk a quick gain in altitude, perhaps enough to get him over the tree, but it would inevitably be followed by a sudden plunge into the jungle.

"Call upon me in the day of trouble . . . " This time there was no hesitation. Ralph called upon Him. The airspeed crept past eighty-five. Then over ninety. The tree was there, and Ralph pulled back hard on the stick. The faithful Duck responded. The banana pontoon reached out and snatched for the branches, but the plane swooped upward, clearing the tree and heading out toward the rapidly clearing afternoon sky.

Ralph wanted to cheer. Instead of the plane ruling him, he was now ruling the plane. He could feel the controls responding to his touch. He breathed, luxuriating in the feeling of dominion. But instead of cheering, he spoke that name which had meant so much to him in times past, the name to whom all the glory of his salvation belonged.

"Jesus!"

It was not enough. He said it again and again. "Jesus! Jesus!" It was not an oath, as his old buddies back in the Canadian Air Force had used it. It was not an exclamation of amazement. It was a deep, reverent utterance to the one whose hand had borne him up lest he dash his foot against a stone. "Jesus!"

Climbing up to the safety of five thousand feet, he spotted the serpentine maze far to the south where the Ucayali and the Marañón Rivers merged. Strange, he thought, that the world was still the same outside the clouds. He pointed the nose of the plane south toward the slow moving flood of coffee brown which he recognized as the mighty Amazon. He knew that there, on the banks of merging rivers, was the tiny village of Nauta. With night fast closing and the magnificent Amazonian sunset coloring the western sky with streaks of burnished gold and brilliant red, he would be safe, welcomed by old missionary friends who lived in a cabin on the river. They all could spend the night there, praising the Lord. Then, in the morning, while the jungle still dripped with dew, they would again crank up the old Duck and, bellerin' and blattin', roar off the river to their destination of Iquitos. It would not be as good as spending the night at home, but it was a million times better than disappearing forever into the vines and swamp of the jungle.

As the Duck settled down into the water of the Amazon, the nose of her pontoon still bearing the telltale signs of her near-fatal joust with the giant jungle tree, Ralph finally relaxed in his seat. Taxiing toward the bank where his missionary friends who had heard his approach were already standing and waving, he let his mind play on the words quoted at the Sunday assembly last week at Yarinacocha. Words from Paul's letter to his friends in Philippi. "In nothing I shall be ashamed . . . with all boldness Christ shall be magnified in my body, whether it be by life, or by death" (1:20).

As the plane nosed gently against the riverbank, Ralph slid back the canopy and patted the old Duck on the fuselage. "Good girl," he said gently.

Below him, Ernie Rich slowly opened the little door in the side of the fuselage and crawled out. His face was still white, drained of color, but he looked up at Ralph and managed a crooked grin.

"Enjoyable flight, Cap'n."

With that, he stepped off into what he thought was an inch of water and sank to his thighs in sticky mud. Ralph leaned back and laughed uproariously. It was a good sound.

Chapter 2

Never Say Can't

It's hard to be an agnostic up here in the *Spirit of St. Louis,* aware of the frailty of man's devices, a part of the universe between its earth and stars. If one dies, all this goes on existing in a plan so perfectly balanced, so wonderfully simple, so incredibly complex that it's far beyond our comprehension — worlds and moons revolving; planets orbiting on suns; suns flung with apparent recklessness through space. There's the infinite magnitude of the universe; there's the infinite detail of its matter — the outer star, the inner atom. And man conscious of it all — a worldly audience to what if not God?

— Charles A. Lindbergh

On January 8, 1956, the world was stunned by word that a savage band of Auca Indians, the fiercest of Ecuador's aborigines, had fatally speared five American missionaries and ripped their tiny plane to shreds.

Following the sensational publicity that circled the globe, most people forgot the incident. But one of those who did not forget was Rachel Saint, sister to Nate Saint, the pilot of the group. His spear-punctured body had been found floating in the jungle river near his destroyed "wood bee," as the Indians called the yellow Piper cruiser.

Rachel, a member of the Summer Institute of Linguistics (SIL) in Quito, Ecuador, bravely set out to carry "God's carving," the Bible, to the men who had murdered her brother and his friends. Gradually, over the years, Rachel was accepted by the Aucas and had not only reduced their tongue to writing, but had successfully translated some of the New Testament into Auca language. Ten years after the massacre, Rachel took two of the Auca converts with her to Berlin to testify before the World Congress on Evangelism. Recently, there was a meaningful ceremony on the banks of the same river where the bodies of those missionaries were found floating face down. Phil Saint, another brother of the famous family, came in from his missionary post in Argentina and baptized some of the very men who had thrown the spears. The Word of God had done its work.

This word was planted by SIL, the visionary product of William Cameron Townsend — "Uncle Cam" to his friends — who had spent more than half a century among the Latin American Indian tribes. I first learned of Uncle Cam through jungle pilot Tom Smoak.

While on summer vacation in my hometown of Vero Beach, Florida, I slipped into the Wednesday night service at the First Baptist Church. Tom, a young pilot, was sharing his testimony. I was fascinated by his story. A former Air Force pilot, Tom was in his B-47 when it had exploded over Little Rock, Arkansas, three years before. Covered with burning jet fuel, his parachute in flames as he plummeted out of the sky, he was miraculously saved. After long months in hospitals recovering from his burns, Tom was now preparing to give his life as a missionary pilot.

After the service, I chatted with Tom and his pretty wife, Betsy, a registered nurse. A few days before, they had been flying an old Luscombe from Miami to Richmond, Virginia, Tom's home. Stopping over in Vero Beach for fuel, Tom had picked up a huge gust of wind on landing and ground-looped the plane, ripping off the landing gear and part of one wing. It looked like his fuel stop was going to drag out all summer while he repaired his plane.

I made some inquiries about this couple who seemed to accept their abrupt change in plans with such peace and joy. I learned that Tom had just finished a mechanic's course in Miami in preparation for his appointment as a pilot with JAARS, the flying arm of the Wycliffe Bible Translators. I knew nothing about either organization, but was interested in planes — and especially interested in this young man who seemed so dedicated to the task of going to the missionfield as a jungle pilot. I asked Tom if I could see his wrecked Luscombe. I knew a few people in town who might be able to help get it repaired.

Standing in the July heat in the old military hangar at the Vero Beach airport, sniffing the familiar fumes of dope, gasoline, and that unique odor that seems to exude from all small aircraft, I looked sadly at the wrecked plane. I had owned one exactly like it, and it pained me to see it lying there, like a wounded bird with white bones protruding through the fabric of a broken wing, its legs twisted and bent under the sagging fuselage. I looked up at Tom, shaking my head.

"It'll never make it back in the air," I said. "It just can't be done."

Tom stroked his scarred face with a hand that had been burned and twisted in the raging fire that almost took his life. "Maybe so," he said softly with a faint grin, "but I doubt if Uncle Cam would ever talk like that."

When I looked blank, he said, "You should meet Uncle Cam. He's a man who never says 'can't.' "

Tom did fix his airplane, and eventually wound up in Colombia as a JAARS pilot. And a year later, standing in the hangar of the JAARS Center at Waxhaw, North Carolina, I met Uncle Cam. I was only ten minutes into our conversation when I realized Tom was right. This was a man who never said "can't."

Over the next several years, traveling the world in search of stories relating to JAARS remarkable group of pilots, mechanics, and radiomen, I learned a great deal more about Cameron Townsend. The flavor of his positive personality, his infectious faith, and his total dedication to the cause of taking the Bible to the Bibleless tribes of the world seemed to permeate every jungle base I visited.

Back in 1917, when he was twenty-one, Cameron Townsend left Occidental College in Los Angeles, packed a trunk with Spanish-language Bibles, and headed for Guatemala. While there, he found that more than two hundred thousand of the people were Cakchiquel Indians who could not even write their *own* language, much less read a Spanish Bible.

One day an Indian blurted out, "Why, if your God is so smart, hasn't He learned our language?"

Cameron Townsend took the challenge, and for the next fifteen years lived with the primitive Cakchiquels in Central America, eating their food (one diet item: toasted ants), mastering their difficult language, and gradually reducing it to written form. Slowly, with great pains, he developed a simplified method for teaching *any* phonetically written language. In 1931, the Cakchiquels received the entire New Testament in their own tongue. God did speak their language after all. He had just been waiting for the man who never said "can't" to be His mouthpiece.

21

The organization that grew up around Cameron Townsend was named after John Wycliffe, condemned in the fifteenth century as a heretic for daring to translate the Bible into the English language. Now the largest independent missionary outreach in the world, Wycliffe has bases wherever there are primitive tribes whose language has never been reduced to writing. From these bases, more than three thousand highly trained men and women, many with PhD degrees in linguistics and anthropology, work toward translating the Bible into the languages and dialects of hundreds of tribes.

Working as independent "faith" missionaries, the translators, pilots, mechanics, and other support personnel first obtain promises from persons in churches at home to send enough money through the Wycliffe headquarters in Huntington Beach, California, to support them while they are on the missionfield. There are no salaried positions, not even Uncle Cam's. Before going to the field, the missionaries are put through a strenuous linguistic course at one of the several universities where the Summer Institute of Linguistics offers such training.

Next come three months of rugged "survival" tests at a jungle training camp. Here both men and women must prove themselves able to make their own jungle huts — using only bamboo and leaves — make rafts, and handle dugout canoes through the raging rapids and crocodile-infested rivers, cope with wild animals and giant reptiles, and find their way on a thirty-mile hike through the unmarked jungle — living off the land. Even though some of the candidates are past fifty years of age when they enter the program, and others have infant children along with them, more than ninety percent pass the rigorous test and are finally assigned to a foreign base.

Although every thirteen days someone from the Wycliffe Bible Translators tramps back into some remote jungle village and begins translating the Bible into a new language, it is still estimated there are at least two thousand tribes who have never read the Gospel in their own language. It is the task of the Wycliffe Bible Translators to reach them, teach them, and leave them — leaving behind the Word of God in their mother tongue.

To speed this seemingly impossible task, Cameron Townsend dreamed of using airplanes to carry the translators over impassable mountains and across the impenetrable jungles to the remote tribes of the world. He estimated that in one minute a plane could travel the distance it would take a man one hour to travel on foot. With two thousand tongues to go, they needed all the speed they could muster.

As early as 1933, Cameron Townsend tried to put his dream into practice. It was premature, like trying to pluck a fetus from its mother's womb only days after conception. The old trimotor Ford crashed in the jungles of Central America, but Townsend and his volunteer pilot were spared. The pilot, however, had all he wanted of jungle flying and quickly returned to the States.

Townsend went through the next seventeen years "expecting." He knew that sooner or later, in God's time, his idea would emerge, not as a premature baby needing the care of an incubator, but as a live, healthy idea ready to grow to maturity.

A six-man Board of Directors was formed, and word of Townsend's achievements through SIL spread to South America. In the summer of 1945, at the invitation of the president of Peru, Manuel Prado, Townsend spent several months surveying the Peruvian jungles.

Years later, I spent the night in Townsend's modest home at Waxhaw, just outside Charlotte, North Carolina. The next morning, I sat in his kitchen while he cooked breakfast. "Just tell me how you like your eggs," he grinned as he manipulated the frying pan like a French chef. Although nearing eighty, he was still active. In fact, he had been studying Russian in anticipation of starting SIL work in the Caucasus. Unlike most older people, Townsend preferred to talk about the future, while I was eager to hear his stories of the past. Over coffee, he finally relented and shared a few things about those early days of pioneering in Peru. "Groups of so-called savages speaking scores of languages dotted the entire inland empire of Peru," he said. "Some were on the big rivers and could be reached in only a few days by steamer or launch. Most were much harder to reach, living along the several million miles of *irarapes* — passages through swamps and woods, often concealed by overgrowth, which were penetrable only by canoe."

While on his tour, he stopped in Iquitos and asked his guide, a vintage Peruvian pioneer, how to get to one of the tribes which seemed nearest to civilization. The Peruvian smiled.

"That tribe is easy to reach," he said. "You go down the Amazon from here to the Nanay by launch, then up the Nanay for two days by motorboat — if you can get one — then two days more by canoe, and from there, it's only a day's walk through the jungle to their village. It's quite near."

Townsend calculated the tribe was only a few minutes from Iquitos by air.

Leaving Iquitos, Townsend flew up the Napo River over the vast expanse of dark green jungle, broken here and there by clearings and Indian settlements. He knew it would be impossible for young women translators and families with small children to live and work in the tribal areas without air service. As he flew over the forty or more tribes of Indians buried in the dense jungle below, he envisioned a network of two-way radios linking the remote locations to a central base where planes could be available in time of need. Travel by dugout canoe, or endless treks through the jungle, were out of the question. His linguists would spend all their time going and coming — or simply trying to stay alive — and would never have time for translating the Bible.

"I saw why missionary work had been so hard in the jungle," Townsend continued. "One missionary told me she and her husband and daughter spent twenty-five days on a raft covering a stretch which by government plane took us only two hours. The only way the forty tribes in the jungles of Peru could hope to receive the Scriptures would be through the use of airplanes."

But the translators, who had heard God's command, "Go ye," and had caught Uncle Cam's positive faith, were not to be held back. In 1946, twenty-five eager linguists, fresh from jungle training in Mexico, arrived in Peru. The first pair of girls to go up the treacherous Urubamba River to the Machiguenga tribe spent seventeen days in a canoe, traveling through water inhabited by boa constrictors and alligators. The need for an airplane was acute.

Three months later, Townsend was in Lima when a phone call came from a young lieutenant in the U.S. Army Air Corps who was training Peruvian pilots.

"Would SIL be interested in purchasing a Duck for three thousand dollars?" he asked.

"That sounds like a mighty expensive duck," Townsend replied, wondering just what kind of nut he had on the phone.

The lieutenant, Larry Montgomery, laughed and explained that he was talking about a Grumman Duck, a single-engine amphibious biplane. The U.S. Marines were getting ready to send it back to Panama, but they would sell it if anyone was interested.

"See if you can hold the plane in Peru for ten days," Townsend said. "I need to send some telegrams."

Broke, as usual, but trusting God, Cameron Townsend wired three friends back in the States, asking them to pray. Two wrote back saying they were praying, but Harry Rankin, the third man, sent a return cable — along with three thousand dollars.

Townsend's wire, Rankin said later, was a direct answer to prayer. He was the owner of a department store in Santa Ana, California, where his employees had been threatening to strike. He asked God to divert the strike, promising to give Him the money saved if He did. The Lord had just seen him through his crisis, saving exactly three thousand dollars.

Townsend, however, knew there were more expenses involved in owning an airplane than the mere purchase price. He began praying the Lord would send funds for the repair of the old plane, as well as operation funds. Three days later, he attended a farewell banquet for the Peruvian Minister of Education, Dr. Valcarso, who was leaving for Mexico. By coincidence (Cameron Townsend is one of those people who believes that every "coincidence" is God's arrangement), Uncle Cam found himself seated beside the Minister of Health, a man who was known for his anti-American views. During the dinner conversation, Townsend told the Minister how he was serving Peru by helping the Indians. The man was highly impressed and asked what he could do to help. Very few gringos, he said, came to Peru for such a high purpose.

Townsend, recognizing that God had ordained this conversation, told the Minister about the availability of the Duck. Besides the three thousand dollars which he had, he said, it was going to cost a good bit to put the plane into service once it reached the jungle.

"Well, my department, the Ministry of Health, can help with that," the Minister said graciously.

Before the evening was over, someone asked, "Will the plane serve everyone, or only those of your group?"

Townsend knew what the government official was driving at. For years, there had been a running battle between the Protestant minority and the strong Roman Catholic leadership in Peru. The Archbishop of Peru had taken a strong stand against all evangelicals. In return, most evangelicals would not even associate with Roman Catholics except to try to evangelize them — and fellowship with priests and nuns was strictly taboo. Would Wycliffe be willing to fly Roman Catholics on the plane?

"Of course," Townsend answered with a disarming grin. "Jesus didn't heal some and leave the others unhealed because their doctrine was different. The Gospel says He healed them all. As representatives of Jesus, we shall serve all."

There were many smiles and a warm *abrazo* from several of the government officials. By the end of the evening, the Ministry of Education, the Ministry of Health, and the Summer Institute of Linguistics had entered into a partnership and become joint owners of an old Grumman Duck, bellerin' and blattin' and ready to fly across the Andes.

Two important policies were born that night, policies Cameron Townsend has never regretted. The first had to do with service without discrimination. The second was dependence on the local government.

"There is a tendency on the part of gringos," Townsend told me, "to try to be independent, self-contained. Such an attitude has caused only distrust and hatred by the Latin Americans. But we are dependent upon the government in whose country we operate. We tell them we need them, that we can't get along without them, and they break their necks trying to help us."

Townsend recalled a particular incident when this came into focus. "I was ushered into the presence of the new Minister of Aeronautics, General Odria. He stood tall and erect, glaring at me, and said, 'I am a descendant of the mighty Incas.'

"Well, I was scared," Townsend said. "I'd never heard a government official speak that way. But I respected his heritage and quickly told him so. I told him I was honored to be in the presence of a descendant of the mighty Incas, and that I needed his help. I wanted to teach other less fortunate Indians how to read. He grinned, warmly shook my hand, and was my friend for many years."

Uncle Cam chuckled as he remembered something. "An old pioneer missionary once told me that the way to deal with big shots is to think up some way to get them to help you do something. From then on, they will be on your side."

Knowing the Latin American's penchant for ceremonies, Townsend arranged an inauguration ceremony for the old plane. As a diplomatic gesture of goodwill, it was a *coup de maître* — a master stroke. Cameron Townsend knew how to touch the heart of the Latin American people. And they loved him for it.

Betty Greene, former Woman's Air Force Service Pilot (WASP), was in Peru flying for a group known as Missionary Aviation Fellowship (MAF). Townsend persuaded her to take a temporary leave from her organization and fly the Duck until Larry Montgomery could get out of the army and come as their first full-time pilot. Betty agreed, only to find that the U.S. general who was Montgomery's boss had prohibited him from going up in the Duck to give Betty a check ride. She had never flown a Duck before, but Larry briefed her on the ground as much as he could, and then prayed for her as she taxied down to the end of the runway and took off. The old general looked over at Townsend and growled, "May the Lord take care of you. He'll sure need to with a woman flying that old crate."

The Lord did take care. Not only did Betty become the first woman in history to fly over the Peruvian Andes, but she continued to pilot the aged Duck for more than a year until Larry Montgomery took over as chief pilot for the one-plane operation — a plane that stayed in the shop far more than it did in the air.

Often Larry had to depend on native mechanics who had never worked on such a plane to do his mechanical work. Parts were difficult to get. Just when the plane was most needed, it seemed, it would be sitting in the makeshift hangar in the jungle, cowling off, with some Peruvian mechanic standing close by scratching his head.

The matter reached a crisis in late 1946 when Titus and Florence Nickel went into the Aguaruna tribe on the Marañón River, expecting the Duck to make regular trips out to them with food and to check on their needs. After eight months in the tribe, their food supplies were exhausted. The Nickels had no way of knowing the Duck was laid up again while Larry tried to get parts. Florence was expecting a child and was in need of medical attention. The Nickels knew but one thing to do: they started out of the jungle on foot. Florence later wrote down her experiences of that jungle nightmare.

We tried to find some Indians who would take us upriver to the place where the trail began, but they didn't want to go because it was the rainy season, and the river was high and hard to travel. Besides, they don't like to go very far away from home because they can never tell when they are going to run into some enemy and meet a sudden death. But the Lord intervened for us. He sent a Peruvian trader up our way, which is something quite rare. This trader had a large canoe with a motor on it. He agreed to take us with him up the river to the place where the trail started.

The second day out, the river which had been swollen by rains began to rise, and the boatman got drunk. That was a bad combination. He wasn't handling the canoe very well. About four-thirty in the afternoon, the motor ran out of gas. We stopped to refill it, and the propeller fell off and down to the bottom of the river, so we couldn't go any farther. A kind Indian woman in a little, dirty hut took us in. We stayed there until the boatman went down the river where he had another propeller, and then he took us on.

We reached a place where the river is forced through a narrow, rocky gorge, and the water was just roaring through. We could see whirlpools forming, and big trees and logs were dashing down in the water, being tossed around like matches. Titus and the boatman decided that we would walk around the spot — and the boatman and two Indians went through the whirlpool in the canoe.

After two weeks, we got to the place where the trail started, and I thought the worst part of our trip was over. But I didn't know what was ahead of me. We had four days of jungle hiking to do. At the end of the first day, we were both very tired, and at night we were so stiff that we could hardly turn over on our air mattresses.

At the end of the third day, my legs were so stiff that it didn't seem possible to crawl over the trees and up and down the hills and wade through the streams anymore.

When we got to the end of the walking trail, we were able to get mules to ride for a day and a half — a luxury to us. After that, we came to the road where we got a truck that took us to the coast. We arrived on the coast the afternoon of Christmas Day. It was a strange Christmas Day to us, but a very happy one because we had reached our destination. We have been traveling twenty-one days.

Cameron Townsend wept when he heard what had happened to his translators. "No more translators should go into the jungles of Peru until they can be assured of adequate transportation service," he declared.

Still brooding over the situation in Peru, Townsend took his wife Elaine and their six-week-old baby and left Lima for the jungle training camp in the southern part of Mexico.

After a good visit with Harold and Juanita Goodall (Harold was later to become director of the Peru branch of SIL and the first Executive Director of JAARS), Cam radioed Tuxtla for a plane to take them on to Mexico City.

Since Cam and Elaine had both worked in Mexico before going to Peru, they were eager to show off their firstborn child to their friends in the capital. Word was sent ahead to Mexico City of their estimated time of arrival, and quite a crowd gathered at the airport to welcome them — a welcome that never took place.

The Mexican pilot arrived in a little Piper Super Cruiser, circled the dirt strip, and finally landed.

(*Two Thousand Tongues to Go,* by E. E. Wallis and M. A. Bennett. New York: Harper & Brothers, 1964. Pp. 157-158.)

"Buenos días, señor," he smiled at Uncle Cam.

Elaine climbed into the back seat of the three-place plane, and Cam handed her the Mexican straw basket that contained their six-week-old baby. The basket was lined with the baby's spare diapers, to save space and give her added padding and protection in flight.

Cam squeezed into the back seat beside Elaine, the baby's basket stretching across their laps. The pilot grinned again, waved at the crowd gathered to watch the takeoff, and climbed in the front seat of the fabric-covered plane. Slamming the door, he waved again. Harold Goodall walked around in front of the plane, put his hands on the wooden prop, and gave it a pull downward. It started on the first spin, and the little plane taxied and turned into position.

Cam and Elaine waved happily at the crowd. *"¡Vamanos!"* the pilot shouted and gave the plane full throttle. With that, they were bouncing down the rough runway.

In hot muggy air with a full passenger load, the MAF pilots always flew far down the valley, perhaps three miles, in order to gain sufficient altitude before attempting to turn back out over the jungle. The Mexican pilot, who had landed the plane empty, misjudged the additional weight factor. As soon as his wheels left the ground, he spotted a gap in the tall trees to one side and started a steep left-hand turn, climbing out over the jungle. It was a tragic mistake. Only forty feet off the ground, with barely enough flying speed to keep it in the air, the heavily loaded plane began to settle. Cam could see the trees rushing by on either side and at the same time felt a tremendous tearing jerk as the rear stabilizer caught on an outcropping branch. Instantly, the plane dropped, hit the edge of a small ravine in a jarring, teeth-rattling bounce, and then skipped to the other side of the ravine where the nose jammed into the rocks and dirt, one wing shearing off, and the plane tipping up on its side.

All was quiet. No sound of the engine, no whistling of air

around the windows. All gone. Nothing. The pilot was slumped forward against the smashed instrument panel. The only sound was the steady drip, drip, drip of gasoline as it dribbled from the overhead wing tank and splashed into the baby's basket, narrowly missing her eyes.

That diaper-lined basket, which Cam and Elaine had been holding in their laps, had cushioned the heavy impact, protecting the baby from any injury, but Cam's left leg was jammed under the pilot's seat, and blood was soaking through his pants around his hip.

Elaine's left foot and ankle were almost severed, the foot dangling by just a little bit of flesh. Just before she passed out, she heard her husband praying, "Lord, let there be no fire."

An Indian who had been plowing in a nearby field was the first the reach the plane. Cam handed the little baby to him through the broken window. "Take her quick — before the plane explodes," he said.

The crowd which had been waving such a fond farewell only moments before was now frantically running through the field and clambering across the ravine to the wrecked plane.

Someone reached in and turned off the switch. Then began the tedious work of removing the three badly injured people from the demolished plane. The jungle survival training the men had just completed paid off. Someone brought an army blanket. Someone else quickly cut two saplings. Elaine was lifted onto the makeshift stretcher, and four men carried her back to the base.

By coincidence (remember that word?), living at the base that summer was Dr. Paul Culley, later to go to Columbia Bible College as their staff physician. Dr. Culley was soon at the scene, black satchel in hand. He directed that the Mexican pilot, still unconscious, should be the next to be placed on the stretcher and carried across the ravine and back to the base, several miles away.

Townsend, his leg broken and his hip badly mangled, was

made comfortable on the ground to await the return of the men who would finally carry him into the camp. Two hours passed, and during that time, as Cam waited, alone with God, JAARS was born. It was not enough to own an airplane, Townsend realized. They also needed to thoroughly train their pilots in jungle flying, they needed to do their own mechanical work, they needed to take care of their own radio equipment. God had spoken, clearly, through the earlier circumstances surrounding Titus and Florence Nickel, and now through this.

By the time the men returned for him, the concept of a division of aviation for Wycliffe had formed in Cam's mind. During the long months of recuperation that followed, as he hobbled around on the rustic crutches Harold Goodall made for him out of jungle materials, and as he kept vigil by Elaine's bed, a bed Juanita had fashioned for her from small trees, Cam made definite plans for the Jungle Aviation and Radio Service. He could hardly wait to get back to California and present his idea to his Board of Directors.

But the Board was simply not interested in Cam's vision about an aviation division for Wycliffe. They heard his arguments, but they were all strong-willed, expert linguists, eager to get on with the job of translating two thousand unknown languages, and not the least bit interested in pilots, mechanics, and airplanes.

"I'll not be responsible for sending young people out in the jungle any longer unless we have our own air arm," Townsend said, his eyes flashing. "We may not have any money, that is true, but God can give us whatever is needed to get His Word to the tribes. We need reliable air transportation, and I believe God has the power to provide it."

But the other five men were not persuadable, insisting they were a linguistic organization, not an airline.

Townsend slammed his hand on the table. "It is impossible to do our job without planes — properly run and serviced. If you insist on your approach, you can just find someone else to take charge of our advance into the Amazon jungle. I shall not be responsible for the hardships you are forcing on these men and women who are giving their lives for Christ."

Two of the men, seeing the determination in Townsend's eyes, backed down, but the other three remained in firm opposition.

Seeing the situation, Cam waited patiently. Several months later, Townsend called another meeting and took a vote. This time the count was four to two, in favor of beginning a flying arm. JAARS was official.

One of Larry Montgomery's first flights as the official chief pilot for JAARS was to return Titus and Florence Nickel — and their first-born son — to their home among the Aguaruna tribe. Although it had taken them twenty-one dangerous and agonizing days to walk and paddle out of the jungle, Larry and the Duck returned them safely in one hour and fifty-five minutes. They thanked God for a man who never said "can't."

Chapter 3

Emergency Landing

The chart read "heavily wooded" but a glance at the solid green mantle five thousand feet below proclaimed this as a gross understatement. It had been an hour since the two small float planes had left the Urubamba River and started following a small tributary eastward. Now the river had disappeared into the green of the Peruvian jungle, and the only sign of water below was an occasional glimpse where the sun happened to peek through the towering trees and catch a reflection of the stagnant water on the jungle floor.

Jim Price was at the controls of Number 277, an Aeronca Sedan he had ferried from the States four years before. The other Aeronca, Number 255, was at four o'clock high and was being piloted by Merrill Piper. The two planes had left Atalaya in the foothills of the Andes, their destination a small Indian village in the watershed of the Rio Purus. Jim's plane was loaded with cargo which the translators needed at their Indian village, while Merrill was carrying the translators themselves, a young couple with two small children.

From five thousand feet, the cloud-speckled world looked like a green quilt from which a mischievous child had pulled countless tufts of wool. For more than an hour, the two planes had dodged rain squalls following the serpentine course of the rivers. Now, over the jungle, they were looking for the first signs of the headwaters of the Rio Purus.

Below them, and stretching out as far as the eye could see, was the illimitable Amazon basin. Within its more than two million square miles spread the largest tropical rain forest on earth. A hotbed of competing life forms, more than one hundred thousand different varieties of animal and plant life, teemed in the steaming swamps below. The waters of the rivers and streams swarmed with countless species of fish: some armored, some fanged, some stunningly colorful, some man-eating. Reptiles — snakes that climbed, swam, slithered, and choked their prey to death; alligators, crocodiles, and other armored lizards — all lived and died by the jungle law of the survival of the fittest. There were giant worms that reached five feet in length and burrowed into the putrid mulch, as well as the smaller grubs and leeches that would get under a man's skin and wriggle and crawl into his intestines or vital organs. But it was the insects — biting, stinging, disease carrying — who were the actual rulers of the realm. Voracious hordes denuded fields and forests and tormented settlers and Indians alike. The Amazon basin remained a region dominated by nature, its vastness dwarfing the most ambitious works of man to tame it.

Jim shaded his eyes against the brightness and looked down. Ahead and to his left he saw the glint of sun on water. It was the beginning of the Rio Purus as it started its two thousand miles of twisting journey through Peru and Brazil toward the Amazon.

He picked up his microphone and called Merrill in 255, telling him he had spotted the river. He waited for an acknowledgment, but there was none. He keyed the mike again.

"255, this is 277. Rio Purus ahead at eleven o'clock."

Again there was nothing, only the steady roar of the engine in his lap.

"255, this is 277, do you read me?"

The speaker was silent.

Looking back and above, Jim could see the other Aeronca in level flight off his tail. "255, this is 277. If you read me, wiggle your wings."

Jim grinned as the other plane did a sudden, graceful imitation of a butterfly.

"Okay, Merrill," Jim said into the microphone, "I guess I've got a bum receiver. I hope you're in contact with Yarinacocha and can let them know our position. According to my calculations, we still have an hour to go before we reach Rio Curanja."

Shaking his head, Jim slipped the mike back into position. Something was always going wrong, it seemed. He remembered Paul Wertheimer's report to the Moody Bible Institute. "JAARS is a flying junkyard," he had said. "They are robbing one airplane to pay another."

Wertheimer was right, Jim thought. It was 1953, and they still didn't have a spare set of sparkplugs, nor the money to buy them. Jim had brought down a barracks bag of fabric scraps and five gallons of surplus dope when he arrived four years before. That, plus some scrap rivets and some tools owned by Les Bancroft and Ernie Rich was about all they had. Everything was handled on a shoestring. The pilots weren't even allowed to circle the base when they came in to land — it used up too much gas. If they didn't know the wind direction, they had to guess at it. They were forever moving boxes around in the dingy old hangar at Yarinacocha, trying to find some spare part to fix one of the always-broken airplanes.

Yarinacocha was one of Uncle Cam's dream places. A four-hundred-acre slash in the jungle, the base was located on what used to be the mainstream of the Ucayali River, just twelve miles from Pucallpa. However, during a high flood, the Ucayali had changed its course, having found an easier way through the jungle. This left behind the huge curved lake, now almost separated from the river although filled with bounding porpoises, alligators, and the ever-present piranhas. For years, Uncle Cam had seen Lake Yarina ("cocha" means lake) as an ideal spot to base a float-plane operation. Now, gradually, the base was beginning to take shape.

The hangar itself was a miracle. Larry Montgomery had told Uncle Cam that in order to accommodate the Duck they needed a hangar at least fifty feet wide and seventy feet deep. Uncle Cam had gone into a lumber mill near the base and asked for lumber to build the trusses. The man, a Spaniard, had laughed at him. As usual, Townsend returned home and prayed. Several weeks later, when he and Elaine started looking for scrap materials to build their own house at Yarinacocha, he returned to the lumber mill to scrounge around in the high grass to find slabs to use for siding. Walking through the high weeds behind the mill, he stumbled on a pile of old trusses. Cam knew they needed eight trusses at least fifty feet long. He counted them. Eight. He stepped off the length. Fifty-four feet. Some of them were even put together with bolts, and all were cut and fitted perfectly. They had been lying in the weeds for over a year.

Townsend went to the yard owner and said, "Thanks so much for getting our trusses for our hangar at Yarinacocha."

"*Your* hangar?" the Spaniard said. "See all that machinery rusting out there in the rain? I'm saving those trusses for a roof for my sawmill."

Cam went back to the base and continued praying. This time, he enlisted some help from the others. A month later, he returned to the sawmill and told the owner he had come for his trusses. To his delight, the owner told him to take them away. He probably would never get around to building his sawmill shed anyway.

Yet even with a good roof, the hangar at Yarinacocha still had an uneven dirt floor which turned to mud when it rained — which seemed to be all the time. There was a rickety, badly warped workbench leaning drunkenly against one of the walls. The hangar was surrounded with cane walls on three sides which bowed out crazily. And in the middle of the thing was the old Duck, the engine sitting on the floor, the wings off and leaning against the wall, stripped of their fabric. Larry Montgomery had landed the Duck on a jungle river, not knowing that one wheel was dangling down. The plane had flipped over on its back, almost drowning Larry in the open cockpit. Later, they had put the remains of the plane on a balsa raft and floated it down the river to the base — in pieces. Les Bancroft, who was the first full-time mechanic in Peru, and some of the other pilots had put the thing back together — partially. They were now waiting for additional parts and new fabric to finish it.

Jim stretched his legs in the Aeronca and managed a crooked grin at no one in particular. He had already had three forced landings in the jungle during his four years of flying in Peru — all caused by lack of funds to supply the proper parts. Fortunately, this time it was only the radio receiver which had gone bad.

Hmm! The tachometer showed the engine RPMs were at 2100. Just a minute before, it had been at 2250 — the usual setting for economy cruise. Jim wrinkled his brow. It seemed that every time he flew a float plane over trees, the engine seemed to go into "automatic rough" — at least until there was water under his floats once more. This time seemed different, however. He applied carburetor heat and a mixture change. The reading remained the same.

Odd. There shouldn't be any carburetor ice below eight thousand feet, at least not at this latitude. Besides, there was some hint of exhaust fumes in the cabin. Suddenly it was more than a hint. The cabin was filled with smoke, eye-burning, choking smoke that swirled from under the instrument panel and instantly filled the entire cabin area.

Jim glanced at the tach. The RPMs were down another fifty. He opened the window to blow out the smoke, which seemed to be thinning, but no amount of control settings could coax more power out of the Continental 145 up front.

The smoke was gone, and the engine had settled down to a rough, though steady, five cylinder 2050 RPM. All instruments indicated normal operation, all but the rate-of-climb indicator. That bothered him. He was descending at the rate of a hundred feet per minute. He couldn't stay in the air.

Jim bit his lip, picked up his mike, and informed Merrill in 255 that he was going to set down on the first stretch of good usable river which showed. Thirty minutes passed, and he was only seven hundred feet off the trees with no possibility of pulling up to go around. The Purus, by this time, was good-sized, but coiled like a snake. If there was a straight stretch for a few hundred yards, it was full of sandbars or fallen trees.

In approaching for a landing, the pilot must first consider obstructions that may protrude into his planned path. He must also note the runway surface condition and accommodate his plan to wind and weather conditions. Since in the jungle there are no weather stations — not even a wind sock — wind direction and speed is determined by watching the way the banana leaves blow, ripples on the water, or in times of good fortune, rising smoke.

Fortunately, in jungle flying, once the plane is below the tree line, wind is not usually a determining factor; and when landing on a river, there really isn't much choice as to runway selection anyway.

As Jim fought to keep the plane from descending into the trees, Merrill, in the other Aeronca, was winging his way ahead, trying to find a suitable landing spot on the river. Down below the treetops, following the course of the river like a roller-coaster car follows the rails, he was praying desperately — knowing that behind him 277 was steadily losing altitude. The encroaching trees kept reaching out to brush the wings at every turn.

Suddenly there was a clear curve followed by a straight stretch which opened up with a sandbar on one side and deep water on the other. Jim immediately banked his plane in the direction of 255 and skimmed in over the river. Easing back on the power, he allowed the plane to settle. At normal landing speeds, water becomes nearly as hard as concrete, but Jim wasn't worried about jarring his spine. If he didn't get it on the water this time, there would be no second chance. There was no way to pull up and go around. He was committed.

The plane was too high, but there was no time to think about that — the jungle wall was coming at him through the windshield. Cutting the power, he pulled the wheel all the way back into his lap. The plane shuddered into a stall and dropped, the stall warning blaring. White spray cascaded up around the windows as the floats smacked into the sluggish current of the river. Jim released his pressure on the wheel, allowing the nose of the plane to rock forward. For a second, he thought he would go all the way over into the water, nose first. But the Aeronca righted herself and sat rocking, back and forth, on the surface of the river.

Engine off, Jim opened the door and crawled out onto the left float. The plane was drifting toward the sandbar on the inside of the curve. Apart from the metallic slap of waves against the floats, there was no sound except the high-pitched salute of a band of monkeys, high in the limbs of an overhanging tree. Obviously, they were not accustomed to such strange intrusions into their jungle home and were putting up quite a fuss about it. Attaching a line to the floats, Jim jumped across to the fine sandy beach and pulled the plane to a secure position. The other Aeronca pulled up, circled, and came in for a landing from downstream.

Merrill had made radio contact with the base at Yarinacocha.

The Duck, of course, was still scattered all over the floor of the hangar, so the two pilots and their passengers spent the night on the sandbar. While the translator family slept in the two planes, the pilots spread their mosquito nets and wiggled their way into the sandy beach for a comfortable night's sleep.

Morning showed the usual jungle fog hanging in the trees, with the hot sun trying to break through. The beach around them was covered with tracks, indicating they had been visited by both alligators and tapirs during the night. And the markings on the sand gave unmistakable proof that some kind of huge jungle snake, probably an anaconda (a water boa constrictor), had crossed the sandbar during the night on its way to the jungle. The width of the markings in the sand indicated it was almost as wide as Jim's body. Both men shuddered, and Merrill said audibly, "Thank You, Lord!"

Jim removed his tools, a must in jungle flying, from the rear of the plane. Soon he was digging into the 277 while Merrill loaded up his passengers and as much cargo as possible and took off upstream for Curanja. By the time he returned, Jim had discovered the cause of all the smoke the day before, a hole about the size of a fifty-cent piece in the top edge of a piston. Further inspection showed no other damage except a cracked cam follower. After cleaning the screens and the lines and as much of the crankcase as possible, he reassembled the cylinder except for the valve push rods. Hoping to be able to coax the plane off the water with five good cylinders, he started the engine. But it was no go. The best he could get was 2000 RPMs, which was not enough to pull it up onto the step for takeoff.

Merrill put in another radio call to Yarinacocha, asking Les Bancroft to send a complete cylinder assembly to Atalaya by TAM Airlines. By Friday afternoon, Merrill had delivered the rest of 277's cargo to Curanja, flown up to Atalaya, and was back with the cylinder. Once again, the two pilots bedded down on the sandbar with the 'gators and snakes.

Saturday dawned with a solid low overcast, which was welcome as far as working on the plane was concerned. They soon had the jugs changed, and a run-up showed everything normal. It certainly sounded much better with all six working. A check of the screens showed very few metal particles in the oil, so they replaced the cowl. They were ready to fly as soon as the ceiling lifted a bit. Jim wasn't about to fly an ailing engine over the watershed without plenty of altitude.

Sunday morning was, if anything, worse than Saturday, with low fog which lifted a little to a solid overcast — a dark, scuddy one at that. The two men resigned themselves to spending another day on the sandbar. This in itself wasn't too bad, but they knew the planes were needed back at the base. Translators were waiting to go to the tribes. Others needed to come out. Supplies were needed in northern Peru, and no one knew when an emergency would come up and a translator would need to be flown out of the jungle on short notice. Yet, the weather had them boxed in.

Since it was Sunday, it seemed appropriate to have a church service. Merrill reminded Jim of Jesus' words that where two or three gathered in His name, there He was in their midst. Certainly He had been with them so far, and both men felt they should take a few moments on that Sunday morning for a time of formal worship and praise — if you can call a service "formal" when the choir is made up of a batch of screaming, chattering monkeys hanging by their tails from a nearby tree, the ushers are four lazy old alligators sleeping in the mud on the far side of the river, and the congregation is composed of two bone-weary, unshaved, homesick pilots praying for the weather to lift so they can rejoin their wives and families back at jungle base.

About two o'clock, Jim looked over at Merrill Piper, who was half asleep, leaning against the front tip of the pontoon pulled up on the beach.

"If we're going to make Atalaya before dark, we've got to take off no later than 2:30."

Merrill cocked an eye toward the sky, which was right down near the treetops, and said, "Take off? In this?"

Jim grinned. "That's a faith statement. I've asked God to clear the sky by 2:30. That means I'd better be packed and ready to go."

Faith was no empty word to either of these men. Merrill yawned, stretched, and got to his feet. "I'll be ready at 2:30," he said. As he began to pack his gear in the plane, he cast another look at the sky. The mist was still swirling just above the treetops.

At 2:20, the sky suddenly started to clear in the west, and through the overcast, both men could see tiny patches of blue. With a whoop, Jim grabbed the rest of his tools and slid them into the back seat of the plane. After a quick check of the water rudders, and twanging the rigging to make sure everything was on tight and straight, he helped Merrill push both planes off the sandbar until they floated free in the water. Cranking up, they did their engine run-up as they floated downstream, checking mags, RPMs, oil pressure, temperature, and going through the other normal cockpit checklist procedures. While Merrill swung his plane into position for takeoff, Jim followed through on the final point of his checklist — an open-eyes prayer, asking God to lift them up with wings as eagles as they broke the bonds of earth to fly skyward.

Merrill took off first. His plane broke water, soared out over the trees, and was immediately swallowed up in the gray overcast. Jim followed. Pushing his throttle all the way forward, he felt his engine roar to full power. Great clouds of spume shot up and out as the airplane sat back on its haunches in the narrow river, nearly touching the water with its tail. The lazy alligators scurried for deep water, and the jungle birds flapped their wings in startled flight. Out of the corner of his left eye, Jim could watch the wake move back along the float to a point just even with the door. He relaxed his back pressure on the wheel, and the plane was on the step, skimming along on the top of the river. From step to flyaway was only a moment, as he once again eased back on the controls, and the little plane broke free from the water's surface and pointed its nose into the swirling gray mist of the jungle overcast.

At six thousand feet, Jim broke out on top of the overcast and spotted 255 less than a mile in front of him, winging its way westward. He switched on his radio, and out of force of habit called Merrill on the plane-to-plane frequency. Instantly, his receiver crackled to life as Merrill's cheery voice responded.

"How about that!" Jim almost shouted back. "My receiver's working. I guess that pancake landing must have jostled something into place. I'll recommend that procedure to the radio boys when I get back to base. No sense in buying a lot of expensive parts when all you have to do is take the thing out and kick it a few times to make it work."

Three hours later, just as the sun was setting over the dark, forboding jungle, both planes swished down on the Ucayali at Atalaya. Jim gave a sigh of relief.

Monday morning, with 255 filled with passengers and 277 hauling cargo, the two planes headed for Pucallpa.

Two and a half hours later, both planes took off from Pucallpa for the six-minute flight over the trees to Yarinacocha and the SIL base.

That night, when Anita Price asked Jim about the flight, he shrugged his shoulders and said, "Routine, I guess."

"Routine?" Anita almost shouted. "Down on a sandbar for almost a week, all of us praying our heads off, and you call it routine?"

Jim winked and reached out to run his fingers through her hair. "Well, routine if you consider the same plane, the same routes, the same rivers, the same trees, and the same endless jungle which stretches forever and ever. But," he added seriously, "when you stop and consider the grace of God in getting me there and back — well, that's never routine."

45

Chapter 4

The Flight of the Cat

In the spring of 1950, Uncle Cam and Elaine were in California to edit the film *O for a Thousand Tongues,* the story of the Wycliffe Bible Translators. The work was being done at Irwin Moon's Moody Institute of Science Studies at Santa Monica. One afternoon, during a break in the film editing, Moon cornered Townsend in the studio.

"Ever since I came back from Peru, I've been convinced SIL needs a big airplane — one that will carry two tons of freight as well as a full load of passengers. Last week I was out at Clover Field and saw a Catalina amphibian which had been modified to use on fishing expeditions and executive vacations. I wish you'd go out and take a look at it."

One of the things that destines a man for greatness is his capacity to dream. Another is his ability to discern between a wild idea and a vision from God. Townsend had both vision and discernment. That afternoon, he picked up John Crowell, who was at the studio making a Moody Institute of Science film, and asked John to accompany him out to Clover Field.

There on the parking apron of the airport, its sleek aluminum sides shimmering in the California sun, was a war surplus PBY Catalina. The big Cats, high-wing, twin-engine patrol boats, had become famous during World War II in the Pacific campaigns as well as on submarine patrol in the Atlantic. Now many of them were being mothballed.

"That's what we need in Peru, all right," Townsend said, "something that can land on water and land and carry as much as you can stuff in it."

Crowell shook his head. "You're too much of a visionary, Cam. Your American backers are upset enough over that Duck you have down there in Peru. Most of them think you should stick to little four-place planes, nothing bigger. The twins are too expensive, too hard to maintain, and too dangerous. Now you've got your mind set on buying a flying boat."

"Not buying, John," Townsend said with a twinkle in his eye. "Let's pray and see if God won't *give* us one."

Shaking his head in dismay, John Crowell joined Cameron Townsend under the sun-baked wing of the silver amphibian. With the heat waves rising around them in ghostly configurations, Cam Townsend reached up and asked God to give JAARS such a plane for the work in Peru.

One of Cameron Townsend's secrets of answered prayer was patience. Once the prayer was prayed, he left it alone. He didn't rush out and try to bring it to pass. He believed that if a thing was of God, God would open the doors. His job was to be quick and alert to sense when the door swung open, and to step inside before it closed again. Six months later, in the fall of 1950, Townsend was back in Mexico to visit his old friend, Dr. Ramon Beteta, Mexico's Minister of Finance, when the subject of airplanes came up. Always alert and sensitive to the timing of the

Holy Spirit, Uncle Cam asked Dr. Beteta if Mexico would be interested in giving SIL a Catalina in memory of Professor Moises Saenz, the man who had originally invited Townsend to work among the tribes in Mexico.

"Why don't you speak to Aaron Saenz, Moises' brother," the Minister of Finance suggested. "If he likes the idea, I shall call a meeting of the right people, and we will discuss it."

Aaron Saenz was in favor of the project, and a meeting was held in Dr. Beteta's office. All the important dignitaries present were enthusiastic, stating that the contribution of the Summer Institute of Linguistics to the literacy work among the Indians was so meritorious that a grant from the Mexican government to buy such an airplane for the work in Peru was highly justified.

"My family would like to underwrite a third of the cost of such a plane," Aaron Saenz said with a large smile. "We are honored that it would carry the name of my late brother."

As the meeting broke up, Dr. Beteta wrote out a personal check for $1,000, and Aaron Saenz handed Townsend a check for $2,000.

Henry C. Crowell, John Crowell's father and vice-president of Moody Bible Institute in Chicago, who had already helped provide substantial funds for the JAARS program in Peru, sent a check for $5,000 to pay for conditioning the plane and ferrying it to Peru. In the letter that accompanied his check, he stated his opposition to large airplanes in the jungle, but said the current project was so worthwhile as a diplomatic gesture that even if the plane were flown into the jungle, tied to a tree, and forgotten, his money would have been well spent.

Once the plane was ready, Larry Montgomery and Paul Carlson flew it to Mexico City where the crossed flags of Mexico and Peru were emblazoned on its nose. President Miguel Alemán, who had agreed to finance the rest of the plane, had arranged an impressive ceremony at the airport. There, amid waving flags and a military band, he personally delivered the plane to the Peruvian ambassador, charging him with the task of turning the plane over to his president in Peru for the SIL work under the Ministry of Education in the Amazon.

Two days later with Larry Montgomery, Joe Qualm (United Airlines pilot), and Omer Bondurant as pilots, the big plane headed for Lima. Aboard as special passengers with Uncle Cam and Elaine were Dr. Ortiz Tirado, Mexican Ambassador to Peru, and Vasquez Benavides, Peruvian Ambassador to Mexico.

Upon their arrival in Lima, the group learned that the archbishop of Lima was planning an all-out attack against the work of SIL, hoping to run them out of the country. The archbishop had personally advised President Manuel Odriá against participating in the ceremonies to receive the plane from Mexico. However, when Vasquez Benavides told him that the president of Mexico had personally turned the plane over to him for presentation to the president of Peru, and not some lesser official, the Peruvian president decided to participate in the ceremony.

President Odriá made a flowery speech and received the plane on behalf of the Peruvian government as a gift from the people of Mexico. General Juan Mendoze, the Minister of Education who at one time had studied for the Roman Catholic priesthood, made a stirring speech accepting the plane. Using terms familiar to the Catholic church, he said that the great plane had been *christened* in Mexico with water dipped from the mighty Amazon River and now, in Lima, they were *confirming* it for its "Christian and missionary service on the other side of the Andes."

Henry Crowell had been right about one thing. The move was of tremendous diplomatic value. In fact, the archbishop had to call off his attack for two years — and by that time SIL was so thoroughly accepted by the Peruvian government (as well as by the governments of many other South American countries) that the attack was scarcely noticed. Larry Montgomery and Omer Bondurant flew the huge silver bird over the Andes, landed it at Yarinacocha, and tied it to a tree. For a while, it looked as if Henry Crowell was a prophet about that, too.

Festooned with spider webs on the inside and covered with bird juice on the outside, the sad hulk of the once proud Cat remained under the mahogony tree at Yarinacocha simply because JAARS did not have enough money to put it in the air. In fact, supplies were so short there was not even enough gas to put in the engines to fire them up occasionally. More and more, the big plane became an embarrassment to the JAARS people who had to walk around it everytime they went to the hangar.

Finally, Les Bancroft and Ernie Rich got tired of seeing the plane corroding in the Amazon weather. They began to put pressure on others in the organization, and after many months, the plane was completely overhauled. Using a big pair of tinsnips and a hacksaw, Les cut off the nose turret and replaced it with a beefed-up clipper bow capable of withstanding the rough handling it was bound to get when one of the pilots rammed it into the mud bank of a river or bounced it off a submerged tree on landing. Bancroft and Rich were aided in the monumental task of rebuilding the plane by pilots George Insley and Omer Bondurant, who, for once, had to take orders from the mechanics.

Later, with Bondurant and Ralph Borthwick doing most of the flying, the Cat helped open up the Wycliffe work in both Ecuador and Bolivia. One afternoon, far south on the Urubamba, Omer had just flown in a group of translators and all their gear. On the shore, a small group of Indians were taking their first look at the plane and its crew. Soon the village chief broke the silence. The translator accompanying the plane interpreted the chief's remark to the pilot: "When that bird lays an egg, bring it here to hatch. I'd like to have a bird like that."

Flying almost every day, the Cat was sometimes gone from base for more than a week as it picked up large groups and carried them from one place to another in the jungle. Therefore it became necessary for one of the mechanics to accompany the pilots as a flight engineer. A new relationship was forming in JAARS, that between the jungle pilot and his right arm, the jungle mechanic.

There is a bond, unlike any on earth, between pilot and mechanic. Even though it is the jungle pilot upon whom all eyes are focused as he climbs into his plane and roars off over the "green hell" on a flight into the savage past of tribes unknown, it is the mechanic who holds in his grease-stained hands not only the success of the flight, but the very life of the pilot and his pasengers. One careless twist of the wrench, one tiny nut left unturned, one glance in the wrong direction while a part is being replaced — these and a thousand other factors could mean engine or structural failure at some critical moment, and an expensive plane (which can be replaced) and human lives (which can never be replaced) are snuffed out in a fiery crash or sucked under the savage greenery of the grasping jungle.

Since the modern airplane is a labyrinth of electrical, hydraulic, and mechanical combinations, all of which must function with scientific reliability, the mechanic must be an expert in all areas. The pilot understands this, and his relationship with the mechanic is based on professional respect as they see each other as members of the "body of Christ," each with a task to do, each indispensable to the other.

On the other hand, the non-flying public traditionally drapes the pilot with tinsel and completely ignores the mechanic or the radio technician. Seldom does the mechanic, with his overalls splotched with paint and his hands black with grease, make the headlines — unless he makes a mistake. When he comes home on furlough to make his report to the people and the churches who have supported him financially during the long years he has been in the jungle, he finds it difficult to say, "My task on the mission-field is to spend all day working on airplane engines. No, I've only seen the savage Indians twice, once on a brief trip into a village and once when I had to go out and help a pilot untangle his plane from a waterfall." Immediately, the faces in the congregation fall. They expected their evening speaker to bring them thrilling tales of witnessing to headhunters, flying through the skies, dodging thunderstorms, landing on roaring jungle rivers, or making daring rescues of linguists about to be eaten by cannibals. But few mechanics can tell such thrilling stories. Their function in "the body" is to tighten bolts, replace faulty altimeters, and straighten a propeller bent when some pilot couldn't stop in time and tried to harvest a mango tree with his prop. The mechanic falls into the category of the lowly blacksmith who did nothing but nail horseshoes for the flashing cavalry—yet for the want of a nail, even a war can be lost.

So the mechanic continues on, day after day, with his unglamorous job of overhauling engines, replacing tires, welding broken landing gears, and patching holes in pontoons where some pilot has inadvertently hit a snag or log. And he does so with joy, for he knows the responsibility that God has placed in his skilled hands. The bond between jungle pilot and mechanic remains strong, unbreakable.

In no instance, however, is the bond as evident as when the mechanic joins the pilot in the air as his flight engineer. As the Wycliffe program extended into Ecuador, Bolivia, Brazil, and finally Colombia, the trips of the Catalina, carrying both pilots and mechanic, became more frequent, and the importance of teamwork between the two was suddenly brought into bold relief.

Ralph Borthwick was in the left-hand seat of the big Cat that October morning as they took off from Yarinacocha on their way to Miami. The Catalina had already made eight trips from Peru to Miami to haul cargo and pick up Wycliffe personnel who were streaming into the jungle now that the bases were opening in other countries as well as Peru. Total round-trip time was thirty-eight hours. No other airline in the world made as many stops at as many places and still provided prayer on takeoff and a smile on landing.

Omer Bondurant, chief pilot on the Catalina, had volunteered to fly copilot that morning, and Paul Bartholomew, tall, balding, outspoken mechanic, was the flight engineer. The Wycliffe advance had just begun in Colombia, and Uncle Cam was interested in starting a jungle base at a place called Lomalinda, in the hill section of the country. JAARS Director Bernie May wanted to see if the Catalina could safely land and take off from a nearby lake or if they would be restricted to wheel planes in Colombia. Bernie had asked Ralph to check out the lake on the way up.

Taxiing out into the middle of Lake Yarina, Ralph finished his cockpit check. As flight engineer, Bart (or Black Bart as his friends affectionately called him) was standing behind and in-between the pilots' seats. From this vantage point, he could call out the airspeed so the pilots could tell when to pull the big flying boat off the "step" and into the air.

The radio operator gave them takeoff clearance, and Ralph pushed the throttles forward, listening as the sound of the engines changed from a steady "thrummm" to a deafening roar that echoed off the trees on either side of the long, curved lake and rumbled out across the jungle. Water cascaded down the hull and poured over the two glass "bubbles" on the side of the fuselage as the two big twelve-hundred-horsepower Pratt & Whitney R 1830 engines pulled the plane across the lake.

Bart automatically looked out the overhead windows above the pilots' seats to check the engines, then shifted his gaze to Ralph as he leveled the plane off at four thousand feet. Ralph was unlike Bart in every way. Quiet, seldom speaking unless spoken to, reserved — he was the epitome of the cool, efficient pilot. Bart, on the other hand, was quick-tempered and highly opinionated, fortunately cooling off as fast as he flared up. He loved to make a demonstration. In the back compartment of the plane, he had a remote control, gasoline-powered model plane. Whenever they would land at a jungle village, he would crank up his model plane and fly it around the runway, much to the delight of the entire tribe. He was a one-man public relations firm for JAARS. He and

Ralph were opposite persons — with affable, efficient Omer acting as the balance between them. They were quite a team.

Nodding to Omer in the right-hand seat, Ralph took his hands off the control yoke and reached into his shirt pocket, bringing out a small packet of Scripture memory cards. Ordinary commercial pilots and mechanics might choose to relax with tobacco — the JAARS men preferred to do it with the Word of God.

Bart took a seat directly behind Omer and leaned his head against the vibrating bulkhead. Habit, a leftover from the times when the engines on the JAARS planes were literally held together with screws and prayers, caused him to listen constantly to the steady throb and roar of the big motors, always straining his trained ear to pick up the slightest murmur of trouble. Perhaps it was simply the ancient art of self-protection. Or maybe it was more. Maybe it was stewardship, knowing that even though God was in control of all situations, He had left him, Paul Bartholomew, in charge of those two engines. It was the mark of a good flight engineer.

Bart wondered if the two pilots gave as much thought to the sound of the engines as he did. After all, both of them were mechanics also. Yet they were concerned with their flying, and if one of the engines should fail, the big Cat could safely fly on the other as long as the landing gear stayed up to keep the drag to a minimum. Otherwise, she would slowly settle to the earth. But with the broad Ucayali below, giving them a constant liquid landing strip, there would be no need to even lower the gear. However, Bart's ear never quite shut out the sound of the big engines overhead.

Ralph was a good pilot. To him, flying a straight course, making a good landing, hitting his ETAs on time, comforting a scared passenger, helping a sick translator out in the jungle, and always being prepared for the unexpected was just as much of a ministry as that of a busy pastor back in British Columbia rushing from one appointment to another.

Although Ralph was a seasoned, experienced jungle pilot, Omer Bondurant knew the Cat backward and forward. He had flown it down from Mexico City and had helped rebuild the big machine in the shop in Lima. Bart was impressed with how the senior pilot was willingly taking orders simply because he was sitting in the copilot's seat. Bart, tough and cocky, needed to see this demonstration of submission. He, too, felt in command of the ship. After all, he had taken it apart and put it back together again. But in the air, the plane belonged to the pilots, and in particular to the pilot on the left. Even if they should experience an emergency, which was unlikely, Bart knew that Omer would continue to take orders from Ralph — whether Ralph was right or wrong. Little did Bart know that they were only hours away from a time when an emergency situation would arise and life and death — for the plane and for Bart — would hang on Ralph's decision.

Ralph began his letdown toward the little lake which sparkled in the bright sun. The jungle was gone now, and beneath them were the strange grass-covered lomas of central Colombia. These huge mounds of soil rose in odd configurations out of the plains, looking like gobs of dirt dropped without order or reason by some giant hand. Most were treeless, and some were as much as two hundred feet high. Lomalinda, a Spanish name meaning "beautiful hills."

Ralph made three passes at the lake, from different directions — each time barely skimming the keel of the Cat on the mirror-surface before pulling up over the high trees at the end. Omer was shaking his head.

"It's too marginal, Ralph," he said. "If those trees were down, we might be able to make it. As it is, I'd be afraid to land and then take off."

"Let's make one more pass from the other side and then head out," Ralph said. He put the plane in a gentle bank and came in low. Cowl flaps open to keep the big engines from overheating,

Ralph cut the power and let the plane settle until it barely skimmed along the water.

Bart was leaning forward between the seats, calling out the airspeed: "Eighty . . . Seventy-nine . . . Seventy-eight . . ."

Omer shook his head. If the big Catalina were to sink into the water, she'd never make it up over the trees at the end of the lake. Ralph nodded. Pushing the throttles all the way forward, he applied full power and pulled the plane up so they could clear the rapidly approaching trees.

Suddenly Bart heard it. Or maybe, out of years of experience and listening, he only sensed it in his soul. Deep inside the starboard engine, there was a murmur. Something was wrong. Turning his head from the instrument panel, he looked upward through the overhead window at the big Pratt & Whitney. For a moment, he froze.

Where moments before the engine nacelle had been glistening clean in the noonday sun, now there was a frothing gusher of black oil. It was not oozing from around the cowling or making tiny streaks on the nacelle as nearly all engines do at one time or another. Black oil was vomiting out from under the cowl. It gushed back and splattered against the leading edge of the inside wing.

That black oil was the blood, the life stream, of the engine. Without it, the engine would seize solid in seconds, the propeller would tear itself away and come slashing right through the cabin. Even if the prop missed the fuselage and spun off into the air, a flaming inferno was almost certain.

There was no time to explain.

"Oil!" Bart shouted. "The starboard engine!"

With lightning speed, Ralph yanked on the right throttle and propeller control. It was a drastic maneuver, to pull the power on one engine with the plane in a critical climbing position. The relationship between pilot and mechanic had met its most decisive test. The Catalina yawed to the right as the engine subsided, and Omer backed Ralph up, action for action, holding the staggering airplane on course. During the most critical moment of the plane's existence in the sky, on takeoff, both men had acted on the judgment of their mechanic. Such pressure either binds men together or splits them asunder — and over the lake at Lomalinda, these three men were one.

The big plane was at two hundred feet, and Ralph pushed the nose over into level flight and cut the fuel mixture on the starboard engine. Omer was waiting for Ralph's nod, and as soon as it came, he reached up over the windshield and punched the engine feather button. By now the oil had stopped its gushing, and Omer cut the right ignition switch. The engine was dead in the air. Ralph, still struggling to keep the heavy plane in level flight, was working hard on the trim tabs. Glancing back, he gave Bart a questioning look, as though the very presence of a mechanic should have prevented any such rebellion on the part of one of the big engines.

"I don't know why," Bart shrugged, sweat glistening on his forehead. "Suddenly she just blew oil all over the place. Fractured main bearing, broken oil line, cracked cylinder — it could be a hundred things." Whatever it was, it had almost certainly drained the engine of oil, and Bart was only thankful he had seen it before the engine seized completely and burst into flames — or threw the spinning propeller through the fuselage.

"I saw it here," Omer said quietly, pointing at the oil temperature gauge on the instrument panel. "Just as we started to pull off the lake, the starboard oil temperature pegged at 120 degrees centigrade."

Ralph reached for the mike and punched the button with his thumb. There was no telltale click in the earphones. He switched the dials on the radio back and forth. Nothing. The radio was dead. Bart checked the fuses, but the trouble must have been in the set itself. Ralph set a course for Villavicencio, thankful he could fly the entire thirty-minute flight at 200 feet since the tall trees of the jungle were now behind them.

Bart was impressed with the calmness of the two pilots. It was their job to keep the heavy old plane in the air. Yet there was not a suggestion of fear in their faces. They were good men with whom to share a crippled airplane.

Ten minutes passed. Fifteen. They were halfway to Villavicencio. The left engine had been getting baby-care attention from the three men, and it seemed to be working perfectly.

Ten minutes out of Villavicencio, they were faced with a new problem. The right engine supplied hydraulic pressure for the landing gear. That meant the gear would have to be lowered by hand, a long, hard, tedious process. With both pilots needed at the controls, it was up to Paul Bartholomew to ease his lanky frame down into the wheel well beneath the wing pedestal and crank down the gear manually.

The airport at Villavicencio was dead ahead. "Lord, just keep other airplanes out of the way, 'cause we're going to have to make a straight-in approach — downwind," Omer prayed silently.

Then, more trouble. As the gear went down, slowly, it greatly increased the drag on the big plane, causing it to lose altitude — altitude that they needed more than anything else just then because even with Bart's long arms cranking furiously, the gear was by no means down.

Even though they were settling rapidly, Ralph decided to circle the field. If he could possibly hold the plane in the air, if Bart could possibly get the gear down, they could land without ripping the bottom out of the big seaplane. Otherwise, they'd have to pancake on the paved strip — with disastrous results for plane and crew — especially for Bart.

It was a life or death decision. Omer realized it the moment Ralph swung the Cat to the right to start in on his downwind leg. He knew Ralph was trying to save the ship. It was a valiant, courageous move — but it was bound to fail. They simply did not have enough altitude, and the plane was sinking fast. Omer's hands jerked automatically toward the controls. But years of discipline in authority and submission — words the Bible used long before he heard them in the military — forced Omer's hands back to his lap. Ralph was the captain of the ship, even if he flew it straight into the ground. At treetop height, with one engine dead, the other going full blast, the big plane started its final turn on the base leg. It wasn't going to make it. Whether the gear was down or not, they were going in — straight across the runway.

Ralph and Omer were both fighting the yoke, trying desperately to keep the big plane in the air. The trees were rushing by the windows, the runway dead ahead — at a ninety-degree angle. A dry riverbed appeared, the rounded rocks laughing at them from below. Ralph dropped his right wing slightly and started what was obviously a futile turn into his final approach. There was no way to turn the plane in the air and line it up with the runway before they smashed into the ground.

For a brief second, Ralph thought about Bart, deep in the hold of the ship, cranking desperately. If the wheels were not locked into place, the gear would give way the moment they touched the ground. The heavy plane would smack in on its underside, skid across the runway, peeling the bottom off, and nose into the deep ravine on the other side. The belly of the plane could give way, and Bart would be crushed to death. Ralph breathed a quick prayer for him — and them.

A chain link fence appeared in front of them, the side boundary to the runway. Simultaneously, Ralph and Omer hauled back on the control yokes with all their strength. The plane pulled up a few inches as it roared across the top of the fence, then dropped heavily toward the runway — crossing it at a forty-five degree angle.

The main wheels clicked into place. And locked down. The left wheel hit first and snagged on some rocks on the side of the runway. The big plane jerked around in a partial ground loop, straightening up with the runway just as the right wheel hit. They bounced once and came to a screeching halt — safe in the middle of the runway. It was a perfect aircraft-carrier landing.

Brown-skinned Colombians came running from all directions. "*¡Magnifico! ¡Magnifico!*" they shouted as they poured out of the hangar and ran down the runway. Perhaps they thought Ralph and Omer were just showing off. Whatever their thinking, none doubted it was the most remarkable landing they had ever seen.

Ralph and Omer, sitting in the cockpit high above the ground, shook their heads and said, almost in unison, "Thank You, Lord!"

Quickly unbuckling his harness, Ralph slipped from his seat and pulled his way through the first compartment toward the wheel well where Bart was just emerging — his shirt ripped by a piece of sharp metal, his face white and dripping with sweat, his hands torn and bleeding from his frantic work on the crank. Ralph reached down and pulled him to his feet. In a moment of deep gratitude, he threw his arms about the tall, exhausted man in a warm — and very sweaty — *abrazo*. It was a perfect demonstration of the relationship that existed between pilots and their mechanics.

A telephone call that night to Uncle Cam in Bogotá set off a chain of events which culminated in a gift from the Colombian Air Force of a new engine, sent on a truck over the mountains, along with six men to help install it.

It was thirty days before the engine change was complete and the Cat took off on its final leg of the flight to Miami. Ralph, Omer, and Bart were unperturbed. In Latin America, everything is *mañana-mañana*.

But that's better than no tomorrow at all.

Pilots, mechanics, radio personnel and translators turn out for the dedication of the Evangel at Lomalinda, Colombia. House on hill (loma) in right background is home of Tom and Betsy Smoak.

Soft landing on the Mitu airstrip - Colombia

Fill 'er up. Columbia

The Catalina flying over the edge of the jungle in Peru.

Jim Baptista delivers Bibles from helicopter to the Waffa people in New Guinea.

Fasten your seat belt, please *(Strange Passengers)*

Dr. W.A. Criswell, pastor of First Baptist Church of Dallas, Texas, carried out of jungle stream after Floyd Lyon landed his Helio following an engine failure in Peru. *(We're Going Down)*

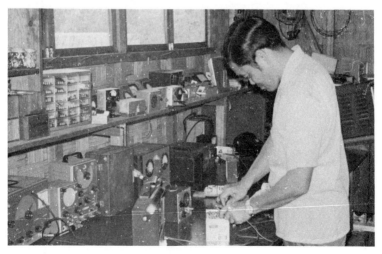

George Ehera, native of Hawaii, works on radio equipment in the radio lab at Nasuli, Philippines.

"Walking the plank." Translators leave the Norseman in Peru to enter an Indian village.

Bernie May, now Executive Director for JAARS, is shown loading polio vaccine aboard a Helio Courier in Peru prior to taking off to deliver it to an Indian tribe.

Tom Smoak and Paul Witte prepare for early morning takeoff in Andoke Land—
(Bloom Where You Are Planted)

Author (left) with Paul Bartholomew pump fuel from the Cat on the
Camasea River in Peru.*(To The Uttermost Part Of The Earth)*

Ken Kruzan and Shirley Abbott at Nasuli, Philippines. *(Land Of Promise)*

Betsy Smoak and the kids wave goodby to Tom at Lomalinda.

The old Duck, bellerin' and blattin'.

No room on this Philippine mountain airstrip for a mistake.

Chapter 5

Miracle on the River

Sometimes the world from above seems too beautiful . . .
too wonderful . . . too distant for human eyes to see. . . .
— Charles Lindbergh

It was early Sunday morning, and the dawn sky over Miami was rapidly changing from gray to rose to robin's egg blue. I had just strapped myself tightly in the right-hand seat of the brand-new Helio Courier sitting on the apron at Miami International Airport and was watching the sun, like a reluctant ball of fire, peeping over the skyline of the still-sleeping city. The morning cumulus clouds, which had huddled together like sheep on the eastern horizon, were now rearing their blue and purple heads only to melt and fade before the golden rays of the sun like piles of sidewalk snow in springtime. It was going to be a beautiful October day — a beautiful day to fly across the Caribbean Sea and on to South America.

Orville Rogers, who would be at the controls, was wiggling into his bright orange life vest. Orville — quiet, always smiling, and fiftyish — was president of the JAARS Board of Directors and a senior captain with Braniff International. It was on his invitation that I was making this trip. Our final destination, still two days off, was Bogotá, Colombia, where the single-engine plane would be turned over to the Colombian government and then flown on across the Andes to its new home at Lomalinda close by the northern extremities of the Amazon jungle.

Orville made a final walk-around inspection of the little plane, wiping some of the collected dew from the windshield, and then climbed in behind the wheel. "In case we have to ditch in the ocean," he said nonchalantly, "you can get the life raft out of the back while I get my door open and work the radio."

I glanced toward the back. Where four seats were usually located, there was a huge auxiliary gas tank, strapped into place with nylon seat belts. I breathed a quiet prayer that in case we did have to make an emergency landing, that tank wouldn't break loose and come smashing forward. Strange, I thought, how pilots never get away from constantly planning what they would do in case of engine failure.

Orville was buckling his seat belt and calling the Miami tower. I had a deep feeling of trust in this quiet man. Still vivid in my mind was his expert approach into the sprawling Miami airport the night before. From my seat, I had alternated watching the huge DC-8 that roared by us in the moonlight, and looking down at the shadow of our own tiny plane as we raced the moon through the spider-web lace reflections in the swamp waters below. It was good to be flying with a man who knew what he was doing. When Orville said I would have time to get the life raft out of the back in case we ditched, I believed him.

"Of course," Orville grinned, as we taxied out toward the end of the runway, "no one really knows what a Helio would do if it landed in the water, since one never has. Some say it would immediately sink to the wings. Others say the big engine would pull the nose down and it would flip over on its back. Let's just pray we don't have to find out."

I nodded vigorously.

I remembered my first flight in a Helio. Bernie May, the dedicated young executive director of JAARS, had picked me up at the Charlotte, North Carolina, airport to fly me down to JAARS Center at Waxhaw, just a few minutes away. Instead of taking off like a normal pilot in a normal airplane, he requested permission from the tower to take off at the runway intersection. With full throttle into the wind, we were airborne after a roll of only thirty feet — the length of the airplane. Needless to say, I was impressed.

I remembered hearing Bob Griffin, veteran JAARS pilot, tell of making what he considered a routine landing on a tiny jungle strip in Ecuador — a strip only two hundred yards long, bounded by tall trees on each end. Bob said the closer they came to final approach, the more the translator in the seat beside him stiffened. Finally, as they cleared the trees at the end of the strip, the translator screamed, "Bob, it won't fit!"

Seconds later, the trees were flashing by the wingtips, and their wheels were rolling on the spongy sod. The plane really did fit. Easily. In amazement, the translator walked back to step off the touchdown roll. Only eighty-four paces. They had used less than half the six hundred feet JAARS requires for a Helio landing field.

Top-rated plane of the JAARS fleet, the Helio Courier is a five to six place, high-performance machine with exceptional short takeoff and landing (STOL) capabilities. If the early JAARS pilots had designed a plane to do everything they wanted a plane to do, they would have come up with most of the specifications now built into the Helio.

The Helio story began when Uncle Cam began praying for a plane that would not only cruise at very slow speeds for jungle surveys, but would race across the sky on emergency flights, one that could land on small, muddy jungle fields and take off with maximum loads.

"There is no such plane," his friends all told him. But the man who never said "can't," just kept on praying.

One day in 1955, driving through Tulsa, Oklahoma, he saw a strange plane "hanging in the sky" over the highway. Hurrying to the airport, he saw this same plane take off at a breathtakingly sharp angle and speed away across the countryside. His prayers were answered in detail. That fall, JAARS took delivery of the first of what would become a fleet of more than twenty Helios to be based all over the world: New Guinea, Nepal, the Philippines, South America.

The Helio is a first cousin of a helicopter. It will fly safely and under full control at the astonishingly slow speed of 30 miles per hour, but has a top speed of 160 miles per hour. Not only that, but the movable slats on the front edge of the wing enable it to make steep banks at these low speeds so that a tailspin, the nemesis of many "low and slow" pilots, is impossible. Helios were used extensively in Vietnam, where their cockpit, surrounded by tubular steel, prevented fatal accidents even though many of them were flown into trees or the sides of mountains. Despite landing on short airstrips flanked by tall trees, sides of mountains, or tops of twisty mountain ridges, in their millions of miles of jungle flying, JAARS had "totaled" only one Helio. Even then the pilot stepped out of the demolished plane with only a minor bump over one eye. "Cabin integrity," a term used by JAARS when they talk about that remarkable quality of the Helio to protect it passengers, was a comforting thought as we prepared to fly overwater to South America.

I thought of something George DeVoucalla, a pilot-mechanic from Colombia, once told me. He said the word "helio" comes from a Greek word meaning sun. And "courier," in Latin, means one who runs with a message. Very literally, the Helio Courier was bringing light to those who dwell in darkness.

Our two-day trip to Bogotá, with an overnight stop in Barranquilla, was no disappointment. Weather perfect, we landed on schedule and were met by several JAARS and SIL people waiting for us at the airport. The messenger of light had been delivered.

It was two o'clock in the morning, and I was suddenly awake

in my bed in the Wycliffe Group House in Bogotá. Something was wrong. It was an eerie feeling, as though someone was in the dark room with me. I couldn't get my breath. At first I thought I was having a heart seizure. Then I remembered I was at 8,600 feet, and my lungs just weren't getting enough oxygen. After several minutes of deep breathing, I was able to get back to sleep; but it was a drastic reminder of the dangers of high altitude for a flatland tourister like me.

The next morning, Don Weber, former JAARS pilot and now Travel Manager for Wycliffe in Bogotá, briefed me on the problems of altitude. "Don't exert yourself. Don't carry anything heavy. Don't run. Take deep breaths. Otherwise you'll get *soroche* — mountain sickness."

I had heard of *soroche,* and I had no desire to experience its headache, nausea, and general misery. With that warning still ringing in my ears, I started the second lap of my trip to Lomalinda — this time in a rickety old taxi which would take me on a four-hour ride across the Andes to the village of Villavicencio — "gateway to the *llanos* (plains) ." There, hopefully, I would make contact with a JAARS plane and be flown on down to the SIL base at Lomalinda. Rich and Karis Mansen and their two children had just come in from the Guajiro tribe in the extreme northern part of the country and were returning to their home at Lomalinda after a six-months' absence. I was glad to have their company in the taxi.

Roaring out of the city, our taxi driver seemed to be trying to build up enough momentum to actually leap his ancient vehicle through the twelve-thousand-foot pass in the mountains. Driving first on the left side of the road, then the right, and often in the middle, he whirled around hairpin turns, barely missed oncoming cars, and swerved — with horn blaring — through flocks of sheep and goats that occupied the sometimes paved, sometimes gravel highway. I was busy with my camera out of the car window until we disappeared into the clouds at the ten-thousand-foot level. Then I had to content myself with looking at the road through a huge rusted hole in the floorboard directly under my feet. We skirted precipices hundreds of feet above rushing mountain streams, and just as we crested the pass and started down, we met a truck coming from the opposite direction that failed to honk as it rounded a curve. We skidded to a wild halt barely a bumper's width apart. Slowly we scraped by each other, our outside wheels (on my side) crumbling away the very lip of the cliff which dropped almost a thousand feet to a roaring river in the bottom of the rocky ravine.

Rich Mansen's running commentary didn't make me feel any more comfortable. As we started down the mountain, he pointed out the place where a taxi filled with Wycliffe personnel had gone over the edge of an eight-hundred-foot precipice. JAARS mechanic Ken Huber, his wife Gloria, and their small children were among the passengers packed in the old car as it toppled over the side of the mountain. The driver was badly bruised, Gloria's neck was broken, and everyone else horribly shaken, but thankfully, no one was killed. The small white crosses along the side of the road, however, indicated where many others were not so fortunate. I found the trip to be an excellent stimulant to prayer.

We arrived at the village of Villavicencio late in the afternoon. A radio message was waiting at the airport — the same airport where the Cat made such a *magnifico* landing — that bad weather at the jungle base would delay the plane until the next day, so we returned to the village and found rooms in the local hotel. My tiny third-floor room had a steel cot and a screenless window overlooking the maze of tin and tile roofs of the little town squeezed between the base of the mountains and the encroaching jungle.

We spent the evening wandering through the mud-coated streets with the Mansens. The tile-roofed dwellings protruded like a rash from the green hide of the jungle. We browsed in dimly lit shops and rubbed elbows with short, brown-skinned people who turned to stare at my blond features. Poverty and filth were abundantly evident. After a meal of chicken, rice, and *Coca-cola* (only a fool drinks the water), we returned to the hotel, and I bade my friends goodnight.

Outside my window, the full moon reflected against the dark, towering Andes. Part way up the mountain, overlooking the city as if to protect it from the evils of this world, was a magnificent Catholic cathedral, built with inlaid marble and gold. I breathed a prayer of thanksgiving for the "new wind" that had blown through the Catholic church since Pope John had thrown open the windows of the Vatican. The days of Catholic colonialism seemed to be at an end. Catholic persecution of evangelicals had been more severe in Colombia than in any other country in the western hemisphere. Recent stories, however, of fellowship between some of the Wycliffe translators and Catholic priests offered evidence that the century-old walls were breaking down.

I leaned against the window sill. Below me were the courtyards and alleys of the little village from which the sounds of goats, pigs, chickens, and playing children wafted up to my window. How I admired and respected men and women like Rich and Karis Mansen who were giving up the comforts and luxuries of their North American homes to bring light into this dark land.

The screams of a parrot in the rubber tree outside my window wakened me at dawn. The eastern sky glowed amber. I dropped back off to sleep, only to be wakened again by the soft padding of footsteps in the room. A young woman, her light brown skin accenting a beautiful set of flashing black eyes, was standing beside my bed.

"*Buenos días, señor,*" she smiled, handing me a glass of freshly squeezed nectar, and backing out of the room, closing the door behind her.

I slipped out of bed and stood at the window, sipping the juice and looking at the shades of the morning sun dancing off the beautiful towering mountains covered with lush green foliage. Below my window, an old woman was chopping wood behind her adobe hut. A brown, barefoot child, hardly four years of age, was gathering eggs under a bush. A rooster crowed somewhere nearby, and a light breeze bent the dark green leaves of the banana trees. A new day had begun in Colombia.

The turbo-charged Helio Courier sat at the end of the airstrip at Villavicencio. Ron Ehrenberg, former Air Force pilot, reached up and twisted the handle which extended the flaps on the wings. The little plane was loaded to capacity and would need all the lift available to pull it off the runway in the thin mountain air.

Weight is always a critical factor in jungle flying. Moments before, as we stood on the apron near the hangar, Ron had pulled out a hand-held scale and, after jotting down each of our personal weights, began to weigh our luggage.

"Sorry," he grinned as he finished. "We're fifty-four pounds over the limit. We could take off, but it would put us over the maximum on landing, and we might break the landing gear. Start sorting." This is standard procedure for the translators, who have learned to expect to leave things behind.

We weighed again and made the limit. Our excess items were stored in the radio shack. Another flight would pick them up later in the week.

Thirty minutes and seventy miles later, we were circling the tiny mission settlement at Lomalinda. Little houses, each one the home of a SIL family, sat on top of the lomas. Ron pointed out a larger building as the dining hall where single missionaries ate, and a nearby building as the Linguist Center, then other central buildings as a clinic, radio lab, school, and a dormitory for school-age children who did not accompany their parents when they lived with the tribe.

Betsy Smoak met me at the hangar. Tom was out on a flight and would be back at dinner time. Since I last saw Betsy, she had borne six children — including a set of triplets the year before. Caring for tiny children in the jungle — without washing machines or pediatricians — didn't seem to faze her. She was just as beautiful as ever, and she showed great wisdom in putting me in the base guest house rather than rearranging wall-to-wall babies to provide a place for me at home. However, she insisted I eat my meals with them, because she wanted to show off the new house a carpenter friend of Tom's had helped him build.

That night, after a delicious steak dinner at the Smoaks (steak is the most inexpensive meat in Colombia), I sat on the steps of Tom's little house. It was almost dark.

Directly in front of me was the grass runway. Beyond it was the open hangar where the three blue and white Helios were tied down. There was no breeze, and the fat, swarming termites were coming out of their odd-looking dirt mounds and flying in circles around the black cones. Inside the house, I could hear Tom's shortwave radio as he picked up a news broadcast from America. A familiar voice was coming across the thousands of miles. "Good evening, Americans, this is Paul Harvey . . ."

The past and present were blended in a moment of timelessness on the edge of the jungle.

Looking at the little houses sitting on top of the strange grass-covered mounds, seeing the runway and the hangar, the radio tower and the yellow lights from the various buildings supplied from the chugging generator, I tried to imagine those early days of the Colombian advance — only ten years before.

Ralph Borthwick, chief pilot in Peru, had volunteered to come up and help get the program started. Two days after Christmas, 1962, Ralph, his pregnant wife Vera, and little daughter Heather left Yarinacocha in a Helio equipped with wheels and crossed the Andes into Bogotá. The Colombian advance had begun.

Cameron Townsend, Clarence Church, and a few other SIL members were already in Bogotá. On January 3, the Borthwicks, Reggie and LaVerne McClendon, and two single women translators — Birdie West and Betty Welch — moved down to San

Martin, a small western-type village below Villavicencio, to start a temporary base to serve the tribes until the program could get underway at Lomalinda.

Early the next morning, Ralph loaded Birdie and Betty into the Helio and took off from San Martin for Mitú, near the Brazilian border. The territory was all new to Ralph, and the jungle was filled with countless tributaries of many colors and unfamiliar names. After almost two hours in the air, flying dead reckoning across the jungle, he realized that even the Vaupes River was charted incorrectly. Finally finding the channel, he followed the black waters downstream to Mitú, where he landed on a dirt strip formerly used by an oil exploration team. It wasn't the rivers that were marked on the map that bothered Ralph, however, it was the ones that weren't marked. Vast areas of the chart which was spread open on his lap as he climbed to four thousand feet were simply marked "unexplored." Dotted lines ran across the white space indicating where the map-makers thought the rivers might be.

Leaving the two girls to head on out to the Tacuno tribe where they had already started work, Ralph spent the night and picked up two more translators, Stan and Junia Schauer who had started work with the Yucuna tribe. Previously, the only way the Schauers could get to their tribe was by boat, which was a thirty-day trip down one river and then back up another. In anticipation of the plane, however, they had hacked a two-hundred-meter strip out of the jungle before returning to Mitú. Now they were ready for their first flight into their tribal strip.

Ralph's taste of the inaccuracy of the charts was still sour in his mouth. He knew he was flying into an area where very few white men had ever gone. After filling his tanks with gas, he checked the plane thoroughly, and with Stan and Junia strapped in, took off about noon to try to find the tiny jungle strip on the uncharted Miritiparana River. He estimated it would take him about one hour flying time.

Some things are drilled into a pilot from the first day when he sits nervously in the seat of a tiny trainer with an instructor at his side. Besides fastening his seat belt, which is automatic, he learns to shout "clear prop" when starting engine, even if he has just landed in a vacant field. He also learns to make a pre-flight check of his aircraft every time he gets into it, even if he has just taxied up to the gas pit in perfect condition. A good pilot automatically spins the adjustment knob on his direction gyro after setting the needle to line up with his compass. Many a novice has followed the needle on the gyro compass, congratulating himself for flying such a steady course, only to find (after he's hopelessly lost) that he forgot to uncage the gyro and has been flying a needle that was still locked in one position. A final "automatic" for the trained pilot is to always believe the map — even when your instincts tell you it is wrong. It is at this point that the jungle pilot has to break from his training, because jungle maps are notoriously inaccurate. Rivers change courses overnight, or sometimes dry up completely. Indian villages are often picked up and moved miles downstream. Clearings grow over with underbrush and disappear in thirty days. Airstrips are often entered on the chart while they are nothing more than a good intention in the map-maker's mind — or they are left on the chart years after the jungle has moved in and occupied the runway. Therefore Ralph knew that even though he had the latest chart in his lap, he should use it only to confirm what he saw on the ground — not as an accurate guide across the endless tract of jungle.

With a direct tailwind out of Mitú, Ralph roughly calculated his ground speed to be 145 miles an hour. He checked over three rivers, all of which seemed to be on the map, about ten minutes apart. However, all these checkpoints came up about four minutes early, so he re-figured his ground speed to be higher than his original estimate. All was going fine, and he estimated he should be coming up on the big Caquetá River in about ten minutes.

He would then turn upstream for a few miles, find the conflux of the Caquetá and Miritiparana and have his translators on the ground in just a few minutes.

The thin overcast at six thousand feet had grown more solid, and Ralph could hear the sound of rain hitting the windshield. Like scattered lead shot, the drops formed instantaneously into tiny streaks and chased themselves to the side of the plexiglass. Suddenly the plane was slammed with a mighty jolt of turbulence. At the same time, a wall of water completely obliterated forward visibility.

Ralph quickly put the plane in a steep bank. The memory of his experience in the old Duck was still very much alive. Stan, in the seat beside him, was wiping the inside steam off the windshield as sheets of rain pounded against the nose of the plane with the force of jackhammers. Suddenly, they were back in the clear, with only a sprinkle of rain still peppering the windshield. Stan relaxed in his seat and reached back to grasp the hand of his wife. Their first plane ride was turning out to be quite an experience.

Ralph grinned and nodded toward the cloud they had just left. "It's moving away from the river," he said. "I think we'll be able to make it."

Sure enough, as the cloud moved rapidly across the jungle, they could see below them the large river. "That must be the Caquetá," Ralph said. "We should be only a few minutes from your strip."

Making a giant circle while the weather moved away from the river, Ralph flew back over the basin, and then headed confidently upstream to where the smaller river should branch off to the right. The tribal strip would be only a few miles from there.

But after thirty minutes of flying, the conflux of the two rivers had not appeared. Something was wrong.

"If we miss the mouth of the tributary," Ralph had assured Stan, "I can always fly on upstream to Puerto Leguizamo."

Leguizamo was a port of entry to Colombia from Peru, and Ralph had flown there several times. This time, however, he was already far north of his intended path — on a river that looked exactly like the one he thought he was on, but was another river entirely. The next village he would see would be Florencia — three hundred miles away.

An old pioneer aviator once said, if you ask an airline pilot if he has ever been afraid, his answer is bound to be, "All the time." Of course, that is a distortion of the truth.

The same question is often asked of jungle pilots, especially those who fly over the vast uncharted regions of the earth where the lines on the maps may be hundreds of miles wrong, or the area into which he is flying may simply be blank with the words "unexplored" stamped across it in red letters. Pilots, whose humor tends to run dry, will simply shrug and say, "Only a fool is never afraid."

The jungle pilot, while he may not be *afraid* all the time, is *wary* all the time. From the moment he leaves the ground until the second when he reaches forward, leans out the engine, and shuts off the master switch at his destination, he is constantly watching. He is looking for that spot where he could land his plane in case of an engine failure. He is checking and rechecking to make sure he knows where he is. Nevertheless, in spite of every precaution, the Amazon jungle is sprinkled with the bleached bones of pilots, some of whom were on God's missions.

Flying over the mountains and jungles is like walking on thin ice in the springtime. The wise man knows that each step is a potential disaster — therefore, he is constantly looking for the telltale cracks which signal danger. So it is with the experienced pilot. Even though he may be carrying on a running conversation with his passengers, his ear is always tuned to the engine. The slightest sputter, hesitation, or murmur of complaint will be caught immediately. His eyes are constantly darting from the gauges on the instrument panel to the ground below, to the weather ahead, to the map of the area. The slightest flicker of the needle on the oil pressure gauge. An increase in the cylinder-head temperature. A build-up of clouds. An inconsistency between the map and the terrain below. A tiny loss of RPMs, and the pilot is all business. Frightened? Sometimes. Wary? Always.

Gradually, Ralph realized he was lost. There was no feeling of panic. It was simply a matter-of-fact situation. After a total flying time of four hours, the river had become so small Ralph knew it could not possibly be the Caquetá. With only an hour of gasoline left in his tanks, he was far past the point of no return. Obviously Puerto Leguizamo was somewhere other than where he thought it should be.

Reaching for the mike, Ralph called Bogotá radio, several hundred miles away. Surprisingly, his signal was heard. The radio controller suggested he "fly south," but Ralph was too wary a pilot to leave the safety of the riverbed and strike out across the uncharted jungle in hopes he would find the larger river. Bogotá radio said they would stand by, and at the same time, they would send a military plane out to try to find him.

Ralph glanced at the fuel gauges. They were already on reserve. He had no choice but to begin to look for a place to land. Without floats, that meant he had but one option — a sandbar, or *playa,* in the river. However, they had been over the river for the last two hours, and he had not seen a single sandbar. Still, the river was fast disappearing under the trees in the direction they were going. They had no choice but to turn back. A landing on the water would be better than going down in the trees.

Putting the plane into a sharp bank, and heading back downstream, Ralph told Stan and Junia of their plight. Stan got on the radio to the Catholic bishop of the area whom he had met when he first came to the tribe to begin his translating work. Bishop Conyas was unable to tell from Stan's description where they might be. He said he would be praying.

Ralph looked over at Stan. "How about leading us in prayer here in the plane?"

The prayer was brief, but packed with meaning. Stan asked specifically for the Lord to direct them to a *playa* that would offer a safe landing and takeoff. It was quite a bold prayer, since they had already flown over the river without seeing a single sandbar. As he finished his prayer, he reached into his shirt pocket and pulled out a small Bible. He opened it to the book of Job and read, "I would seek unto God, and unto God would I commit my cause: Which doeth great things and unsearchable; marvellous things without number . . . that those which mourn may be exalted to safety" (Job 5:8-11). They had done their best; they would let God do the rest.

Almost immediately, there was a feeling of peace that filled the cabin of Helio 457. Junia began to hum the tune of an old Gospel song, and Stan relaxed in his seat, smiling. The God who opened the Red Sea and gave dry ground for His people to walk on could also open this river and provide a landing strip for the tiny mission plane.

The plane was at four thousand feet and the gas gauge was knocking on empty when ahead of them, in the river, appeared a huge sandbar. All three of them saw it at the same time, though none of them could remember it being there earlier when they flew up the river. Breathing a sigh of thanksgiving, Ralph picked up his mike and called Bogotá radio once again. He told them he was landing on the sandbar and asked the controller to contact Cameron Townsend at the *Instituto Linguistico de Verano*.

"Señor Townsend has already been notified," the operator said. "He said to tell you he has been praying for you."

"That means the others in Bogotá are praying also," Stan said with a smile. "Between them and the bishop, we're pretty well bracketed."

Ralph nodded, hung up the microphone, and cut the power on the engine. Coming in low over the sandbar, he saw it was totally free from obstructions. In fact, it seemed to have just been formed. Smooth, hard-packed gravel, it was at least 1,200 feet long, 250 feet wide, and 10 feet above the water. As they slowly buzzed the strip, all three of them could see the gravel looked as if it had been sized and packed — the closest thing to a concrete landing strip imaginable. They touched down on the hard-surfaced runway, five hours after takeoff from Mitú.

Before leaving the plane, the three entered into another praise service, and once again Stan read from Job about the faithfulness of the Lord which doeth great things, marvelous things without number.

While Stan and Junia explored the *playa* which had so miraculously appeared out of the jungle, Ralph called Bogotá again and told them that a military Beaver or other STOL aircraft could easily land on the *playa* and bring them gasoline.

If ever a place was made to order, this was it. The jungle was far enough away to give the impression of surrounding them with a virtual Eden of lush green. The river ran between two hill formations at that point, and the water was swift, although not rapids. The sandbar had no vegetation on it, but the wings of the plane were adequate to provide shade during the day.

As the sun set over the jungle, Ralph and the Schauers realized there were no mosquitos or bugs on the *playa*, another miracle in the jungle. There was plenty of food, since they were flying supplies out to the Schauers' tribal home. A magnificent equatorial sunset appeared in the western sky, then quickly faded into inky blackness. A billion stars twinkled overhead, and the soft yellow glow in the east indicated there would be a full moon in the cloudless sky. Ralph built a small fire, and after supper they found they could soften the gravel with their feet and shape it to the contours of their bodies, making a comfortable bed. Since there was no need for mosquito nets, they spread the blankets on the ground, and with Ralph under one wing and Stan and Junia under the other, they spent a beautiful night on the jungle river —

sleeping on a sandbar which God had obviously formed just for their comfort and safety.

The next morning, after brushing his teeth in river water and running his wet fingers through his gray hair, Ralph got busy with his maps. Checking his flight log, he concluded they were probably on the Apaporis River and notified Bogotá of his approximate position. Bogotá radio said a Colombian Air Force Beaver on floats was searching the Caquetá River and would probably not be able to get to them until the next day.

Ralph helped Stan unload and set up the Schauers' radio, an eleven-pound set developed by Jim Baptista while he was on furlough from Peru. The radio had a range of more than five hundred miles. Within minutes, they were in contact with Uncle Cam at the SIL office in Bogotá and with Reggie McClendon at San Martin. Townsend told them a U.S. Geodetic Survey plane and another Beaver were searching for them. That evening, Ralph and Stan went swimming in the swift current of the black water, and later the three of them spent more than an hour reading from the Word before bedtime.

The following morning, January 17, Bogotá radio informed Ralph that an Avianca DC-4 would be flying its regular run from Bogotá to Letecia and would arrange to pass over the area where they were thought to be. If the pilot could locate them, it would help in the search. The DC-4 arrived on schedule, and Ralph talked to the pilot on the Helio's radio. Bogotá assured them that help would reach them the next morning.

The third day, January 18, a brown and green camouflaged Colombian Air Force Beaver arrived overhead at 9:45 A.M. After circling the area, it landed on the water and unloaded half a drum of aviation gasoline. Five minutes later, the U.S. Geodetic Beaver roared in and landed on the *playa* and unloaded another drum of gasoline.

After expressing deep gratitude to the crews of the two planes, Ralph watched as they took off. The Geodetic plane continued

77

to circle overhead until the Helio was safely off the *playa* and headed toward its intended destination at the tribal village of the Yucuna Indians. One hour later — three days late — the Helio touched down on the jungle strip. Ralph helped the Schauers unload their cargo, waited out a rainstorm, and then took off for San Martin.

It wasn't until he arrived back at San Martin that he began to realize all that had been going on while he was on the sandbar. Uncle Cam called by radio to congratulate him for his safe arrival home and to tell him about the big celebration that was to be held in Bogotá in honor of the rescuers.

"Celebration?" Ralph questioned. "But it was just a routine search and rescue."

"Routine?" Townsend laughed. "You should have been up here while it was going on. After Voice of America and the Associated Press picked it up, the entire world knew that one of our planes was lost in the jungle. The U.S. Geodetic Survey plane couldn't find you. The Colombian Air Force couldn't find you. Even the Catholic church was in on the act."

Even though some of the Wycliffe officials thought the entire matter should be quickly hushed up and forgotten, Townsend — in typical Townsend fashion — saw it as a wonderful opportunity for a celebration. A large testimonial banquet was held honoring the president of Avianca Air Lines and the captain of the Avianca DC-4 Number 180 who had spotted the Helio and radioed back their exact location; General Alberto Tau and Captain Marino and their staff in the Bogotá radio tower; Dr. Alberto Llyano, Raoul Manco Garcia, and Bishop Conyas of the Catholic church for their untiring standby at the radio during the time the plane was on the *playa;* the crew of the Colombian Air Force plane with Captain Tieniente Montenegro at the controls; and the crew of the U.S. Geodetic plane with Major Weston and Captain Nathan in command.

Major Weston testified that the *playa* was the only sandbar he saw the entire length of the river. He added that only God could have worked such a miracle at a time when the Helio was running out of gas.

Townsend then announced that in honor of all those who had worked together, the Colombian legislature had by special decree given the *playa* an official name, a name which from that time on would appear on all the world maps. The name: Point Cooperation.

Ralph Borthwick, in typical conservative fashion, made an entry in his logbook in which he noted the location of Point Cooperation: 72 degrees, 22 minutes west longitude; 1 degree, 5 minutes north latitude — just a few miles from the equator. He then added that it was an excellent place to spend a vacation and thoroughly recommended it for any tourists who might be passing that way.

Chapter 6

Bloom Where You're Planted

When the cloud is scattered
The rainbow's glory is shed.   — Percy Bysshe Shelley

Breakfast was over, and Tom Smoak, sitting at the end of the table, picked up his Bible. I looked at the six children who were in high chairs or sitting on back issues of Sears' catalogs. With necks bibbed and faces jellied, they were paying as much attention as small children can. Betsy was hovering over her brood from behind, as a mother hen keeps her chicks in line with the brush of a wingtip.

"How do we praise God?" Tom asked, after reading Psalm 150.

"We sing," young Tom-Tom said.

"And by not hitting the other guy when he makes a face at you," five-year-old Jonathan added.

"How do the flowers praise God?" Tom asked.

Betsy answered softly. "They bloom where they are planted — even if it is only God who sees their beauty."

A prayer time followed. Tom prayed for the children's safety and for Betsy's strength and health. Betsy prayed for our safety as we left on our jungle flight. Then, after hugs and kisses (jelly and all), we left the house armed with sandwiches and a thermos filled with lemonade. Tom and I made our way down the steep side of the loma where the wet grass soaked our shoes and wet the cuffs of our trousers. Picking our way across the mud at the end of the runway, we walked up the steep path to the hangar.

Our flight that morning would be over the Mazarena mountain range to the village of the Coreguaje tribe. Our passengers were four Indians: father, mother, and two small children who had come out of the tribe more than a month ago to help Carolyn Muller and Dorothy Cook with their translations. Such Indians were called "language helpers" and were supported by the translators out of their regular donations from the States. Since there was no "slush fund," every expense had to be carried by someone. The morning's flight into the land of the Coreguajes would be paid for by the two women translators — at a price that exceeded twenty dollars per hour flying time. The fee was determined by figuring the actual cost of keeping the airplane in the air — parts, gasoline, insurance, etc. All labor, of course, including the pilot's time, was donated free as part of their ministry. Since I was going along, I would pay my share of the ticket — in this case, one-third.

Dorothy and Carolyn were at the hangar to make sure their Indian family was safely tucked in the back seat of the plane. The Indians were scared. Their only other experience in a "flying machine" was in coming out of the tribe a month ago. At that time, they all got airsick and blamed it on the evil spirits in the clouds. Even though they were eager to return to their tribe, they did not look forward to the plane ride.

After a brief cockpit prayer at the end of the field, Tom waved to Betsy and the children who were standing in front of the house overlooking the runway. I logged our time off the Lomalinda strip at 0810 as Tom pushed the throttle all the way forward and the big prop pulled us into the air. We would be at the tribal village in a little more than an hour.

Climbing to five thousand feet, we crossed the rolling lomas and flat stretches of the Colombian plains, broken only by an occasional red streak where a lone road wound its way to an isolated hut in the middle of a field. Ahead of us, I could see the edge of the jungle, and beyond that the *Serrania de la Mazarena,* a small, odd range east of the Andes about one hundred miles long that rose from the jungle to five thousand feet.

"The natives are afraid of the Mazarenas," Tom said. "They say they are haunted. Even the Colombian pilots refuse to fly over them."

Finding a pass between two peaks, Tom threaded the plane through the high valley and dropped down on the other side of the mountain range. "I don't want to fly into the clouds if I can help it," he said. "It really scares the Indians."

I turned and looked at our back-seat passengers. Both small children were asleep. The little Indian mother, fear written all over her face, was staring straight ahead, but the squat man gave me a crooked, toothless smile in return for my "How are you doing?"

Below us now was the jungle, stretching as far as the eye could see. Like a flat green carpet it was an awesome spectacle that never failed to send a shiver up my spine. "The jungle," the Indians say solemnly, "eats the planes." I knew they were right.

Tom called the base every twenty minutes just to check in. He also called as soon as he safely touched down on a jungle strip, when he was ready to take off, and after he had cleared the field and was safely in the air. Any interruption in this pattern meant something was wrong and would start an immediate search from the base. No pilot was ever on his own as long as the radio end of JAARS was functioning.

Tom changed his heading. From now on, he'd be flying dead reckoning toward another river fifty miles away. Since he had no way of estimating the speed or direction of the winds aloft, he deliberately flew to the north of his intended destination on the river. After hitting the river, he would turn downstream until he found the village and the airstrip. It was a trick used by many of the experienced jungle pilots. Otherwise, he might hit the river and not know which side of his destination he was on. By deliberately plotting a wrong course, he would know which way to fly to correct himself.

The green below was punctuated by tiny clearings with a thatched hut in the middle, surrounded by hundreds of dead trees, some of them standing, some of them lying on the ground. Here an isolated Colombian family had hewed a place for themselves in the jungle. Tom explained the procedure. A man and his wife, or perhaps two couples, would make their way by footpath into the jungle until they found a piece of high ground. They would clear the small underbrush and chop down as many of the trees as possible. The trees would lie where they fell, and during the dry season, the men would set the clearing on fire. The underbrush would burn away, and the big trunks of the forest giants would be left to char and rot. The ashes would fertilize the jungle soil which, contrary to popular opinion, was notoriously weak in nutrients. Between the fallen trees, the family would plant corn, manioc, beans, sweet potatoes, squash, peppers, and tobacco. With pointed sticks, the woman would poke holes in the ground, and the man would follow, dropping seed in the holes and tamping the soil flat with his bare foot. Then would come the battle against the insects, animals, and weeds. If the family was fortunate, and if they did not get bitten by one of the countless specimens of poisonous snakes that live in the tall grass, they might harvest enough to keep their family alive. Since there was no way to preserve meat, they would have to rely on fresh fish or wild pigs and monkeys. Indians were deadly accurate with blow guns and bows and arrows and could kill a swinging monkey or a swimming fish with a single shot.

Tom finally decided that despite the Indians' fears, we were going to have to climb to escape the rough air which was bouncing us all over the sky. Making a deliberate effort to keep from going through any of the white puffy clouds, he climbed back up to four thousand feet, where we found smooth air on top of the scattered cloud formations. The Indians in the back seat smiled as we leveled off — they would rather run their chances with the unknown evil spirits than have the very real nausea brought on by the bumpy air beneath the clouds.

Landing at the Coreguaje village, we were met by the entire population. Our Indian passengers, who had not spoken a word the entire flight, were out of the plane and chattering a mile a minute. The little children from the village, some naked, some wearing only a dirty T-shirt, and all with runny noses which had collected a full deposit of dirt and dead insects, scampered around the plane. They would timidly touch the tires and then jump back, giggling and squealing in delight. I let one of the boys listen to my wristwatch, holding my arm close to his ear. He listened seriously for a few seconds, and then his face broke into a huge grin. "Ticky-ticky!" he shouted, and motioned for all the other children to come listen.

Immediately, there were about thirty children of all sizes and with varying amounts of dirt on their bodies, who queued up in a giggling, laughing line, waiting to listen to my watch. I noticed that after they had taken their turn, listening seriously, giggling, and shouting "Ticky-ticky," they ran to the back of the line to start all over again. I finally had to break away and hold my hand behind my back as a sign of "no more." By that time, an enterprising boy — one of the few with shirts and pants — had wrapped a small vine around his wrist and was dashing from one child to another, holding his wrist against their ears. All were laughing and shouting "Ticky-ticky." Soon a dozen children had vines wrapped around their wrists and were running up and down the runway shouting "Ticky-ticky" to anyone who would listen. They no longer needed me. They had learned to tell time by themselves.

The women of the tribe, some with suckling babes at their breasts, stood back shyly watching us unload the plane. Most of the men were out of the village on a hunting expedition, but a few of the younger men eagerly helped us unload the translators' cargo which would be stored in their little hut until they returned to the tribe.

We rolled a gasoline drum out of a thatched hut, and Tom crawled up on the wing. I poured the gas into a bucket and passed it up to him where he poured it through a funnel and a paper filter. We had to change filters three times, since there was a lot of water and rust in the gasoline. The wing was blistering hot and the stinging gnats were swarming in their batches. Both of us were wringing wet with sweat when we finished. Jungle flying was fast losing its romance.

One of the young men told us that two white rubber-hunters, armed with guns — *malo, malo, muy malo* — had been through the village the night before. They had stolen most of the things out of the translators' hut, including many of the tapes the girls had made of the various tonal sounds in the Indians' language alphabet. We knew it would be a terrible setback to the translation of the Bible into Coreguaje. Tom radioed the bad news back to the base at Lomalinda, and before long Carolyn Muller was on the radio. She gave Tom a detailed description of all the things they had left behind — clothing, personal articles, a typewriter, and a big trunk full of books and papers. Nearly all had been stolen. With the men out of the village, the Indians had been able to do nothing against the guns. They could only watch helplessly as the men looted the hut and then returned to their boat. Two of the young men had started after them, but a warning shot scared them back to their huts.

We also learned that the old chief, *El Capitan,* one of the girls' first converts, had been taken by dugout canoe to the hospital in Florencia — a sizable town about seventy-five air miles away. The Indians said he was *muy grave* — in a very grave condition.

In the Indian language, there was only one word for sickness, the same word used for death. All sickness, to the Indians, was unto death. Very few ever recovered from such minor diseases as measles, dysentery, or even the common cold. When it had become obvious the old chief was dying, the younger men had put him in a dugout canoe and taken him to Florencia to the hospital. The chief was no stranger to Florencia. In fact, he had been honored by the mayor and district governor when he had stopped a tribal war. The young Indians rightly assumed the Colombians would take care of him during this time of great need.

The chief's old wife told us she was preparing to leave that day by canoe to see him. He had been gone for a month, and she did not know whether he was alive or dead. It would take her almost a week to make the trip by water and on foot. We could fly it in thirty minutes. Tom radioed Carolyn back at Lomalinda and asked her advice. She urged us to fly the chief's wife into Florencia, saying the flight could be charged to her account.

Tom helped the old woman into the back seat of the plane and strapped her down. She had all her belongings slung around her neck in a woven net bag. Her grandson, a half-naked nine-year-old child, was begging to go. He was standing outside the window of the plane, tears making little streaks in the dirt on his face.

His grandmother explained in her own language that he could not come, but the little boy, holding on to the handle of the door, continued to weep brokenheartedly, begging to come along.

Something in me let me understand how he felt. His grandfather, the chief, had been taken away, maybe dying. Now his grandmother was strapped in the back of a strange silver bird that would roar off into the sky. Panic, terror, fear, and loneliness — I could read them all in his eyes as he huddled against the fuselage, wetting the Plexiglas window with his tears.

Unbuckling my seat belt, I slid out of the cabin and bent over the crying child, putting my arm around his bare shoulders. I prayed softly, in a language I couldn't understand. It lasted only seconds, but when I finished, the child turned and looked up in my face, his eyes filled with wonder. Pulling away, he ran to the edge of the grass strip to join the others who were waiting for the takeoff. I rejoined Tom in the cabin, and we taxied to the end of the strip, gunned the engine, and released the brakes. As we roared into the air, I saw the little boy clutching the skirt of an Indian woman and waving at the plane — his face wreathed in smiles.

It was a deeply moving experience for me. God's miracles were not limited to creating gravel landing strips in the middle of rivers, nor to answering the prayers of jungle pilots with dead engines. God could also dry the tears of a heartbroken Indian boy. I sat back in the seat and relaxed as we skimmed over the treetops toward Florencia. I was no longer concerned that the rubber hunters could thwart God's plan for translating the Scriptures into Coreguaje. Not even the gates of hell could withstand the force of prayer.

We found *El Capitan* drinking a Pepsi-Cola on the village square in Florencia. He had been released from the hospital just that morning. He and his wife decided they would return to the village by canoe, so we left them behind, slipped across the tops of the haunted mountains, and touched down at Lomalinda just before a torrential rain flooded the field. Borrowing an umbrella, I made my way through the mud to my guest room. I desperately wanted a cold shower — maybe three or four of them. Tom and I were to leave early the next morning for an overnight flight south of the equator to pick up an independent translator family on a charter flight.

Paul Witte had spent eight years studying to become a Roman Catholic priest. Then, just before he took his final vows, he fell in love. His bishop wisely advised him to marry and seek some other way to serve God than through the priesthood.

Paul chose to become a Bible translator in the tiny tribe of Andoke Indians in southern Colombia, and Cameron Townsend encouraged him to seek appointment as a Wycliffe Bible Translator. WBT had never appointed a Roman Catholic. However, Uncle Cam believed having a Catholic translator on the SIL staff, especially in Colombia where Catholic persecution had been so fierce, would go a long way to break down the crumbling barriers.

Paul and his pretty wife, Genny, went through the regular Wycliffe program — language school at the Summer Institute at the University of Oklahoma, and jungle camp in Mexico. Then he ran into his first real problem. He naïvely tried to raise his financial support through the regular Wycliffe channels, the Protestant churches of America. Evangelicals, it seemed, were very reluctant to give money to support a Roman Catholic faith missionary — especially one who was identified with the Catholic Pentecostal movement. Despite Paul's contention that he would not be teaching doctrine, only translating the Word of God and letting the Holy Spirit do the teaching, he was unable to raise support among evangelicals. He finally received promise of minimum support — less than two hundred dollars per month — for his wife and two small children through a small group of sympathetic believers in Philadelphia. However, when the time came for final appointment, the WBT Board of Directors outvoted Uncle Cam and refused to appoint Paul as a Wycliffe translator. They might have been able to go along with Townsend's crazy dream twenty-five years ago that planes could be used in the jungle, but they could not catch his vision of Protestants and Catholics working together to translate the Bible. It was one of Cameron Townsend's bitterest disappointments in his long years of service and ministry.

However, the refusal of the WBT board did not dissuade the tall, blond Catholic scholar from the task he felt God had called him to perform. Taking the training they had received from Wycliffe, and believing God would support them through their friends back home, Paul and Genny packed their belongings and set out by boat and then canoe to make their home among the Andoke Indians on the Aduche River two degrees south of the equator. It took them almost a month to reach their new home, traveling by canoe up the Caquetá River. Without radio contact with the outside world (the lifeline of the SIL program), even without the vital prayer support which undergirds all the other Wycliffe translators and support personnel, Paul, Genny, and their two small children had begun their task. They built their house, and using Wycliffe methods, began to learn the language and start their grammar write-up. The SIL people in Colombia seemed to have a high respect for Paul and Genny, and when a JAARS flight was going their way, the pilots would drop a packet of mail and circle their clearing to see if they were alive and well.

When the Wittes learned they could charter a JAARS plane to fly them out of the jungle (at slightly higher rates than those charged the regular Wycliffe translators), they hacked out an airstrip and sent word out — by a JAARS pilot who landed to check on them and spent the night due to bad weather — that they would like to be picked up on October 19. That day had now arrived, and Tom and I were on our way south, not knowing for sure whether the Wittes were even still alive in their isolated jungle village. This was the way it used to be for the Wycliffe translators before they had radios to make regular skeds with their home base, Tom said. I shuddered.

Our first stop, after two hours of flying south, was on top of a huge mesa deep in the heart of the jungle. With sheer rock sides, it rose starkly out of the jungle like a shoe box sitting on the living-room carpet. The year before, JAARS mechanic Marcus Lauver, Ken Yoder, a SIL agriculture expert, and Fred Chambers, an American Airlines pilot from California, had parachuted onto the isolated plateau to build an emergency landing strip. They had cleared about two hundred meters, enough to enable Ron McIntosh and George DeVoucalla to land. They then extended the strip to nine hundred feet before flying back home. It had not been landed on since, and Tom wanted to check it out.

It was a strange sensation. Here we were in the middle of the Amazon jungle, just a few miles above the equator, sitting on the top of a rock mesa. The plateau, which was obviously the result of some gigantic earth upheaval centuries before, was about three miles square with vertical walls which fell away almost one thousand feet to the jungle below. The thin soil on top of the mesa could support only stunted underbrush and a few wild flowers. One of them, a beautiful star-burst on a long stem, was called *estrellita del sol* — little star of the sun. Tom told me their agriculture expert said this was the only spot on earth where this particular flower grew. Tom picked some for Betsy, and I plucked a handful, hoping they would dry so I could carry them home as a reminder of this beautiful solitary place where flowers bloomed where they were planted — for the glory of God alone.

Two hours later, we were on the ground in Andokeland. Paul Witte heard us coming and ran the quarter mile from his tiny hut to the landing strip. Lanky and muscular, Paul looked more like an offensive end on a professional football team than a Catholic scholar and Bible translator. He greeted us warmly and helped us carry our bags back through the waist-high grass which grew between the felled trees in the open field.

It was impossible to comprehend, from the air, what a near-impossible task it was to clear a landing strip in the jungle. Trees, two hundred feet tall, several times thicker than a man's body, and the hardest wood in the world — ebony, teak, ironwood — had to be cut down and then burned or rolled to the edge of the field. Paul said it took one man with an axe working two days without rest, to cut down one tree. Yet that was nothing compared to the task of digging up the stump — which took three weeks. And that was just one tree. Later, they filled the holes with dirt and cut more trees at the end of the strip to give clearance for landing and takeoff. Altogether, it took Paul and his Andoke helpers a full year to clear a two-hundred-meter landing strip which was used, at the most, three times a year. Yet the plane saved them almost a month of ground travel each time.

Climbing over the dead trees that stretched out like bleached skeletons in the blazing sun, we made our way to the little thatched bamboo hut on stilts where Genny and the two blond, blue-eyed, laughing children were waiting for us.

The Wittes' hut was exactly like the Indian huts, the nearest of which was another quarter of a mile away. Two tiny rooms — built high off the ground to provide protection from roving wild boars and boa constrictors. One room was a bedroom, where all four of them slept. The bed consisted of a wooden platform covered with a thin cotton mat. The other room was a combination kitchen and study where after dark, by the light of a gasoline lantern, this brilliant linguist spent hours listening to the sounds the Indians had made on his tape recorder and then translating these sounds into written words.

Genny, sparkling and full of life, was delighted to receive the mail Tom had brought.

"We never got the last mail pouch you dropped," she said.

Tom was dismayed. "But there were at least thirty letters in the envelope," he said. "And some of them must have contained money. I buzzed the house so you'd see me and then threw the packet out right over the field. It had a long red streamer attached, and I know it hit right in the middle of the runway."

Grinning sadly, Genny explained what had happened. "Paul saw you make the drop and started running toward the airstrip. But by the time he got there, one of the cows that belongs to a nearby Colombian patrón had eaten the packet, letters and all. Paul arrived just in time to see the last of the red streamer going down."

I was horrified, but Paul was smiling. "That's just part of jungle life. The first week we were here, Genny washed my clothes and

91

hung them out to dry on lines attached to the stilts under the house. The cows ate them, too. They liked the taste of soap."

Later in the afternoon, Tom, Paul, and I made our way to a quiet stream where we bathed our hot bodies in the cool water. Having heard stories of the tiny armored catfish, the candiru, which swam into people's ears and other body openings and then had to be removed surgically because of barbed gills, I was hesitant to venture into the water. However, Tom assured me that the stream was free from such creatures. It wasn't until after I was immersed that Paul added, grinning, "No candiru. All we have are a few piranhas."

But I was so hot and sweaty that even the thought of a nipping flesh-eater didn't prevent me from luxuriating in the cool water which ran brown over the smooth white rocks like tea over sugar cubes. Bird calls beckoned us from the other side of the stream where the bank was littered with ripe mangoes and hundreds of big, buttery avocados. Sitting on a rock to dry off before putting on my clothes, I was suddenly enveloped in a cloud of yellow and black butterflies. At first I thought they were cute, but the swarm grew so thick, I decided I'd be more comfortable back in the water until they flew away into the jungle looking for some other white meat to flutter against.

Darkness came quickly on the equator. At 5:45 the sun was already below the trees. We ate supper by gasoline lamp, seated at a bamboo table. Genny had cooked on a one-burner kerosene stove and served us a meal of fish soup, yucca, fried bananas, and paca. Paca, I learned after supper, was a jungle rodent, like a rat only larger. I was thankful it was already down and well on its way to being digested when I learned its identity.

Afterward, we sat in the dark on the porch, high off the ground. Paul talked softly about the subject that was closest to his heart.

"In 1910 there were ten thousand Andoke Indians. Their nation stretched all the way from Florencia to the borders of Brazil. They were peaceful and knew nothing about war or killing. In the thirties, white Peruvian rubber hunters came in and made slaves of them, slaughtering them just for the fun of it. They raped the women and then cut their arms off. At night, for recreation, they sat around their camp fires and poured gasoline on the Indians. Then they would set them afire, watching and laughing as they ran screaming and flaming through the woods. For that reason, the Andokes still call all white men *duiojo* — people who burn. Today there are less than one hundred adults left in the tribe."

"Why did you choose to spend your life with such a small tribe," I asked, "especially since most of them speak Spanish anyway?" I knew that many of the Wycliffe translators had made similar choices, and I wondered why.

"Spanish is only a surface language to them," Paul said thoughtfully. "Man can understand the deep things of the Spirit only when he reads them in his mother tongue. Genny and I are here so the Holy Spirit can speak to these for whom Christ died — and speak to them in the language of their hearts. Most people go through life and never win a single soul to Jesus. We are claiming this entire tribe — what's left of it — for Him. We believe the Word will win them once it is translated into their language."

I probed to find if there was any bitterness over Paul's rejection by WBT because he was a Catholic. I found none.

"We're grateful for the training we received and especially thankful that we can call on the Lomalinda people for help. It just wasn't God's time for us to come with SIL. One day, that door will open. Until then, we believe God is still in control, and we will serve Him right where we are."

We took to our hammocks early. Tom tied his jungle hammock under the house. I stretched out on the porch in a woven palm Indian hammock provided by the Wittes. How quiet it was in the jungle. Slight rustles heralded the arrival of night-prowling monkeys. In the shadowy gloom, they leaped and cavorted like a troupe of clowns. A margay—a small, spotted jungle cat—dashed through the clearing beside the house. Vivid in my mind were the stuffed tiger's paws Paul had given me to take home to my children. The animal had been shot by an Indian with a bow and arrow only yards away from where I was swinging in the hammock. Soon, I heard the splash of raindrops on the thatched roof over the open porch. The temperature dropped rapidly, and before long I had to scrounge around in my bag and come up with a plastic raincoat to wrap myself in. Even so, I shivered until the first rays of the sun peeked through the huge vine-covered trees, and the jungle came alive with the sounds of daybreak.

I rose early, unaccustomed to being bent all night long to the shape of an Indian hammock, and brushed my teeth in the creek. Tom followed me down the jungle trail to the edge of the water. He said he would have slept fine except for a cow who kept trying to crawl into the hammock with him.

Tom and I helped the Witte family carry their earthly belongings the quarter of a mile through the tall grass and mud, clambering over the fallen trees — some of which were shoulder high — to the plane. By seven o'clock, I was already drenched with sweat and longing to take one final plunge in that cool brown stream where the piranhas swam.

One of the things the Wittes left behind was Paul's expensive concert accordion. He had brought the instrument with him so he could play hymns for the Indians and entertain himself and his family in the evenings, but it had lasted only a few weeks in the sultry jungle. Mold and mildew had formed on the stops and base buttons, and the bellows had quickly rotted in the humid air. Paul left it behind along with his expensive German camera which had also fallen victim to the jungle's corrosion.

The airplane loaded, we roared out over the tree tops and headed back toward civilization.

The Wittes asleep in the back seat, each one holding a child, I turned to Tom. "Paul and Genny must be a special breed of people."

"No, very ordinary folks," Tom said. "With extraordinary faith."

The he grinnned, nodding down toward the mesa in the jungle with the airstrip and the little flowers. "They're like the *estrellita del sol*—just blooming where they've been planted."

Tom didn't seem to realize it, but that's exactly what he and Betsy were doing also. Just exactly.

Chapter 7

The Gooey Bird

The big DC-3, engines stopped, had been sitting at the end of the abandoned grass runway at the village of Puerto Lleras for almost five hours, waiting for the rain to stop. Pilot Roy Minor and copilot George Fletcher were pacing up and down the steeply slanted aisle, obviously as restless about the weather as I was. We were headed to Bogotá. From there, the DC-3 would go on to its base at the SIL center at Limoncocha, Ecuador, and I would catch the airlines for Peru — if we ever got off the ground in this miserable weather.

Unable to land on the short strip at Lomalinda the night before, Roy had landed the big plane on the longer commercial strip at nearby Puerto Lleras. A former Air Force bomber pilot with graying hair, Roy now held the position once held by Bernie May, who had since moved to North Carolina as the executive director for JAARS. George Fletcher was on loan to JAARS in Ecuador — to learn to fly the DC-3 — from his regular assignment as a pilot in the Philippines.

At seven o'clock that morning the three of us had been driven
out to the airstrip in a jeep from Lomalinda, ten miles away, and
left there. By the time we finished the preflight check, which for
some odd reason included George Fletcher kicking the tires on
the monstrous old plane (I used to kick the tires on my old Luscombe, but never did know why), the weather had closed in and
the rain had started. We stood under the wing for a while until
the rain got too hard, and then dashed for the back door, pulling
the steps up behind us. Now it was almost noon, and the rain was
still drumming on the top of the old metal plane in a low, steady
roar.

Because the DC-3 was a tail-dragger, the inside aisle between the
rows of seats was at a steep angle. Soon after we climbed aboard
to wait out the weather, I had discovered that by letting one of
the seats back into a reclining position, I could stretch out almost
horizontally. While Roy spent the time briefing George Fletcher
on the controls and characteristics of the plane, I grabbed a quick
nap. I had never recovered the sleep I lost that night in Paul
Witte's hammock.

I woke from my nap and lay in my seat, watching the rain which
was still falling in a steady drizzle. I could hear Roy's muffled
voice from the cockpit as he answered George's questions about
the various instruments. Occasionally, I would hear the Bogotá
radio reporting the weather.

The DC-3 was a unique kind of airship. No other flying machine
had been a part of the international scene and action so many
years, cruised every sky known to mankind, been so ubiquitous,
admired, cherished, glamorized, known the touch of so many different national pilots, and sparked as many maudlin tributes as
this one plane. It was without question the most successful aircraft ever built.

Eight hundred and three commercial DC-3s were eventually
built, and over ten thousand military versions. They were an easy
aircraft to fly, almost totally forgiving of the most ham-handed

pilots. Their inherent stability made them excellent instrument airplanes, and their low stall speed combined with practically full control response at slow approach allowed the use of very short fields. They could be slipped with full flaps or held nose-high and allowed to descend in a near power stall. In the hands of a skilled jungle pilot such as Roy Minor, the DC-3 could even be landed successfully on many of the muddy strips hacked out of the encroaching jungle.

Like the old Duck, a DC-3 could carry just about anything you stuffed into its hold. What the Catalina could do well, the DC-3 could do better — except land on water and get its nose wheel stuck in a muddy pothole. Before JAARS got its first DC-3, the trip from Limoncocha to Quito took the better part of a week. Now they were able to take a big group up to the capital city in the morning and bring them back in the afternoon.

Bernie May, JAARS Executive Director, had briefed me on this DC-3 before I came to South America. The story actually dated back to the time when Bernie was a pilot in Peru. Just before he and Nancy left to return to the States on furlough, they had prayed with the JAARS team, asking the Lord to provide JAARS with a DC-3. After returning to the States, Bernie was invited to speak to the Sunday school of the First Presbyterian Church in Pittsburgh, Pennsylvania.

One of the secrets of fund-raising in JAARS has been to talk about God's provision, rather than man's need. That morning in Pittsburgh, Bernie refrained from talking about the lack of equipment in South America (including their need for a DC-3), and spent the hour sharing stories of the miraculous way God had already provided. It was a principle which never failed to reap dividends.

Immediately after his talk, Bernie was aproached by Paul Duke, a member of the Christian Couples class at First Presbyterian.

"I'm chief pilot for the Blaw-Knox Steel Corporation," Paul said in introduction. "I don't know anything about your needs in

South America, but my company has a DC-3 which they are getting ready to dispose of. Are you interested?"

Bernie had a three o'clock TWA flight back to Philadelphia, and Paul took him out to the airport and around to the big hangar where Blaw-Knox kept their planes. In the gloom inside the hangar, Bernie saw a fully equipped DC-3.

"Do you think we could get it for JAARS?" Bernie asked, his heart beating wildly, for he sensed God was answering his prayer right before his eyes.

"I'll talk to the people in charge," Paul said. "But you've got to remember. If you get it, it will be because God intends for you to have it — not because Blaw-Knox wants to give it to you. Therefore, it will come to you in God's way."

Safely strapped in the seat for his flight to Philadelphia, Bernie reached in his briefcase and pulled out his Bible. It fell open to Psalm 37. "Delight thyself also in the Lord; and he shall give thee the desires of thine heart."

"Wow!" Bernie said out loud, causing those around him to stop their talking and look. But Bernie was too excited to care. God was speaking — through circumstances and through His Word. It was something to be excited about. He just *knew* God had promised him *that* DC-3.

A week later, Bernie got a call from Paul Duke. "Bad news, Bernie. I've discovered the chairman of our board had already promised the plane to Lehigh University in Bethlehem, Pennsylvania, as a donation."

"But I was so sure," Bernie told his wife, Nancy, when he hung up. "I still believe God is going to provide that plane for JAARS. I'm going back up to Pittsburgh and talk to Paul Duke."

Like Bernie May, Paul Duke was a man of prayer. When Bernie arrived, Paul said. "Let's just commit this entire matter to the Lord." Without saying any more, he dropped to his knees in his living room and Bernie hit the floor beside him.

"Lord," Paul prayed, "I don't believe You ever take anything away after You've promised it unless You intend to give us something better. I don't know what could be better than this DC-3. But whatever it is, we'll thank You and praise You for it."

Rising from his knees, Paul said, "Bernie, why don't you talk to the vice-president of Bethlehem Steel Corporation? He's on the Board of Trustees at Lehigh University. I understand Lehigh is going to sell the plane, and Bethlehem Steel is handling the negotiations for them."

The matter was becoming more complicated by the minute.

"We'll be glad to sell the plane to JAARS," the vice-president said. "Since all the money goes back to the university, we're trying to get as much as possible. Our price is sixty-four thousand dollars."

"That's too much," Bernie said, knowing that not only did he have no authorization to contract a purchase for JAARS, but even if he did, JAARS didn't have any money set apart for such an expensive item.

"Well, make us an offer," the executive said. "We'd really like to see JAARS get the plane."

Bernie stumbled for words.

"How about sixty thousand dollars?" the executive said. "That's really a good bargain."

But Bernie, of course, had no money at all. The more he thought about being there in the office of this industrial executive, trying to buy a plane for nothing, the more embarrassed he felt.

"I'm sorry, Mr. May," the man said, standing up behind his desk and walking toward the door. "We've got an offer from a Canadian outfit who says they will buy the plane at our price. We'd probably be willing to turn it over to you for fifty-five thousand. But if that's too much, you'll just have to lose it."

Bernie returned home, disheartened and confused. He was so sure God had spoken to him saying the plane would belong to JAARS.

A week later he received a call from the assistant to the vice-president at Bethlehem Steel. "Would you believe we haven't been able to sell that airplane?" the fellow chuckled. "God must be on your side. We've had three bonafide offers, all of which fell through at the last minute. Come on up and see us. We're open for any reasonable offer."

Bernie contacted Lawrence W. Routh, chairman of the Board of Directors for JAARS. Routh agreed to go with Bernie to talk to the Bethlehem Steel people one more time.

"What will you give us for the plane?" the vice-president asked after Bernie and Routh were settled in his office.

"We'll give you thirty-two thousand dollars," Bernie said.

Lawrence Routh cleared his throat and looked at Bernie out of the side of his eyes. JAARS didn't have that kind of money. In fact, the JAARS board wasn't even sure they should have a DC-3, and here Bernie May, a pilot from Peru, was obligating them for a small fortune. Mr. Routh started to speak up. He needed to let the executive know that Bernie was not authorized to transact business, but the vice-president was on his feet.

"You've got to be kidding, Mr. May."

"Nope, that's my top dollar," the confident pilot said. "God has promised us the plane, and that's all God is willing to pay."

"Well, since it's God who's going to buy this plane from us, I guess we'd better accept His offer," the executive smiled. "The plane is yours."

Mr. Routh, who had been half-standing, collapsed heavily in his chair.

"Could we pay off the debt over a period of two years?" Bernie asked. He had never transacted any business before, but now, assured God was in control, he was speaking with boldness.

Taken aback, the executive said, "Why, I guess that will be all right — although I hoped you'd be able to come up with the cash."

"How about eight thousand down and eight thousand every six months until the debt is paid?" Bernie asked.

"Yes, that will be all right, too," the executive said, making hasty notes as Bernie outlined God's deal.

"Great!" Bernie said. "Now how much time will you give us to raise the first eight thousand dollars?"

"What!" the executive said, leaping to his feet. "You mean you don't have any money at all?"

"Not a penny," Bernie grinned. "It's all in God's bank account. It will take us a while to transfer the funds, that's all."

"I see," the vice president said, settling gingerly in his chair. From the other chair, Bernie heard a low moan.

"Well, we usually don't handle business this way," the steel magnate said. "However, we have to hold on to the plane until the first of the year so it can count as a tax deduction from the donor. Therefore, if you can come up with the eight thousand by December 31, we'll let you have the plane."

As they walked out of the Bethlehem Steel offices, Lawrence Routh asked, "Where did you come up with that figure of thirty-two thousand dollars?"

"Gee, I don't know," Bernie said, still amazed by all that had taken place. "It was half of sixty-four thousand, and it seemed to be the figure God wanted me to give."

Mr. Routh shook his head. "The JAARS board meets next month. I trust you'll be present and let them know what you've done."

The Board of Directors was divided. Some of them saw the vision and were for it. Others were cautious. After all, they'd never done anything like that before. They told Bernie if he could raise sixteen thousand dollars, twice the amount needed for the first payment, by December 31, they would consider God intended JAARS to have the plane. Otherwise, it was no deal.

But Bernie had heard a word from God. Now all he had to do was trust God to supply the funds. Between Thanksgiving and Christmas, he pulled out all the stops, speaking to everyone he knew about God's promise to provide the plane.

The little Marcus Hook Baptist Church, where the Mays had their membership, joined them in prayer. A group of businessmen in Philadelphia formed a sponsoring committee. Dr. Robert Lamont, pastor of the First Presbyterian Church, called from Pittsburgh, inviting Bernie to speak to a group of businessmen. On a sudden impulse, Dr. Lamont asked the men to make contributions through a freewill offering. Seven thousand dollars came in that morning. Churches, Bible classes, individuals, housewives — all caught the vision of that big plane flying the jungles of South America on a mission for God. And at the watch-night service, December 31, at the Marcus Hook Baptist Church, Bernie stood to his feet and, in a voice choked with emotion, announced that the Lord had sent in twenty-two thousand dollars toward the purchase of the DC-3. By the end of the first six months, the entire thirty-two thousand dollars had been raised, and the plane belonged to JAARS, debt free.

Paul Duke, in reflecting on God's method, reminded Bernie that the Lord had indeed had a better way than JAARS receiving the plane as an outright donation. Had it been given to them, all those people would not have gotten involved as interested prayer partners. Not only that, but additional money to condition the plane to send it to South America had been provided through the drive. And besides, the JAARS Board of Directors had seen the result of faith in action. Because the JAARS team had claimed something from God, and because Bernie and Paul Duke had delighted themselves in the Lord, the desires of their hearts had come to pass.

A special dedication for the plane was held at the Philadelphia International Airport on February 20 of that year. Between seven and eight hundred people — most of whom had made some kind of contribution toward its purchase — showed up to see the plane dedicated for its ministry in South America.

The ceremony over, Bernie and Captain Lynn Washburn from Ozark Airlines climbed into the cockpit.

"Philadelphia ground control, this is DC-3 two thousand Lima, request taxi instructions for takeoff."

"Say, DC-3," the voice came back over the radio, "what was all that celebration going on around your plane?"

Bernie gave the ground control people the full story, how this was a mission airplane on its way to South America to fly Bible translators into the jungle.

"Roger, two thousand Lima. Cleared to runway two seven. Wind: two seven zero degrees at seven knots. Altimeter: three zero zero eight. Have a safe flight."

Taxiing away from the ramp, Bernie heard his radio come to life again. This time a rough base voice said, "Ah, two thousand Lima, this is Eastern Airlines three two seven. We know where you're going and want to wish you the very best."

Moments later, another voice came through the speaker. "Two thousand Lima, this is the United 737 right behind you in the lineup. We want to say our prayers go with you, sir."

One by one, the departing airplanes at the Philadelphia Airport came on the air, all wishing them the best — some promising their prayers.

Finally, as the DC-3 was sitting at the end of the runway, the Philadelphia tower came on the air. "DC-3 two thousand Lima, cleared for takeoff — and may the Lord bless you, sir."

No airplane ever had a finer send-off.

Six years later, JAARS got another DC-3. Again it started with a call from Dr. Robert Lamont, saying he had heard the Koppers Corporation in Pittsburgh was phasing out their DC-3 and replacing it with an executive jet. This time, the Lord, having already tested JAARS willingness to trust Him, gave them the plane. The Koppers Corporation also donated many spare parts, including a spare engine.

"The DC-3 has saved us countless hours," Bernie told me. "We've been able to get all the tribal leaders of an area together and fly them to a teacher-training school. Once we took out all the seats and flew livestock from Santa Cruz, Bolivia, to our base at Limoncocha. There were pigs, ducks, cattle — two of each — a flying Noah's ark."

During the last twelve months, this same DC-3 had hauled a million pounds of cargo, at one-fourth the expense of doing the same job in a lighter aircraft.

I remembered a famous World War II story. A China national DC-3, designed like all the others to carry twenty-one passengers, carried seventy-five people out of China to a Burmese airfield. Among the passengers was a certain James H. Doolittle, who had begun that particular flight aboard the aircraft carrier Hornet, and had arrived in China by the way of Tokyo where he had dropped a few bombs out of the belly of his B-25 before bouncing down on the China mainland out of fuel.

More than a thousand DC-3s took to the air as C-47s on D-Day in 1944, and they were present at all the major World War II engagements. They kept right on flying throughout the Berlin Airlift and continued through the Korean conflict. In Vietnam they were used as gunships. With six-barrel rapid-fire machine guns poking out the doors, they went into the heat of the battle zone to lay down a base of fire. They had been used as makeshift bombers, ambulance litter ships, flying cattle cars, flying pullman cars (sleepers) for the airlines, and missionary aircraft for four decades.

There was no indication that the DC-3 would stop flying before that Great Day when airplanes will be superseded by those rising to meet Him in the air.

Most airline pilots referred to the DC-3 as "the three." Air Force personnel dubbed it the "Gooney Bird." The Navy (with typical dull Navy formality) called it the RD-4, and the British named it "the Dakota." The Russians, who received a great number of DC-3s as gifts from the USA, conveniently forgot the Americans had invented the plane and announced it was a Russian invention called the "Ilyushin IL-2."

Regardless of the label, the Douglas masterpiece was profoundly

105

admired by all those who took to the air. And in just a few minutes, I was about to see still another capability of the big plane which I would never have believed possible. Roy Minor was going to put it through a flying maneuver which I wouldn't even have attempted in my tough little Luscombe. And he would call it routine.

After pacing the aisle and taking about nine looks out the back door, Roy finally said, "I think the weather's lifted enough that we can make it. Once we break through this overcast, we'll be on top and can cross the Andes into Bogotá."

Leaving my reclining bed, I walked forward to the cockpit. Through the windshield, I could see Roy was right. Although raindrops still peppered the Plexiglas, the sky to the north was clear. However, halfway down the grass strip was a lake — a twenty-foot mud puddle — that stretched the width of the runway. Matter of fact, it looked like a small river. It didn't seem deep, but I knew that once the wheels of our big plane hit that water, our takeoff roll would be slowed so drastically we'd never make it over the fence at the end of the strip.

Roy closed the back door and slipped into the left-hand seat. Grinning, he said, "I am about to show you a flying maneuver which can be accomplished only by the marvelous Gooney Bird." Swallowing hard, I decided it would be wise to strap myself tightly into the front seat in the passenger section — and pray for Roy, George, the DC-3, and me.

Starting the engines, Roy ran through his usual cockpit check. Then, with water spewing and the plane shuddering as he applied power, he slowly turned the awkward old flat-wing around on the soggy runway and taxied back a few feet to the absolute threshold. Swinging the plane back into position, he locked the brakes and applied power until every rivet in the aluminum panels seemed ready to pop out from the thundering vibration.

Brakes released, engines at full power, and propellers whining in full pitch, the DC-3 strained forward. Slowly at first, then with increasing speed, we rolled down the squishy runway, water flying in all directions. Through the open cockpit door, I could see Roy apply forward pressure to the wheel. I felt the tail rise. Now we were on two wheels, and the shallow lake was dead ahead. I braced myself for the sudden shock as the wheels hit the water. Instead, even though we did not yet have flying speed, Roy suddenly hauled back on the yoke. The plane was airborne for just a moment, then it settled back to earth with a big bounce and continued on its roll. But we had cleared the twenty-foot mud puddle. Moments later, with no trouble at all, Roy eased back on the wheel, and we were airborne — this time for keeps.

George Fletcher, having received a nod from Roy, pulled the gear lever, and the big wheels thumped into place under the wings. I noticed that his eyes were as wide with amazement as I knew mine were. But four decades of pilots had not been wrong. The DC-3 was quite a plane.

Chapter 8

"We're Going Down!"

Helio 571 rocked gently on its pontoons on Lake Yarina. It was a beautiful clear September morning in 1964. Floyd Lyon, eight-year veteran jungle pilot, was at the controls. In the right seat, dressed in a short-sleeved sport shirt, slacks, and tennis shoes, was the pastor of the largest Southern Baptist Church in the world, Dr. W. A. Criswell of Dallas, Texas.

For three weeks, Criswell had been touring SIL stations in Colombia, Ecuador, and Peru. Impressed by the testimony of two young women translators he had met in Oklahoma — brilliant linguists who were giving their lives to translate the Bible to a small tribe of Indians — Criswell had decided to come to South America to see this work for himself. Due back in his pulpit the following week, he had scheduled a last stop in the land of the Shapras. In particular, he wanted to meet Chief Tariri, former headhunter turned Christian whose life he had seen depicted on a mural in the Wycliffe Pavilion at the New York World's Fair.

Plans called for Floyd and the famous preacher to spend the night in the chief's hut and return to Yarinacocha the next day.

In 1950, the Shapras, vicious killers and headhunters, were among the most feared of all Indian tribes in Peru. Chief Tariri had attained leadership in much the same way the old Roman emperors used to lay claim to the throne. He had slain his predecessor in cold blood and then dared any warrior to dispute his authority. None had.

Then one day Loretta Anderson and her co-worker, Doris Cox, paddled up to his village in a dugout canoe. Climbing the riverbank and ignoring the hostile stares of the armed tribesmen around them, the two young white girls faced the chief. Using a few Shapra words picked up from a trader, plus sign language, they explained to him they had come to live among his people and study their language. One of the Shapra words they had learned was the word "brother." They used it in addressing Tariri. They didn't realize it at the time, but by using that word, they had bound the chief to protect them, since by tribal law Shapra men must defend their sisters.

Years later, during a conversation at Yarinacocha, Tariri told me, "If Uncle Cam had sent men, I would have killed them on sight — maybe shrunk their heads. If he had sent man and wife, I would have killed the man and taken the woman for myself. But what could a great chief do with two innocent girls who called him 'brother'?"

He chuckled as he told me, remembering the instance. But back in 1950, it was no laughing matter. The Shapras still took heads, and Tariri was their vicious leader.

The chief assigned the girls to a hut and then nodded to two older women in the tribe. Tariri charged them with helping the young translators in any way they could.

Remembering those early years, Loretta told me, "We were scared most of the time during the first five months. But when we trembled the most, we prayed the hardest."

One night while the girls were working over their notes by candlelight, one of the old Indian women burst into their hut with alarming news. The Shapra men had been drinking and feasting all day and even now were staggering down the jungle path, intent on raping the two girls. "You must hide," the Indian woman said.

Loretta and Doris fled into the jungle and spent the night there. Next morning, they sneaked back to their radio transmitter and called Yarinacocha, four hundred miles away.

"Bring Tariri to the radio," the base director said.

Shaking, the two girls persuaded Tariri to talk into the radio. The chief, who understood some Spanish, heard a stern voice coming from the strange black box. It said, "You are the chief — and you cannot control your tribe?"

His authority at stake, the short, stocky chief, his head wrapped in folded leaves and feathers, drew himself up to his full height. With solemn dignity he spoke back to the box. "I am the chief," he said. "I promise the señoritas will not be harmed."

That was the last trouble the two young women ever had from the men of the village.

Loretta and Doris buckled down to the tedious task of learning the language. Their job was typical of what all the Wycliffe translators faced as they tried to distinguish one sound from another in the strange jargon that swirled around them. The Shapras, flattered by the girls' sincere love and earnest attempts to learn their language, eagerly helped by giving them words for objects pointed at. The language notebooks, crammed with phonetic symbols, began to fill up. After many months, the girls were able to work out an alphabet. Then came the long task of producing primers and teaching the Shapra children to read and write their own language. Of course, the first thing they translated into the language were verses from the Bible.

During those long months, Tariri was busy with his wars. The girls did nothing to dissuade him, nothing to try to stop his killing or headhunting. They stayed busy with the task God had given them — translating the Bible into the language of the Shapras.

One day the translators looked up from the little group of girls they were teaching and saw the fearsome chief standing at the back of the circle. He was frowning, but listening. After hearing the first Scripture verse translated into his own language, he marched through the children and demanded that the girls repeat the verse, not once, but several times. He stood, face to face, watching their lips and listening intently. Finally, his bronze face broke into a wide grin, the first time the girls had ever seen him smile.

"My heart understands with a leap," he exclaimed.

He turned and started to march away. Then he caught himself and turned back. "When you came, I did not understand why. Now I know. What you are doing makes my people happier and better able to care for themselves."

From that time on, the burly chief appeared regularly at the girls' hut. He would sit for hours, patiently helping them get the exact meaning of words, write down tribal stories, translate more Bible verses. Something was happening to Tariri. That something, the girls knew, was the mighty influence of the Word of God, activated by the power of the Holy Spirit.

It took three years, but finally Tariri called his Shapras together for a dramatic announcement.

"I like the white girls' God," he said. "He has brought us many good things. I am going to stop worshiping the boa."

Tariri's public announcement was backed up by his changed life. Not only did he put aside his snake worship, but he shrugged off the incantations of the witch doctors. He also passed a jungle law that outlawed murder and abolished headshrinking.

In 1955, Townsend took Chief Tariri with him to Lima for a celebration of SIL's tenth anniversary in Peru. Loretta went along to translate, and Tariri talked enthusiastically, not only to the press, but to the president of Peru himself. Every inch a chief,

111

even in the white man's jungle of concrete and high buildings, he held his head high and told Loretta, "Leave out nothing I say."

It was Townsend's theory — confirmed by Tariri's exciting testimony — that jungle Indians are the most curious people alive. Only fear, plus generations of mistreatment by the only outsiders they had met — rubber workers, gold seekers, and those running from the law — had kept them from learning about the mysterious world beyond their jungle prison.

Townsend's aim was not to take the Indian out of the jungle, but to take the jungle out of the Indian. Tariri was living proof that Townsend's aim could be achieved.

When Tariri returned home, his Christian commitment underwent a dramatic test. Attacked by a marauding tribe of jungle killers, he was shot through the chest, and others among the Shapras were slain. Ordinarily, the Shapras, following the age-old jungle law of retribution, would have entered into a bloody war and taken the heads of their enemies. But Tariri's faith in Jesus Christ changed all this. He issued an order for his bloodthirsty Shapras, bent on revenge, to simmer down, and he called the girls to him. "Read please," he said, "where God says, 'Return not evil for evil.' "

Many of the Shapras followed Tariri's example and became Christians. The Gospel of Mark had been entirely translated, and other books of the New Testament, plus some stories from the Old Testament, were almost ready. Tariri had even been to the United States and appeared on Ralph Edwards' "This is Your Life" TV show, along with Loretta Anderson and Rachel Saint from Ecuador. It was no wonder Dr. Criswell was eager to visit the chief in his jungle kingdom.

Floyd Lyon was completing his checklist: engine instruments — in the green; all flight instruments — normal; trim tabs — set; fuel selector — on the mains; boost pump — on; mixture — rich; prop control—full RPM; controls (he wiggled the ailerons and pushed the rudder pedals) — free. Turning to the minister beside him, Floyd grinned.

"The last item on the checklist is prayer," he said. "How about leading us before we take off?"

Glancing at the jungle trees on each side of the lake, feeling the steady rock of the pontoons on the water, and listening to the muted roar of the powerful engine on which they would depend for the next four hours as they followed rivers and crossed the jungle, Dr. Criswell nodded seriously. His prayer was intense as he claimed God's promise of protection as they flew. Neither of the men realized that what both men anticipated to be a routine flight over the jungle was about to turn into what Criswell would later call one of the greatest experiences of his life.

Floyd pushed the throttle forward, eased the float plane up on the step, and then pulled back on the wheel. The Helio responded beautifully, roared off the water and up into a gentle turn over the jungle. Floyd picked up the mike.

"Yarina, five seven one, off the water at oh three (9:03 A.M.). Will fly at six thousand five hundred feet. Estimate Tariri's village in four hours. Over."

Gertrude McGuckin, wife of pilot Jack McGuckin, was standing by in the radio tower that morning, logging 571's position reports. By plotting their position on a map before her, she knew almost to the minute where every plane was — or where they were supposed to be.

The flight that morning would take the two men north, following the Ucayali, and then Floyd would turn on a heading of northwest for a fifty-six mile crossover to another river basin. After an hour of uneventful flying, he picked up his microphone again.

"Yarina, five seven one. Five miles west of Orellana at six thousand five hundred, heading three ten degrees. Estimating over the Huallaga at three five (10:35 A.M.)"

The Helio made a gentle bank to the left and started out over the jungle. It was the only leg of the trip where they would not be over the safety of a river runway.

Criswell tried to keep his gaze inside the cockpit as the little plane droned high across the treetops. He kept remembering those two Ecuadorian Air Force planes that had gone down in the jungle just a few weeks before — swallowed up without a trace.

Floyd used the time to share some of the stories of God's watch-care over the pilots during the millions of miles they had logged in the jungle. Actually, it was a fantastic record. No JAARS plane had ever gone down in an unsafe place. There had never been a fatal accident. No passenger had ever been injured. It was a record unmatched by any other flying organization.

Suddenly Floyd broke off the conversation — stopping in the middle of a sentence. His trained ear had picked up something. Or perhaps it was just the feel in his fingertips as they caressed the throttle and wheel.

Then it happened. A terrific clanging in the engine, the sound of metal parts hitting against one another. Instantly, Floyd pulled back on the throttle. The noise increased, filling the cabin with vibrations. It was 10:15. They were exactly halfway over the cross-over.

More than a mile below them and off to the left was the only clearing in that entire stretch of jungle. It was a small Indian village, just a few huts along a shallow creek that crossed their path at right angles. Without a word to his passenger, Floyd put the plane in a steep bank, intending to follow the tiny stream back to the big river in case the engine did not clear up. Reaching for his microphone, he reported back to Gertrude.

"Yarina, this is five seven one. Engine is suddenly rough. Following Santa Catalina stream back to Ucayali."

"Five seven one, Yarina. Roger. Read you okay. I'm calling the hangar to stand by in case they can help you."

Within ten seconds, however, Floyd's plans to follow the tiny stream back to the large river changed abruptly. The engine gave two violent lurches accompanied by the sound of breaking metal. The entire airplane began to shake.

"What's wrong?" Dr. Criswell asked, alarmed.

Floyd was too busy to answer. He pumped the throttle and worked the mixture control. The engine was gone. Easing the wheel forward, he put the plane in a shallow glide. Fortunately the Helio had a tremendous glide ratio, which gave the pilot precious extra minutes to try to pick some kind of landing site.

"Tighten your seat belt, doctor," Floyd said tersely. "We're going down."

Like all professional pilots, Floyd dreaded using the emergency term "Mayday." Such a term was reserved for use only in the *ultima hora* — the last hour. But such a time had arrived.

Picking up his mike, he said calmly, "Yarina, five seven one. Engine vibrating badly. We will be landing near the village here. Will notify you exact location as soon as possible."

Gertrude's voice, equally cool, came back through the speaker. "Five seven one, Yarina. Roger. You are landing at the village, landing at the village. **Over.**"

The plane was passing through thirty-five hundred feet in its circular glide toward the dense jungle below. What they saw wasn't encouraging. The village plaza, the open place between the row of huts, had at one time been used as an emergency landing strip for JAARS planes. Now, however, it was grown up and pocked with holes. Besides, it offered no hope since the plane was on floats. The little creek wasn't much better. Covered with overhanging trees, the water was so shallow it only trickled over the sand and logs. Even if Floyd could get the plane into the creek bed, it would surely nose over — possibly burn.

In a power-off landing, there would be no room for mistakes. Either the pilot would hit the target on the nose or he'd wind up in the trees or scattered along the riverbank. Flattening his glide and swinging out over the jungle, Floyd estimated his approach pattern into the creek. His power-off landing would follow the same procedure as a normal landing — set the trim tab, roll down the flaps. Only, in this instance, he cut the switch ahead of time. That way, in case he plowed into the ground as he nosed over, the plane would be less likely to burn.

An overhanging tree was blocking half the stream to his left. He couldn't slip the plane very well with the flaps down. He would have to lift the wing, yet keep enough flying speed so the plane wouldn't stall into the ground. He cleared the trees. His wings were level again. Only feet off the ground now. Water ahead, but there were small rapids with outcropping rocks on the right. Hard left rudder and right aileron. He'd have to try to slip the plane anyway. Suddenly a brown-skinned man appeared in front of them, dragging his canoe across the stream. Better buy the canoe than hit the rocks. Floyd pulled the wheel back into his lap. Dr. Criswell braced himself for the crash. The plane shuddered, stalled into the water, bounded over a log, and came to a terrific jolting, grinding halt on a sandbar. Aground in the middle of the jungle. Motionless. Safe!

Floyd turned to the minister and said with an impish grin. "Praise the Lord. We're safe!"

Dr. Criswell answered with a long sigh, and then said reverently, "Let's tell Him about it." And they did, heads bowed in the cabin, both joining in what was no doubt the most heartfelt prayer of thanksgiving either had ever uttered.

As Criswell lifted his head from his extended prayer of thanksgiving, he saw brown faces — a dozen of them — eyes wide, teeth white, peering into the plane from the outside.

Floyd clapped Criswell on the shoulder. "It's okay, doctor. They're friendly. Just curious."

Floyd picked up the microphone. "Yarina, five seven one. We're on the Santa Catalina stream. Plane and passenger okay. Repeat. Everything okay. Everything okay."

Gertrude McGuckin's voice, rippling with joy, came back

through the speakers. "Five seven one, Yarina. Roger, and praise the Lord!"

It had been four minutes since the first sign of engine trouble, but during that period, three people had lived a lifetime—Floyd Lyon, Wally Amos Criswell, and Gertrude McGuckin.

The village leader, a Peruvian, insisted on carrying Dr. Criswell piggyback through the ankle-deep water to the shore. He then told Floyd that the people of the village were at his disposal and assured them the village plaza had been used some years ago by JAARS planes on wheels. Floyd inspected the field and paced it off, finding about 550 feet could be made usable if the holes were filled in and tamped down—holes made by the rooting hogs. He told the villagers what needed to be done, and almost fifty men and boys appeared with pails, basins, and boxes to carry dirt to fill in the holes. The entire operation took less than an hour.

By 2:00 P.M., after Floyd had radioed back to the base, Leo Lance, chief pilot, and two mechanics landed on the plaza in a wheeled Helio Courier. The mechanics stayed behind to begin the engine change on five seven one. It would take them ten days. but at the end of that time, after the entire village helped carry the heavy plane up out of the creek and over to the makeshift airstrip, they would install wheels, and Leo would return to fly the plane back to Yarinacocha. However, the afternoon of the crash, Floyd, Leo, and Dr. Criswell took off for home, and by 5:00 P.M. were safely back at the base. Total round-trip flight time from Yarinacocha to nowhere and back again was eight hours and fifty-seven minutes. Two days later, Criswell returned to Dallas and his grateful First Baptist Church. His visit to Chief Tariri would just have to wait until another time.

117

Chapter 9

Strange Passengers

No one ever got through the hangar at Yarinacocha without hearing of Larry Montgomery's experience with a cat in the cockpit. Larry had been out to a forlorn tribal strip at Yurimaguas in a Helio Courier. David Beasley had asked him to return a pet cat — supposedly fastened in a vine and barkcloth basket — to a friend at Yarinacocha. Taking off on the river alone, Larry was concentrating on dodging several canoes filled with Indians when the terrified cat scratched its way out of the basket.

Scratching and howling, the panic-stricken feline began tearing around the inside of the plane. Larry shoved the throttle all the way forward and pulled the Helio off the water, barely missing a canoe-load of Indians, some of whom threw themselves into the river to keep from being struck by the pontoons. At the same time, the cat was defying all the laws of gravity as he tore around inside the plane, hitting the Plexiglas windshield and side windows with all four feet as he roared round and round the interior. Somehow the cat had enough momentum — like a motorcycle inside a motordrome — to keep hanging on. Yowling at a high screaming pitch, tail sticking out like a broomstick, three times bigger than normal, all fur standing straight out, every few seconds the cat would shoot past Montgomery's eyes, across the windshield — at ninety miles an hour. All this time, Larry was desperately trying to keep the plane from crashing into the trees.

He was finally able to give the cat a mighty whop with his hand and knock it into the back seat dazed, where it calmed down — until they got home. There they had to remove the seat and two side panels in order to pull the terrorized cat out of the hold. From that time on, cats were strictly taboo with Larry Montgomery.

JAARS carried animals in the bigger planes quite often. It was only when a young bull, a crate of chickens which popped open in flight, or a snake wound up in the back seat of a Helio that exciting things began to happen.

Soon after Bernie May arrived in Peru, he made a flight to a tribal strip to pick up Marge Sasnett, wife of JAARS radioman Bill Sasnett, who had been assisting translators in the Chayahuita tribe. Marge and her three children were returning to the base before going home on furlough. When Bernie landed, he found their luggage waiting for him in the high grass near the runway. He loaded the suitcases, boxes, and jungle bags into the back, helped Marge and the children into the plane, and took off for home. Bill would follow the next day.

Thirty minutes later, flying at five thousand feet, Bernie heard the little girl exclaim to her mother, "Look, Mommy, there's a snake!"

Bernie turned around and looked behind him. Sure enough, there was an impressive boa constrictor appearing from under the seat.

Marge screamed and automatically reached for the door.

"Don't get out!" Bernie yelled. "That first step is a big one."

By the time Bernie had calmed the near-hysterical woman, the snake had disappeared. Hoping it had gone to the luggage compartment, Bernie turned to the controls, to get the plane back on course. Suddenly, he felt something nudging his feet. There was the snake — a six-foot boa constrictor — sliding out from under the front seat.

Bernie propped his feet on the instrument panel and started looking for a place to land the plane — immediately. With his feet off the rudder pedals, and his eyes everywhere *but* on the instruments, the plane began to zigzag all over the sky. Bernie's feet remained up on the instrument panel as he continued to shout to his passengers, telling them to remain calm. It was nothing to panic about — only a snake loose in the tiny cockpit.

Finally the teenage boy in the front seat beside him reached down and grabbed the snake and stuffed him into a plastic bag. Bernie put his feet down, and the flight was smooth the rest of the way.

The snake, which had probably crawled up into the the luggage which had been left in the tall grass beside the runway, became a family pet for the Sasnett children. He later accompanied them home on furlough, going through customs in Miami curled up contentedly in the bottom of a suitcase.

As for Bernie May, he added one more item to his checklist: shake all luggage carefully before putting it in the plane.

Most JAARS pilots agree that, aside from the time helicopter pilot Roger Dodson delivered an Indian baby in the front seat of his tiny helicopter while flying over the New Guinea jungle, the greatest cockpit feat was the time Jack McGuckin successfully fought it out with a small tiger in the cabin of a Helio — three thousand feet over the Amazon basin. Jack was on one of his first flights as a JAARS pilot in Peru. He had stopped at an Army outpost near the Brazilian border. There the commander gave him four live chickens, their legs tied together with what appeared to be weed stems, and asked if he would deliver them to an Army colonel at Iquitos — two hundred miles away. Since he was flying alone, Jack simply dropped the chickens over into the back seat of the pontoon-equipped Helio.

Another soldier appeared with two huge land turtles and asked if he would take them to the same colonel. Jack lacked enthusiasm for that cargo, because he remembered Bernie May's story of the time an eighty-pound turtle chewed a hole through the seat of the pants of one of his passengers before Bernie could land the plane. However, Jack made sure the turtles were secure in their box and dutifully put them in the luggage compartment.

Just as he was ready to take off, the base sergeant came running down to the river, dragging a wicker basket made of reeds and strips of bark. In the basket was a live ocelot — a tigrito. The snarling cat, bigger than a North American wildcat but not quite as large as a panther, was plenty mean. The sergeant assured Jack the basket was strong and asked him to deliver the ocelot to an Air Force major in Iquitos. Jack took another look at his plane, rapidly beginning to resemble a flying Noah's ark, but remembered Uncle Cam's philosophy of cooperating with government personnel whenever possible, and reluctantly accepted the cat.

"The tigrito cannot possibly escape from the basket," the sergeant assured him.

Jack put the big basket behind the seat, near the turtles, and took off. Fifteen minutes later, at three thousand feet, he heard the chickens begin to squawk — loudly. A farm boy, Jack recognized the squawking as being the same sound he'd heard when a chicken hawk appeared overhead, or when a fox got into the henhouse late at night. Turning around, he saw the ocelot had escaped. She was climbing over the back seat, hungrily eyeing the chickens.

Grabbing his canteen, Jack threw water on the big cat. She retreated to the luggage compartment, but moments later started over the seat again, her heart obviously set on a fresh chicken dinner.

The chickens were frantic, flapping their wings and squawking loudly. More water. Once again the ocelot withdrew, only to reappear, sharp claws reaching out for a tender drumstick.

Having used up all his water, Jack threw the canteen at the cat. He missed, and the ocelot leaped, landing in the seat beside the chickens. Bedlam broke loose — and so did the chickens. Snapping the weed-stem strings around their feet, they began flying in all directions, wings beating against the windows and in Jack's face as the ocelot stood up on her hind legs, batting and swatting, trying to knock one down. Jack forgot all about trying to fly the airplane and started grabbing for the chickens.

Finally, amid all the squawking and flying feathers and beating wings, the tigrito trapped a chicken on the floor under the front seat. Jack grabbed the microphone to call Yarina. He needed help. Immediately. The chicken, however, had gotten tangled up in the radio wires which run under the seat, causing all sorts of bad connections.

Jack's wife, Gertrude, was manning the tower that quiet, serene morning at Yarinacocha.

"I can barely hear you," she said. "Something must be wrong with your radio. Your transmitter keeps cutting on and off — sounds like you're inside a chicken coop with a wildcat. I'll phone for one of the radio technicians to come to the tower. You can tell him what's wrong, and maybe he can tell you how to fix it."

"Skip it," the befuddled pilot answered. "He'd never believe me. And even if he did, he wouldn't know what to do."

By that time, the ocelot had finished his chicken appetizer and started under the front seat toward Jack. It was time for the main course.

Spotting a small military outpost on the river below, Jack rolled down his flaps and headed down. Kicking the cat with his heels as she reached out for his leg, he finally got the plane on the water and taxied to the bank.

A band of soldiers met him, and Jack shouted out the window. "I have a loose tigrito in here. I need help."

All twelve men jumped on the pontoons at the same time, and the plane started to sink — pilot, tigrito, chickens, turtles, and all. The men jumped off, and finally a sergeant appointed a volunteer to lasso the angry animal and tie her up.

By that time, the base commander had appeared at the river. "We are glad you landed," he said to Jack. "We heard you come over but had no way to contact you by radio. One of our men had a serious heart attack this morning and may die if we cannot get him to the hospital in Iquitos. Can you take him?"

God had used a snarling ocelot — and a scared pilot — to get *His* plane to an isolated military outpost, just in time to save the life of an unknown Peruvian soldier. Less than two hours later, the man was safely in the hospital in Iquitos, the major had his ocelot, the colonel his two turtles and *three* chickens, and Jack was on his way back to Yarinacocha. It was a long time, however, before he agreed to carry anything but people in his airplane.

Chapter 10

Three Feet From Death

Mud unto Mud! — Death eddies near —
Not here the appointed End, not here!

Rupert Brooke, "Heaven"

Chief Italiano Cabrera of the Machiguengas (Mah-chee-gen'-gas) stood, hands on hips, and surveyed with satisfaction the newly completed airstrip that ran through the middle of his village of Tayakome. For many weeks, he and the other villagers, men and women, had been laboriously hacking the strip out of the virgin jungle. More than six hundred feet long, the strip ran directly in front of the row of eleven rectangular palm-thatched huts built on short stilts. On the far side was a low swamp, then the jungle again. The strip came to an abrupt end with a one-hundred-foot drop-off to the Manua River below. Off to one side was another row of huts, one of which was the schoolhouse where Martin Vargas, a government-paid Indian, held classes to teach the Machiguengas how to read Spanish. He was assisted by SIL teacher Harold Davis.

124

These brown-skinned, gentle Indians lived in a pre-stone-age condition in southern Peru, yet had a remarkable ability to provide themselves with all food, clothing, and utensils necessary for existence. Although the tribe used to number in the tens of thousands, now only about five thousand were left, making their homes in ten small villages along the jungle rivers. Small of stature and introverted in character, they had fled to their isolated areas to avoid contact with outsiders who, across the years, had exploited and killed them.

Translators Wayne and Betty Snell had completed the translation of the New Testament in the Machiguenga language, and new readers through the tribe were carrying its message to others. Harold and Pat Davis followed with a bilingual program — teaching the Indians how to read Spanish, teaching them arithmetic (the language had no numbering system), and also giving them names. As with some other Indian tribes, the Machiguengas simply called each other by their relationships — "brother," "sister-in-law," "father's sister," "father's sister's second girl of her second husband." Though the Snells had reduced the language to writing, the Davises were still struggling with conversational Machiguenga even after five years. Verbs were monsters which could be composed of thirty-four letters and twenty-two syllables, all of which had to be pronounced in exact order if the meaning was to be clear.

Example: i-ra-pu-sa-tin-ka-a-ta-sa-no-i-ga-pa-a-kem-pa-ro-ro-ka-ri. Put together, "irapusatinkaatasanoigapaakemparorokari" means, "They will probably turn head over heels into the river upon their arrival."

Since the rivers, for the most part, were too swift and dangerous for travel, the Davises had to travel back and forth to their villages by plane. In the village of Tayakome, Chief Italiano had volunteered to prepare the landing strip. It was difficult to land on the swift Manua River, and even if the plane could have gotten down safely, there was still a wide mud and cane flat between the water and the bank, and then the one-hundred-foot vertical cliff to climb. No, it was much better to spend the time and effort to hack a strip out of the jungle. Now the chief and his villagers were eagerly awaiting the first landing of a SIL plane on their new strip, bringing Harold and Pat back to their home in the tribe.

Back at Yarinacocha, three hundred miles to the north, pilot Don Weber, an eleven-year veteran with JAARS who would later move to Bogotá as the travel chief, was at the controls of the heavily loaded Helio.

Pat Davis, in the seat beside Don, reached back and touched the hand of her husband, who was sandwiched in the back with their five-year-old son Neal, seven-months' supply of food and materials, a special shipment of measles vaccine packed in dry ice, and a pet kitty. (Knowing something of JAARS experience with cats in the cockpit, Harold had promised to keep the kitten under tight security.) Pat entwined her fingers with those of her husband as the plane taxied down the runway toward the end of the strip. They had been away from the Machiguengas for several months. The new airstrip should be completed, and the measles vaccine would save many lives. They were eager to return.

Fleecy white clouds brushed the sides of the plane as they climbed for altitude. From the front seat, Pat watched idly as the shapes of the clouds changed from giants to sheep to elephants. Below them was the Ucayali waterway. Scattered huts and communities along the riverbank, a single motorboat or canoe, a cleared field here and there — all marked pockets of human life. Yet all were immediately swallowed up in the vastness of the Amazon jungle.

"Well, it looks pretty good," Don said, as the plane lost altitude and circled the newly cut airstrip at Tayakome.

Everyone in the plane was trying to inspect the field through the windows. They could see their Indian friends, including Chief Italiano and teacher-preacher Martin Vargas, waving from the side of the strip. The Indians had done a good job and were obviously excited over the arrival of the plane.

Don finished his turn and began to level off over the jungle on the far side of the river. Just as the plane came in over the river, it passed over a small, misty, almost transparent cloud. For a fleeting instant, Pat caught a glimpse of the shadow of the plane on the cloud. Surrounding it was the pilot's halo, that indescribably beautiful full-circle rainbow.

"Thank You, Lord," she breathed, "for safety all the way, and for help for the work You have brought us to do." Then she closed her eyes. She never had gotten accustomed to the sight of the ground rushing up in front of the plane, and the specter of that huge cliff looming up in the windshield was a bit more than she wished to face.

Don intended to touch down just as near the edge of the cliff as possible. That way, he could make a "touch and go" landing, if necessary, taking off soon after his wheels touched the ground and coming around for another try. It was a normal safety precaution used by all pilots. The old adage, "You cannot land on the runway behind you," applied even more so in the jungle.

Suddenly, almost quicker than he could think, the plane was caught in a mighty down draft. Perhaps it was the wind blowing in over the treetops and pushing down into the deep river gorge. Perhaps it was a trick suction caused by air currents over the mud flats. Whatever it was, instead of seeing the strip through the windshield, Don suddenly saw the face of the cliff as the plane was pushed down into the river basin just as they approached the cliff.

Automatically, he shoved the throttle to the firewall and pulled back on the wheel. An ordinary plane would have flown right into the side of the cliff. But the Helio was no ordinary plane. Its nose pulled up. At forty miles an hour, they cleared the front edge of the cliff by inches, and the wheels caught on the tufts of grass that hung out over the river and began to roll forward. The tail assembly, however, was still below the level of the cliff's edge, and with a mighty BUMP! the rear of the fuselage and tail wheel snagged on the lip of the precipice. The entire tail section of the airplane broke off just in front of the tail wheel. The plane rolled forward a few feet on the two front wheels, dragging the amputated stump of a fuselage behind before coming to a quick stop — only feet from the cliff's edge.

"Well," groaned Don, "that's the last of that tail wheel."

He swung out of the plane and stood looking and shaking his head. It looked as if someone had taken a giant can opener and sliced the entire tail assembly off the plane — leaving it to drag along behind, connected only by the cables and a few shreds of metal.

The Indians were racing down the runway, shouting, "Why did you land on the bank? We built the strip down here."

Chief Italiano, panting and sweating from the long run, came up to the open door of the plane, his face furrowed with concern.

"Didn't we make the strip right? We saw you go down just at the last and were sure you would all be killed."

Don reached out and put his arm around the bare shoulders of the worried chief. "Of course you made the strip right. You did a magnificent job. It was just an accident. We praise God we were not all killed by the wind."

Don pointed out to the Indians where the front tire tracks began, only scant inches from the edge of the cliff. With his hands, he showed them how the down draft had forced them into the gorge, and how the hand of God had picked them up just as they were about to smash into the cliff.

"We were only three feet from death," he said solemnly.

The Indians helped Harold and Pat unload the damaged plane, leaving a heartsick Don Weber to try to figure out what to do next. There was no time to waste. The measles vaccine, eight-five doses of it, would last only as long as the dry ice held out. While

Pat and little Neal gulped some water, rummaged for a sandwich, and accepted the boiled yucca and tapir meat which Martin Vargas' wife offered, the men supplied Don with all the tools they had to fix the plane — a barrel on which to rest the damaged fuselage, and a rock to pound out the dents. It wasn't much, but it was a start.

Harold went right to work with the vaccine. Taking it directly to their hut across the landing strip, he pushed their baggage toward the edge of the porch, brushed the dust off the table, and officially opened the clinic.

The entire community turned out — nearly one hundred people. Men and boys filled the porch, spilling out into the front yard. The women, more timid, took refuge under the teacher's tall house next door where they could remain inconspicuous yet still obtain a good view of operations. Children whined in anticipation, and proceedings were relayed from the ringside occupants to those behind, liberally sprinkled with comments. Harold and Martin laid out the supplies.

The measles vaccine required an accompanying injection of gamma globulin, administered in the other hip. Joking, commanding, and definitely in control of the situation towered Chief Italiano, conspicuous in his black feather headband. In deference to his position, Harold delegated him to line the people up as Pat called their names and swabbed each hip with alcohol.

"Okay," she said. "Here we go. Agosto," she called, "have you had measles? No. Well then, you first."

Three hours, eighty-five bottoms, and many jokes later, the job was done. The community filtered back to its own campfire, grateful that never again would they have to face the dreaded measles, which often wiped out entire villages. Harold rummaged for the kerosene Aladdin lamp and the hose with which to fill it. Pat made a dash for the bedrolls, hoping to get the mattresses laid and the mosquito nets hung before darkness and the night insects complicated the work to the point of impossibility.

However, before the job was done, Martin Vargas arrived with an unusual invitation. Would the Davis family and Señor Weber come to his house for supper? The people at Tayakome, although they had expressed love to the Davises, had built them a house and welcomed their help, had always been shy—afraid, perhaps, their gifts might be rejected, their invitations turned down. Tonight, they knew, there had been no time for the white people to fix their own supper. Thus for the first time they knew they could offer an invitation without having to run the risk of rejection — the ultimate embarrassment.

Martin's cookhouse, located behind his sleeping house, was a twelve-by-fifteen rectangle, raised three feet off the ground. There was an enamel washbasin, a water pail, a shelf which held the standard enamel plates and stainless-steel spoons, a few blackened aluminum pots, and three scooped out gourds. In the middle, a fire blazed cheerily, set upon a heap of earth and ashes to avoid burning through the floor. As a special gesture for the honored guests, Martin had lighted his Coleman gasoline lantern. Although it drew the flying and crawling insects by swarms, it made it easier to see what was being eaten.

As was customary, all the relatives who formed the eating group crowded in together — ten children and six adults — the men and boys grouped on the floor on one side, the women and smaller children on the other. Martin's wife, Teresa, began to serve into the enamel plates from the large kettle set by the fire — a stew of yucca and tapir meat. Her brother, Cesar, had gone hunting the day before to furnish them with fresh meat for the feast.

"Are you thirsty?" Teresa asked. "We have boiled water for you." It was the epitome of hospitality.

Pat began a series of questions concerning the village events during her absence. "No, there has not been any serious illness. No one has been bitten by a snake. . . . Yes, several have traveled downstream. . . . Yes, traders have been here. . . . And two new families have been added to the community, coming out of the jungle."

After supper, the men of the community gathered at the equivalent of the old-time cracker barrel — a platform fifteen feet long just outside the teacher's cookhouse. Harold and Don joined them, while Pat walked across the new airstrip in the dark to put Neal to bed by flashlight. She just had him settled when there was the shrill sound of a referee's whistle. Martin was calling the community for the evening church service.

The schoolhouse was crowded that night. The benches were filled, and women squatted on the floor along the back and stood looking in over the half-walls which formed the sides of the school building. The form of the service was basically the same each night. Two or three hymns, followed by a prayer. Martin's lengthy sermon was, as usual, addressed to one man. This night it was to Chief Italiano and turned into a running conversation between Martin and the chief, who replied in the affirmative or negative, repeated information, or professed lack of understanding. All the others sat in silence, heads bowed, as if they were too embarrassed to look up while the two men were talking back and forth in the feedback sermon. Then another hymn was followed by a challenge.

"Who knows a memory verse?"

Feet shuffled, but the heads remained bowed.

"Come on, you all knew one last night," Martin coaxed.

Finally one, then another, started calling out Scripture quotations. Eventually, everyone had a turn, and the meeting became a discussion of community affairs, with the chief presiding. There had been an argument between two men over the ownership of a field, and the chief made a decision which seemed to be acceptable to all present. It was obvious these people were not playing church — it was an integral part of living.

After the meeting, Harold, Pat, and Don returned home. Like the other Indian houses, the Davis house was rectangular with a palm-thatched roof, and was divided into three areas. The back of the house was Harold's study, a roofed-in area without floor or walls. In the middle was a bedroom/storage room, enclosed with loose-fitting palm-bark walls that let in air, light, and insects, yet afforded a semblance of privacy. The storage shelves in the bedroom were made of native cane tied with vines. The beds were of springy palm bark, resting on huge balsa logs. This part of the house was off the ground about three feet and floored with more springy palm bark. On the front was a roomy porch, open around the sides but also off the ground with a palm-bark floor. The porch served as the kitchen-dining room, guest room, and clinic/store for the entire community. The only "imported" furniture was one bench and two tables, prepared at Yarinacocha by the base carpenter and assembled after it reached Tayakome. Except for the beds (the Indians all slept on the floor) and the shelves, the Davis house was similar in construction to all the other houses in the village.

That night, several of the Indians joined them on the front porch, feet and hands drawn into their *cuzmas* (the long robes worn by men and women alike) to protect them from the ferocious swarms of mosquitoes. However, it had been a long day, and soon the Indians were nodding. One by one, they slipped off the porch and drifted back to their huts. Harold and Pat withdrew into their bedroom, and Don crawled under the mosquito net on the porch. He was asleep before he was aware of the uncomfortable palm-bark floor.

Morning came early among the Machiguengas. Well before daylight, Don Weber heard the whish of the black feather fire-fans, as embers from the three large fire logs were coaxed into brisk flame. Here and there, the stillness was broken by the crowing of a rooster, the clatter of a pot lid, or the padding of feet en route to the river for a day's supply of water — carried in a clay pot in a mesh carrying bag suspended on the back by a tump line (forehead strap) .

Lying on the floor, looking up at the thatched roof through the mosquito net, Don heard yet another sound. It was the murmur of hymns, Scripture memory verses, and prayers as Martin and his brother-in-law, Cesar, conducted their morning devotions. He could clearly hear Brother Cesar calling out the names of his family and listing before God, in great detail, the needs of the community. Don could not understand the Machiguenga language, but his heart was deeply touched as he heard this Indian, who could not yet read the Bible, calling his name as one of those he was asking God to bless that day. For a long time, Don lay there, listening. This day, like the day before, was the day the Lord had made. He would rejoice and be glad in it.

Harold and Pat were busy at the house. Even before they finished breakfast, the Indians were around with their usual requests. Harold left to help Martin with his school classes, teaching the Indians how to read and write Spanish. Pat remained at the house to minister to those already lined up at the front porch.

The villagers, unhampered by American time schedules, were free to drop whatever they were doing and come by whenever they felt like it — sometimes staying for hours. Pat had learned to hand out back issues of the *National Geographic Magazine* to all who came (she long suspected this was one of the reasons they showed up to begin with), and used each family duty as a teaching situation with her ever-present Indian company.

"See how I wash Neal's cuts and then cover them with a clean bandage? That's so the dirt won't get in and cause infection."

"See how I wash my dishes with soap and then pour this boiling water over them? That's to kill the germs that make us sick to our tummies."

"That picture? Oh, that's of people who live far away where it is so cold they have to wear the skins of animals to keep warm."

"Your baby died of tetanus! Do you know what the Piro mothers do? They never let the umbilical cord touch the ground, but place it on clean banana leaves and flame their knife carefully before cutting the cord. That way, the germs don't have a chance to get into the baby."

"Yes, it was God who kept us safe when our airplane went down below the bank. Now you see how strong He is, and how carefully He looks after us when we ask Him to."

"You want to buy a spoon? Have you enough money? Let's see if you can count it yourself. One . . . two . . . three . . . four soles? Okay. That's enough. And here's your spoon."

Pat knew it was important to sell things, not only to teach the Indians the importance of money and how to count, but to teach them how to bargain with the traders who came up the river — often to take advantage of the Indians.

The Davises lived their lives as though they were constantly on television, surveyed from all angles of the village every waking moment of the day. Hygiene, geography, simple mechanics, the use of money, child care, and myriad other subjects were taught in their everyday lives. Most of all, however, they prayed they would be able to transmit the reality of faith in a God who loved and sustained them in trials and who was longing to do the same for each Machiguenga.

When Harold and Pat had first moved into their house five years before, the days were hard. Day and night, the Indians were around them. It was necessary for Pat to dress under the mosquito net before sun-up, and impossible to change or take a bath until far after the evening service, when everyone else had gone to bed. Modesty — or lack of it — never bothered the Indians. But the Davises had a difficult time getting used to having people sitting and watching them bathe, undress, or use the toilet. Food was scarce, and the insects so ferocious Pat feared for her sanity. When the jungle behind the house (the village bathroom) was burned down to make a new field, things seemed to have reached the absolute limit of endurance.

Fortunately, as Pat said, the Lord took pity on them. The men were able to give a little time to build walls around their bedroom and to dig a "john" in one corner. In retrospect, Harold and Pat realized that even this adversity had a purpose. When they arrived in the village, most of the people had never seen a white person, although they had heard many tales of the white man's atrocities. They were prepared to believe the worst about Harold and Pat. However, as they watched them living completely in the open, most of these fears were allayed. In the meantime, the Davises had grown accustomed to the lack of privacy. In many respects, they so thoroughly identified with the Indians that their western needs for creature comforts had almost entirely disappeared. The only things that bothered them were the things that bothered the Indians — the insects more than anything else.

By the end of that second day, Don had stored the tail pieces from the plane under the projecting roof behind the Davis home, and, with the aid of his oval stone about the size of a small football, he had pounded out most of the V-shaped bend in the plane's belly.

When evening fell, there was a brief respite from the small, black, biting fly which drew blood, and the large, black triangular horsefly persecutors which were not repelled by any kind of repellent. The slanting rays of the setting sun were pleasantly warm, and a quiet cheerfulness pervaded the village. Don and Harold joined the men in a village soccer game on the airstrip and then went with them toward the river where they all clambered and slid down the steep bank, waded through the stinking knee-deep mud, and finally reached the water for a cooling swim. Then it was back through the mud and up the dirt bank to where they had left their clothes. Don realized he was even dirtier after his swim than before, but at least it was fresh mud. The men scattered to their huts, and Don and Harold made their way back to the Davis house.

Again, pot lids clattered, and pungent blue smoke curled from every cookhouse. Hens clucked their broods home for the night, and Pat trimmed the kerosene lamp. The nightly frog chorus commenced in the pond behind the house. As night descended, they all donned *cuzmas,* Don wearing one loaned him by the chief, and bathed themselves in insect repellent to provide at least partial protection against the clouds of hungry mosquitoes which suddenly surrounded them.

After supper, which was climaxed by Pat's surprise papaya cobbler, Harold went to check on a sick patient. Pat set to work boiling water for tomorrow and cooking a monkey leg so it wouldn't spoil overnight. It looked so much like a baby's hand and arm that Don immediately decided he would have to say he wasn't hungry when it was offered him the next day. Little Neal sat under the lamp, sharing some of the new *National Geographic* magazines with his little Indian friends. Don relaxed on the porch, hands and feet tucked under the *cuzma,* Machiguenga style.

Then "Wheet!" The whistle and time for church again.

While Don had been busy pounding out dents in the plane and learning to become a good Machiguenga, a contingent of technicians back at the base swung into action, calculating the repairs that would be necessary on the damaged plane and assembling men and materials to accomplish them. Mechanic Dick Hudson was assigned the responsibility of the on-the-spot repair job, with the assistance of metal worker Demetrio Mananita, a Peruvian employee who was trained in the JAARS hangar at Yarinacocha. The third day, Dick was flown down to Tayakome to inspect the wrecked plane and to bring Don Weber home.

Dick Hudson decided he should prepare a partial tail cone, fly it and a tail assembly to Tayakome, bolt the pieces in place, and then have a pilot fly the repaired plane home for a complete structural overhaul.

Within a few days, Tayakome was definitely on the map, as planes descended upon the new field with mechanics and supplies. The second weekend, three pilots, two planes, and two mechanics were all weathered-in at the tiny strip. The Indians were thoroughly impressed with all the movement, and volunteered to sleep in the planes overnight to protect them.

Dick and Demetrio put in long hours under a broiling sun, and the staccato of their electric drill and the put-put of the little generator they had brought to power it resounded across the village. Little by little, the airplane resumed its accustomed shape, until at last it was ready for the new tail pieces.

Three and a half weeks after that near fatal BUMP! Superintendent of Aviation Omer Bondurant flew in and returned the Helio nonstop to Yarinacocha without incident. Another chapter on the JAARS safety record was closed

Later, Chief Italiano placed a small stick marker in the ground near the place where the Helio made its maiden landing on his new airstrip. The marker was only three feet from the edge of the cliff. Paraphrasing the JAARS motto, the chief chuckled and said, as he drove the stick into the ground with the flat edge of his machete, "Señor Weber did his best. The Lord did the rest."

Chapter 11

In Furrows of Pain

En surcos de dolores, El bien germina ya.
— from the Colombian National Anthem

Despite all the adventure surrounding the miracles of flying, the real story at Yarinacocha was not found in the drama of near-fatal airplane escapes, but in a different dimension entirely. I sensed it the moment I arrived at the jungle base — a real depth of spirituality. Somehow, these four hundred people in the depths of the Amazon jungle had learned how to live — and how to live abundantly.

The lesson was learned, as so many spiritual lessons are learned, in a tragedy that fell on the base — a tragedy so great it seemed at the time the light could never again shine through the darkness. When I heard the story from Floyd Lyon, JAARS Flight Coordinator, I recalled a line from the Colombian National Anthem: *En surcos de dolores, El bien germina ya* — "In furrows of pain, good now germinates."

The lights went out on Christmas Eve

The base was preparing for a gala Ch
of the translators had come in from tl
days with family and friends. On the
of America transported into the hear
lights were strung in the dining hall, ana
festooned each home. Christmas trees, ranging from tᵢₓ
pines to broad-leafed banana trees draped with colored ᵢₙ
blinked merrily through the windows. The loudspeaker played
Christmas carols; strains of "Silent Night, Holy Night" floated
out over the steaming jungle. It was hot, of course. South of the
equator Christmas falls in the middle of summer.

Shortly before noon on that Christmas Eve, LANSA Airlines
Flight 508, a turbo-prop Electra, took off from Lima to Pucallpa —
475 miles northeast across the high Andes. Among the ninety-
two passengers were five SIL members, eagerly looking forward
to returning to Yarinacocha for Christmas with their families.

On board were Roger and Margery Hedges, a young couple
from the States who had come down several months earlier to
teach in the school. Margery, a native of Tacoma, Washington,
taught first grade. Roger taught music to all the grades and had
just a few days before directed a forty-voice choir in a beautiful
Christmas cantata. Their two children, ages five and seven, had
chicken pox, and had been left with friends at Yarina while their
parents made the quick trip to Lima for Christmas shopping.

Sitting across the aisle from them was David Ericson, nineteen-
year-old brother of Carole Daggett, who, with her husband Jim,
served the Chayahuita Indians. David had been at Yarinacocha
since June, helping to build a tribal airstrip and assist Flight
Coordinator Floyd Lyon at the hangar. Like the others, he was
returning from Lima after visiting friends to spend Christmas
with his family.

Seated next to him was Floyd and Millie Lyon's fourteen-year-
old son, Nathan. Nathan was not supposed to have been on that

ar flight. He had been in Lima for two days, visiting with Peruvian friends. He was scheduled to have returned to nacocha the day before, on his father's birthday. However, traded his December 23 reservation with a translator, and stayed over until Christmas Eve. Nathan was president of his eighth-grade class. Like his mom and dad, he was a licensed ham radio operator, and he was eagerly looking forward to riding his bicycle over the Andes during the Christmas vacation.

The final SIL passenger on Flight 508 was Harold Davis, veteran teacher who had been in Peru since 1957. His wife Pat had stayed on the base with their two children, ages ten and five, while Harold made the quick trip to Lima for a seminar. Harold was accompanied by Haroldo Pascho, an Indian boy who was going to Yarinacocha for medical treatment.

Everything on board the big four-engine Lockheed seemed normal — the takeoff, the climb over the snow-covered Andes, a snack served by the stewardesses, then the green jungle stretching east to the horizon.

Thirty minutes after takeoff, just as the plane cleared the snowy peaks of the Andes and started out over the jungle, visibility diminished. A giant storm had formed over the jungle. From the Andes as far as the eye could see, the air was boiling and churning in gray black clouds. The storm was moving in rapidly from the south, and the pilot thought he could let down through the edge of it and be on the ground at Pucallpa before it hit. He was mistaken. Even at twenty-six thousand feet, torrential rains were beating against the hull of the big Electra. The plane was being buffeted and shaken like a toy rattle in the hand of a playful infant. Trying to escape the battering turbulence, the pilot throttled back and continued to descend. Fifteen thousand. Finally ten thousand. Better to be late arriving in Pucallpa than to be scattered all over the jungle.

Back at Yarinacocha, Floyd Lyon felt uneasy. At home for Christmas Eve, he had been watching the storm from the screened

window of his living room as it built in
over the jungle. Hoping Millie was no'
the next room and switched on his s¹
to monitor the CORPAC channel, tʰ
handled all airplane flights. He lookeu
o'clock, and the rain was just beginning to
should have landed fifteen minutes ago — but there w
from the Pucallpa tower that it had arrived.

"I'm going down to the hangar to see if the planes are all tied down," Floyd called to his wife.

Wrapping a plastic raincoat around his shoulders, he hit the starter on his little motorcycle and pulled out of the path toward the lake. The rain was falling hard now, obliterating the trees on the other side of the lake. Floyd knew all the planes were tied down. He had seen to that last night. He needed to get to the radio in his office at the hangar. Something was wrong. He had been a pilot too long not to recognize the feeling.

Floyd had had that same feeling once before. That was back in 1964 when he went down in the jungle, but then he was in control. Now all he could do was wait.

Neither Pucallpa nor CORPAC had any information on the plane. It had reported in thirty minutes out of Lima and then disappeared. The airwaves were full of calls from Lima, Pucallpa, and Iquitos — all trying to raise the Electra on the radio. No answer. A military jet out of Iquitos said he was at thirty thousand feet and the storm extended as far as he could see out over the jungle. Weather experts later agreed it was the worst jungle storm on record in Peru.

After fifteen years of jungle flying, Floyd Lyon didn't try to kid himself. If the plane went down in the jungle, it would mean instant death for all aboard. He called Eugene Loos, Branch Director, and asked him to ride with him back up to the house to tell Millie. Then of course there was Pat Davis, and the Hedges children, and Carole Daggett.

141

grapevine at Yarinacocha has a way of transmitting in-
tion — rather accurately, too — in an amazingly short
. Within half an hour, everyone on base knew the plane was
st. The base leaders called a prayer meeting. Friends left their
Christmas Eve dinners and flocked to the homes of those in
trouble. It was, in essence, what the Bible called "body ministry"
— the strong holding up the weak.

Early the next day, Christmas morning, a Peruvian Air Force
colonel flew into Yarinacocha to take charge of the search. Floyd
Lyon, along with everybody else who could fly, joined in. There
were commercial airlines, military planes, the planes from the
Roman Catholic missions, a Seventh Day Adventist plane, independent missionaries, and, of course, the planes from JAARS.
All went into the air to begin the search for the lost airliner.

Stories of planes going down in the jungle and being swallowed
up by the trees, never to be seen again, abounded in Amazonia.
But this was the first time a big plane had ever disappeared with
so many people on board. Overnight, the news circled the globe.
Christians everywhere began praying. Many others expressed
genuine concern. But there was nothing anyone could do that was
not already being done. The planes were in the air — looking.
That was it.

The radio personnel at Yarinacocha suddenly found themselves the focal point of inquiries coming in from all over the
world. Millie Lyon stayed at her ham radio continuously for the
first four days of the search. Following a near collapse, she limited
herself to half days. Paul Wyse, a Mennonite radio technician
who had come with JAARS after a stint in Peru helping R. G.
LeTourneau build his colony at Tournavista, was busy eighteen
hours a day on his ham set. Several other ham operators put aside
their regular duties to keep the lines of communication open from
Peru to the outside world.

One of the most amazing developments during this critical time
was the emergence of the brotherhood of ham radio operators

from all over the world. From the USA, England, France, Canada, Iceland, Africa, Australia, the Philippines, and the South Pacific Islands, men and women who had never seen each other, yet who knew one another through the regular contacts via radio, rallied to help their friends in the jungle. At least two men in the USA took off vacation time just to stand by all day to assist the ham operators at Yarinacocha with calls. The little known "Halo Net," Christian ham operators who handled many of the calls from missionaries back to the States, got in on the act. Not only did they set up a nationwide prayer chain by ham radio, but they sent two ham operators to Yarinacocha to relieve those who had been on the radio continuously.

The JAARS pilots canceled nearly all their regular operations and flew steadily for four days before more bad weather set in. During this time, hysteria was building in nearby Pucallpa where the distraught family members of those on board the stricken plane were frantic with fear and anxiety. As the rumors rippled through Pucallpa that the plane had been found, the people of the city piled into their cars and rushed out into the jungle. Every day, hundreds of cars roared out of the city and down the dirt and mud roads only to return sadly at the end of the day. Almost every hour, it seemed, someone was rushing out to the base screaming, "They've found the plane. All are safe." Or, "The plane landed safely in Ecuador." Or, "The plane crashed on the mountains, and there are nine survivors."

Indians in the jungle sent in stories of having heard the plane flying at low altitudes, just above the treetops, during the height of the storm. Reports such as these were heard all the way from the Colombian border to the southern tip of Peru. At least two Peruvians said they saw the plane circling over the southern jungles, hundreds of miles from where it should have been.

A supposedly reliable Indian informant called in one morning on the missionary radio net and reported he had heard a plane circling the jungle at 4:00 P.M. on Christmas Eve. A big airplane, he said. A South American Missions (SAM) station, on a river 150 miles south, called on the radio and said twenty Indians came into their base and testified they had seen the airplane. Although they had never seen a big airplane before, the plane they described was an Electra. The wife of an American pilot, far south on the Ucayali River, said she had gone out of the house at 4:30 on Christmas Eve and heard a big airplane going over. From all over the jungle, reports came filtering in — people saying they had heard a big four-engine airplane flying over the trees. All said it was between 4:00 and 4:30 in the afternoon. Every lead was traced down, but all in vain.

The second day of the search, Jerrie Cobb, famed aviatrix, the first woman ever to qualify as an astronaut with NASA, and long a friend of JAARS, flew her twin-engine Islander into Yarina-cocha. She had heard the news and was coming to offer her services. She and Floyd teamed up together to fly search patterns, coordinated by the efficient Peruvian colonel who was in charge of the search procedure.

After eleven days of searching, it was obvious that no one could have survived the crash. The last place to search was the approach path to the airport at Tournavista. Floyd and the Peruvian comandante flew with Jerrie Cobb in the Islander, zig-zagging back and forth over the jungle. Nothing.

"That's the last clue we have," the comandante said as he got out at Tournavista. "Tomorrow I will go to Lima and tell them that we don't have any more leads."

Floyd and Jerrie flew back to Yarinacocha later that afternoon. After gassing up her plane, Jerrie turned to Floyd.

"Get me six men. I'm going flying."

"But you've been out all day, and there's no place left to search."

"I've still got an hour of daylight, and I'm not going to waste this good weather," the pretty aviatrix said with determination. "Get me some men to look out the windows. I'm going back up."

144

Jerrie was ready to take off when a phone call came into the flight office in the hangar. Floyd took it. It was a phone patch from a radio operator in Tournavista, and the connection was very poor. Floyd could catch only sketches of what the woman was saying.

"LANSA . . . emergency . . . send oxygen . . . Tournavista . . ."

"Hold it, Jerrie," Floyd shouted from his office. "We need you on an emergency flight to Tournavista. Something's going on down there."

It was a twenty-five-minute flight, and after Jerrie took off, Floyd went back to his house. Millie needed him as did their two younger sons, Kelly and Kevin. They had run down so many false leads over the twelve days that he no longer had any hope.

At 5:45, a call came over the radio in Floyd's house. It was from Jerrie.

"I'm taxiing out from Tournavista. I have a survivor on board —"

Floyd looked up at Millie who was standing behind him. Her fist was to her mouth, her knuckles white with tension. "Oh, Floyd — could it be . . . ?"

The two of them stood for a long time, embracing. Praying. Feeling God's presence. One survivor. Who was it? If there was one, could there be more?

Floyd could see the wisdom on the part of the comandante to have the survivor sent to Yarinacocha. They had medical facilities there. A good clinic. Fine doctors. To send the survivor to Pucallpa would trigger the hysteria in the city to catastrophic proportions.

Millie mounted the little motorcycle behind Floyd and tightly clutched his waist as the two of them bounced down the dirt path toward the hangar. Over the sound of his muffler, he could hear Jerrie's powerful Islander coming in on final approach. In a moment, they would know.

In the back seat, eyes bloodshot, face disfigured and swollen out of shape, arms and legs pocked with worm lesions, was a small, slender, emaciated seventeen-year-old girl in a tattered

145

mini-dress. Her name was Juliane Koepcke, daughter of a German ecology professor at San Marcos University in Lima.

As Floyd helped her out of the plane, he asked, *"¿Que idiomas habla usted?"* (What languages do you speak?)

"Hablo español" (I speak Spanish), she answered softly, her eyes darting around at the circle of faces. Then, in perfect English, she added, "I also speak English very well."

Millie could contain herself no longer. "Were there any other survivors? Anyone?"

Juliane looked deeply into Millie's face. "None," she said sadly. "No one but me."

It was Tuesday, January 5 — twelve days after the plane was lost. Millie Lyon thought she had cried herself out, but discovered there were still tears left. She fell weeping into the arms of her pilot husband. Now they would face it. Nathan was dead.

Dr. Francis Holston, one of the base physicians, took Juliane to the clinic. However, the word had already spread to Pucallpa that there was a survivor at Yarinacocha. Cars were pouring out of the town, heading down the dirt road toward the base twelve kilometers away. The police set up roadblocks, but some still got through. Dr. Holston felt it safer to move the girl next-door to the house of Jeanne Lindholm, one of the base nurses. There, with police protection, and under the tender ministry of Jeanne and Don, Juliane got her first night's sleep in almost two weeks. The next morning, she talked quietly to Jeanne, relating the incredible story of what the *Reader's Digest* later called Juliane's "Nightmare in the Jungle."

Juliane, who had just graduated from high school, was flying out of Lima with her mother to Pucallpa where her father would meet them to spend Christmas in their jungle hut. She was seated next to the window in the third row of seats from the rear of the plane. Her mother was beside her. When the seat-belt sign flashed on, she knew they were in for some rough weather. Then came the extreme turbulence which tossed the plane like a leaf in the wind.

The force of the elements was too much for the plane. There was a horrible cracking noise as the metal plates gave way and the wing struts pulled loose. What happened after that was too furious to describe, as all the fury of nature was unleashed against the Electra. With a mighty explosion, the plane disintegrated in midair. The left wing and the front part of the cabin were hurled far off to one side. The tail section, broken from the fuselage, was slung backward as the plane turned upside down. The cabin area was battered into a thousand pieces. Lifeless bodies were strewn from the wreckage to fall through the torrential rain into the soggy jungle below. Some rescuers surmised that Juliane might have ridden the tail section to the ground, but the ones who went in and brought out the bodies said that was impossible. The tail section was torn all to pieces. It was more likely that strapped in her seat, the young girl had free-fallen ten thousand feet into the jungle — perhaps cushioned by air currents. Surely protected by the hand of God.

For many aboard, it was probably the most terrifying of all moments. For a few — including Roger and Margery, David, Nathan, Harold and Haroldo — it must have been the moment of long-awaited glory. As Nan Beasley, a SIL translator, later wrote, "Imagine boarding a plane with the joyful anticipation of joining your family at home for Christmas, and finding that the approaching storm clouds all had golden linings; that you no longer needed to be lifted on silver wings — that the welcoming arms were your Father's!"

Harold Beaty, Base Director, reported that the five "changed destinations en route and went to meet their Heavenly Father instead."

The rain woke Juliane. It was late afternoon, and she was lying under a section of three seats turned upside down. There was no sign of her mother or any other passenger — or of the plane. All she could hear were the frogs croaking and the rain. She took stock of herself and didn't seem to be badly injured, although later medical examinations showed her right collarbone was fractured and she had sustained a severe concussion. Being very weak, she had spent the night lying under the seat half asleep — in shock.

The next morning, she crawled out from under the seat and staggered around in the jungle. She had lost one sandal, her clothes were torn, and she had very little protection from the thick swarms of insects that immediately attacked her, crawling into her cuts and scratches, where they laid their eggs. She wandered about the area for almost three days, finding other bits of wreckage and another section of three seats with three dead girls pinned under them. She knew, from the teaching of her parents, that it was not the big animals that were most dangerous, but rather the snakes and the insects.

Discovering a small stream, she began to follow it. She had heard a man who survived a plane crash in the jungle tell how he had followed a creek downstream until he found help. She knew the rivers in the tropical forest meandered and circled and that she could walk for miles along a bank and advance only a few yards toward her destination. Not only that, but the rivers were alive with mosquitoes — billions of them, all bloodthirsty. And alligators. She also knew the rivers swarmed with piranhas which would be attracted by the blood from her cuts, but she had no choice but to stay with the stream. It was her only hope.

Its banks were overgrown with tangled vines, making each step difficult. Sometimes she waded through the water because huge, rotten tree trunks barred her way. Other times, she swam in the stream.

Nights were the worst. There was always a rustling somewhere. Snakes. Something crawling on her. Spiders. Even the air seemed poison.

It continued to rain off and on, and she was often able to progress only a few hundred yards an hour as she fought her way through the tangled undergrowth. However, she continued to push her way through the vines and bushes, sometimes swimming, sometimes crawling, dodging the alligators, and resisting the delicious-looking fruit that hung from some of the trees. She knew that many things that looked good were poisonous.

A week passed, and her stream widened to a river. Her wounds were getting worse because of infection. Every time the flies — horseflies, bat flies — stung, they laid eggs in the deep sores, out of which maggots hatched. As they emerged with wagging heads out of her raw wounds, she bent her ring and used it to gouge them out of the wounds on her arms and legs, knowing they were literally eating her alive. She had to watch every step so she wouldn't step on a snake or a poisonous thornback crab.

On Sunday, January 2, ten days after the crash, she stumbled across a canoe pulled up on the bank of the river, and followed a path to small hut. On the dirt floor, wrapped in plastic, was an outboard motor. Nearby was a can of gasoline. Surely someone would be back. But when?

Terribly weak from the 110-degree heat and the other rigors of her long ordeal, Juliane spent the night in the shelter. When she awakened the next morning, she found the river had risen so high it was now flowing through the jungle, swirling around the trunks of the trees. It would be impossible to follow the bank any longer. She spent the morning gouging out more maggots with a sliver of palm wood. Then, about midafternoon, she heard voices. Three men burst into the shelter out of the pouring rain. They were hunters and lumbermen who had come after their boat. They knew about the crash — one of them had even flown in one of the search planes.

They poured gasoline in her sores and extracted about thirty white worms from under her skin. They shared some dried yucca with salt and sugar on it, and an egg.

The next morning, they took her on a six-hour ride downriver, through rapids and whirlpools, to the jungle settlement of Tournavista. The men who found her said they came to their hut only about once every three weeks.

Through Juliane's clear recollections, the search narrowed down and intensified the following morning with a number of planes, including Floyd copiloting with Jerrie Cobb in the Islander. Part of the wreckage was finally sighted by a Roman Catholic pilot in a "Wings of Hope" airplane. The following day, Jerrie sighted more of the wreckage, which was strewn over a five-mile area in the jungle. A ground party went in, but the jungle was so dense that bringing out the bodies (all of which were in bad states of decomposition) was very slow and difficult. Despite wild rumors that others survived the crash and lived to write messages on underwear in blood, men who knew the jungle best said it was impossible for anyone else to have survived. Only Juliane was spared.

Broken watches on the wrists of some of the victims indicated the plane had disintegrated in the air at 1:04 P.M. There was never any explanation as to why, all over the jungle, people reported having heard the plane flying at treetop level three hours later.

Don Adams, dentist at Yarinacocha, made positive identification of the five SIL members whose bodies were carried out of the jungle in plastic bags. Nathan Lyon and David Ericson were buried on January 12 in the small cemetery just behind the Lyons' house. Harold Davis and Roger and Margery Hedges were buried two days later. On January 16, 1972, a memorial service was held in the big assembly hall at Yarinacocha. Although the jungle around them was filled with mourning, the Wycliffe Bible Translators were putting into practice the teachings of the Word — that same Word they had been translating for more than twenty years. "In everything give thanks, for this is the will of God in Christ Jesus concerning you."

Following a brief time of remembrance for the passengers who had "changed destinations en route," the group of Translators, many with tears streaming down their faces, joined their voices, and with uplifted heads made the jungle echo with the sound of Handel's "Hallelujah Chorus."

It was the practice of the Machiguenga Indians, where Pat and Harold Davis had spent ten years, to run away into the jungle when a loved one died. Pat Davis changed that practice, however. She contacted the Indians in all the communities in which she and her husband had lived and worked — letting them know that even though Harold's smiling face would not be seen in the villages any longer, she and the two children would not run away. They would stay on to serve the people she loved so much.

In furrows of pain, good was beginning to germinate.

Chapter 12

Jungle Pentecost

Although tales of flying miracles abound in the jungle, none compare to the miracle of the spiritual renewal which took place at Yarinacocha following the LANSA crash.

As Jerry Elder, new Branch Director for SIL in Peru confessed, "For years the Wycliffe Bible Translators in Peru — and I in particular — had been self-reliant people. We were highly trained, skilled technicians. We knew our jobs and prided ourselves that we were the best in the world. Many of our linguists had PhD degrees. Our pilots, mechanics, and radio personnel were the finest on earth. We took pride in saying that we could handle any challenge that arose. If we needed to change an engine on a sandbar, we could do it. If we needed to analyze a new language, we could do it. Nothing was too hard for us.

"The LANSA crash changed all that. During those days of uncertainty, when our men were combing the jungles, hoping against hope our friends were still alive, something happened in the hearts of the people on base. Love, more love than we'd ever dare express, was poured out toward the families of those lost in the jungle. And when the bodies were finally returned to the base, that love increased. It spread to others on base and flowed out into the jungle toward our Indian friends. It leaped the boundaries of doctrinal differences, as we began to love and respect our Roman Catholic friends who were part of the same crisis. For the first time we began to understand some of the things God wanted us to learn."

Jerry told me about an evening communion service held some time after the crash. They didn't get around to serving the bread and wine until after midnight. It seemed that everybody on base — more than four hundred — had something to confess, and wanted to do it publicly. Men, women, and children rose to their feet, tearfully confessing such things as pride, selfishness, haughtiness, intolerance, envy, and resentment. On into the night the service went, until the people of God got right with God — and with their neighbors.

"We discovered," Base Director Harold Beaty later told me, "that we had been trying to do the Lord's work without the Lord's power, and it was killing us in the process. But when the power of the Holy Spirit came, bringing us love, joy, peace, and patience, God's work was no longer drudgery, it was fun."

JAARS Aviation Director Eddie Lind confessed to me there had always been a certain pride among the fraternity of jungle pilots. "We not only considered ourselves professionals, but we prided ourselves in our professionalism as well. Our motto, 'We do our best, and the Lord does the rest,' really meant we thought we could handle most emergencies. If we couldn't, we would call on God. But as the Holy Spirit began to be present in our lives, even the pilots started realizing that our best was not good enough. We were going to have to start leaning on God for everything."

Rister Jenkins, tough, highly skilled Director of Peru's JAARS operation, chuckled as he told me of the change that had swept through the hangar. He said the pilots stopped referring to God as their copilot and started letting Him fly in the left-hand seat. It was the difference between giving God directions and learning to take orders from Him.

At the Yarinacocha Bible conference, there was more confession. People admitted their hypocrisy, they confessed their fears and failures, they publicly cried out to God for help. The base divided itself into small groups, meeting on a weekly basis for body ministry. One day a month was set aside as a day of prayer when all work was kept at a minimum and everyone turned aside to pray for one another. When there was sickness, instead of first calling for one of the base doctors, they called upon God. Even the base physicians began laying hands on the sick — and seeing them healed.

I attended one of these small group meetings one night in the home of radio technician Paul Wyse and his wife Peggy. Also present were Wes and Eva Thiesen, veteran translators with the Bora tribe, and Gene and Marie Scott, translators with the Sharanahua people.

As we gathered that night—two veteran translator couples and a skilled radio technician—in Paul and Peggy's small jungle house, the only sounds were the night noises of the jungle which wafted through the screened windows.

"What's the procedure for the meeting tonight?" I asked.

"Tonight," Scotty said, "we're going to wash one another's feet."

It was the reenactment of the old practice followed by Jesus in the Upper Room on the night before His crucifixion. Seldom had I been in a place where the Holy Spirit was so evident as that night in that jungle house.

"I'm new at all this," Scotty confessed, as he gently placed his wife's foot in the basin. "I grew up a Methodist, and sometimes I thought a handshake was pretty intimate. Now I understand that if I am not willing to kneel before my brother — or my wife — and wash feet, I am not qualified to be used of God in other areas."

The Wyses came from a different background. They were Mennonites. "We used to have an annual foot-washing service," Paul said. "But this is different. This has more meaning; it is an act of love — of giving and receiving love. It's humiliating — but oh, it feels good in your heart."

From the day I arrived at Yarinacocha, I began hearing rumors about miracles among a tribe of Indians that lived along the Amazon River near the Brazilian-Colombian border. I heard sketches of almost unbelievable stories about meetings where the Indians were anointed with tongues of fire, where they spontaneously spoke in unknown tongues, stories of large water baptismal services, and even resurrections from the dead. I couldn't rest until I had checked out the stories.

The translator in that particular tribe, Jay Bruce,* was highly protective of his Indian friends. "They're simple, believing people," he told me. "But if the word leaks out concerning these miracles, the jungle will suddenly be filled with curiosity seekers. I'll let you hear the story only if you promise not to use the name of the tribe."

I agreed.

"I was home on furlough when the miracles started," he said. "However, my language informant, a young girl named Cecilia, was present. If you'll be at my house at four o'clock this afternoon, you can ask her questions, and I'll be glad to interpret for you." That's when I learned what actually happened the night the fire fell in the jungle.

Cecilia's light brown face framed the most beautiful sparkling eyes I had ever seen. Barely four feet tall, she came up to my armpit when we stood side by side. About twenty years old, she was staying with the Bruces while Jay finished some additional lan-

---

*At the request of the translator, this is a pseudonym.

guage study. Her language was quite nasal, and some of her words could be pronounced without opening her mouth — the sounds coming almost entirely through her nose.

"She may be a little shy about answering questions," Jay said, running slender fingers through his curly blond hair.

Cecilia's bashfulness disappeared the moment she began to talk, however. Bubbling over with the excitement of once again sharing what happened during these exciting experiences, she began to talk with such rapidity and animation that on several occasions Jay had to slow.her down in order to keep up with the interpretation.

"When Señor Bruce left our village on the Amazon to return to the United States," she began, "we had only a handful of people who were attending the church meetings at night. Señor Bruce urged us to keep reading our Bibles, to attend the services, and to keep the little church house in good repair.

"He had been gone a few months when on Christmas Eve afternoon, the year of the big airplane crash, three men walked into our village. They first came to the house of our pastor, Leonardo. The leader of the three was an old 'grandfather Indian' who said he could not read or write, but he said he loved the Lord and wanted to preach to the people that night. He said God was getting ready to do a 'great work' throughout the jungle. Leonardo said it would be difficult to get the people together for a meeting in the church house. Perhaps it would be better if they gathered outside on the soccer field.

"The three men left Leonardo and went to where the men were having a big work party. 'What do you say we have a meeting tonight?' the old man said. 'I'll tell you all about God's Word.'

"The people were not interested, and many turned away. Only a few — maybe thirty or fifty — came to the meeting. 'Tonight we don't have many people here,' the old man said. 'But tomorrow night we are going to have a meeting with everybody.'

"Nobody really believed him, and as he began to preach, there was much argument about whether he was preaching truth or not. Some said he was a false preacher. Others said he was preaching the same message that Señor Bruce had taught us. Even though the old man could not read, he had memorized long passages from the Bible — many, many chapters.

"Halfway through the meeting, storm clouds began to gather overhead, blotting out the stars and moon. We could hear the rumble of thunder as the storm moved in from the south. Big streaks of lightning came from the sky, and rain began to fall. Most of the people jumped up and said, 'Hey, I'm going home.'

"The old man turned and held up his hand. 'No,' he shouted. 'Do not leave. God wants to do something here, and that rain isn't going to fall. Let's pray it won't rain.'

"Everyone thought he was crazy. But the old man raised his hands toward heaven. In a loud voice he cried, 'Clouds go away — in the name of Jesus.' Immediately the clouds went away, and the stars and moon came out again.

"When the people saw *that* happen, they knew it was God. They got all excited and started listening to what the man was saying. He told them to come back the next afternoon, and God would really speak to them.

"The next evening, Christmas afternoon, we had another service. Word had spread through the village, and almost eight hundred people came to the meeting. The little church building would not hold us all, so many of the people had to stand around outside. Again the old man preached a very long time, telling the people that a mighty revival would come through the jungle just as it did among Christians in the Book of Acts. As he spoke, many of the people began to weep, feeling sorry they had hated God's Word. The young people, especially, fell to their knees and asked God to forgive them.

"Everyone was weeping and asking God to forgive them when a man sitting beside me suddenly fell off the bench onto the dirt floor. First we thought he had fainted, but then we saw he was not breathing. He was dead. The men carried him outside and tried to bring him back to life. They worked for an hour, but he was dead. We have seen many dead people and can tell if someone is dead or not. His skin was cold, and his arms and legs had begun to get stiff. The men started to take him to a house to prepare a funeral when the old man cried out, 'The Lord is with us now. He is going to perform a miracle so all will believe.'

"The pastor, Leonardo, shouted out also. 'That is right. I believe it, too.' Then he called for the three strangers, and they put their hands on the dead man and began to pray. Very slowly, the man got up. All the people began to praise the Lord. The man said, 'I'm no longer a part of this world. I have been with Jesus.'

"Then suddenly a great star came down out of heaven and broke into many pieces and sat on the heads of many believers. Those who had the fire on their heads began to speak in unknown tongues, praising God with new words. At that moment, the building lifted up and began to shake. Everyone began to dance. Our weeping had changed to dancing and praise.

"The meeting lasted for many hours. Sometime after midnight, Leonardo said, 'We should have a baptismal service tomorrow.' So we had a baptismal service in the Amazon River the next day. Many people came, and over a hundred were baptized, including my father and mother. That night, we had a communion service, and the people spent a long time thinking about God and what God was doing for them. There was such *love* in the village. For the first time, we invited other people to our houses for eating. All over the village, you could hear families singing together and praising the Lord together.

"The young people especially were on fire for Jesus. Six of us took three canoes and went down the river thirty miles toward Brazil to a village where there were no believers. We went to every house in the village and told the people about Jesus Christ. They laughed at us. They threw rotten fruit at us and told us to go home, but we sat up all night in the middle of the village, praying.

We were there four days, and when we left, forty people in that village had accepted Jesus Christ.

"When we returned to our village, we learned that the three men had disappeared into the jungle. They never came back, but ever since then, whenever we pray for the sick, they are always healed."

Cecilia's face was beaming as she told the story. She went on to tell me how Leonardo had become a mighty jungle apostle. He had been used to start many churches and had even come to Yarina-cocha and preached the Gospel to the missionaries.

"The old Indian?" I asked. "What was his name?"

Cecilia thought for a moment and then looked over at Jay as if to ask, "Should I tell him?" Jay nodded his head, and Cecilia spoke again, pausing for Jay to interpret.

"It probably doesn't mean anything; many people have Bible names. He said his name was Gabriel."

Jay's voice was shaking as he finished the interpretation. I stopped making notes and sat, spellbound.

I looked at Cecilia's bare feet. They were thick and club-shaped, coated with the dust of the path. They had walked many miles. Strong feet. With toes spread wide, as human toes were meant to spread. Not crushed and pointed from wearing fashionable high-heeled shoes. For some reason, I wanted to wash them. I saw them as the kind of feet Paul must have been thinking about when he quoted Isaiah's *"How beautiful are the feet of them that preach the gospel of peace, and bring glad tidings of good things!"*

Jay cleared his throat and picked up the story.

"The first night back in the village after we returned from furlough, the bell rang, and we went to church. The village generator was not working, so the lights were very dim. Even so, I could hardly believe my eyes. They had not only widened the building but had lengthened it and put in a new floor. We hardly recognized the place. And it was packed with people, sitting on the floors, standing around the walls — almost nine hundred of them.

And such singing! We had been gone for almost a year, and all this took us by surprise.

"A young man got up to speak and launched into a magnificent sermon on the power of God. I blinked and looked at him through the dim light. It was a little guy who used to slink around the village, so shy he wouldn't even speak to anyone. Now here he was standing in front of this huge crowd, preaching with apostolic authority. He was saying his new power to preach came when he was filled with the Holy Spirit."

Jay paused, obviously flustered, since his theology did not have room for any such experience. However, committed to the truth, he continued.

"I had never believed that healing and the other gifts of the Spirit were for the church today. I still have problems, but I can no longer deny that God is healing the sick — especially in our tribe.

"One day, after church, an Indian I had never seen before came up to me and said, 'Sir, do you pray for sick people?'

"I tried to put him off, but he wouldn't listen. 'I have a sick lady at my house who cannot walk,' he said. 'I'd like you to come and pray that she might be healed.'

"I told him I'd come by the next day, but I didn't go. The following morning, I was at the sawmill helping a group with a new piece of machinery. I looked up and there was that man, just standing there staring at me. He stood there all day. He never said a word—he just stood and looked. At the close of the day, I agreed to go home with him.

"It was almost dark when I reached the house. Inside, I saw an old woman, just skin and bones, crumpled on a palm-thatch mat. They dragged her mat outside so I could see her. She was horribly twisted and crippled by arthritis. The man said friends had dragged her through the jungle for many miles, on a stretcher between two poles, because they heard there was healing power in the village. She had not walked in two years.

160

"I had no faith at all," Jay confessed. "I told the old woman not to be disappointed if she didn't get well when I prayed for her. I told her my mother had arthritis, and the only thing that helped her was heat. After having said all this, I put my hands on her head and prayed a short prayer for healing. Then I left. Quickly.

"Two weeks later, I was sitting in the church building on a Sunday morning when I felt someone reach across the aisle and tap me on the leg.

" 'Hola, hermano' (Hello, brother), a woman said.

"I looked up, and it was that same old woman, smiling a big, toothless smile.

" 'How did you get here?' I exclaimed.

" 'Oh, I walked,' she said.

" 'But it's more than a kilometer,' I objected.

" 'I know,' the old woman grinned. 'But the day after you prayed for me, I felt better, so I stood up. The next day, I took a few steps. Now this morning, I have walked all the way to church. *Jesús Cristo es maravilloso.*'

"Her legs were actually beginning to put on new flesh," Jay said. "Where once there had been only brown, wrinkled skin covering brittle bones, new muscles were growing. Since that time, the village has become known throughout the jungle as a center of healing."

I looked at Jay. "Why do you think such a thing could happen among the Indians, when it so seldom happens in our 'civilized' nations?"

He leaned back in his wicker chair and closed his eyes. "Perhaps," he said slowly, "it is because the Indians are innocent enough to believe the Bible we have translated and left behind."

His conclusion was simple. Coming from the lips of a man who, by his own admission, had trouble believing made it ring with truth. Deep in my heart, I knew he was right. Perhaps when the rest of us believed as the Indians believed — when we became as little children — Pentecost would come also to our jungle.

Chapter 13

The Uttermost Part of the Earth

If I take the wings of the morning, and dwell in the uttermost parts of the sea; Even there shall thy hand lead me, and thy right hand shall hold me.

Psalm 139: 9-10

It was not quite five in the morning. All night long I had slept in the hold of the stuffy seaplane as it rocked gently on the jungle river, tied against an eight-foot mud cliff on the Camisea River near a Machiguenga Indian village. Twice during the night, Paul Bartholomew, flight engineer on the Catalina, had gotten up to check the moorings. The river was rising rapidly, and if the lines were not loosened almost hourly, they could pull the plane under the raging water.

Aside from the lapping water and the occasional CA-THUMP! of a floating log banging against the hull of the plane, the only sound was the heavy breathing of the two men beside me. Dr.

162

Larry Dodds, redheaded young physician with a bushy moustache, was a former combat medic in Vietnam. Now graduated from medical school, he had committed his life as a missionary doctor at Yarinacocha. This was his orientation trip, acquainting him with the various Indian villages and people. On the other side of me, curled up on a bench cushion, was the Canadian, Ralph Borthwick, who, I decided, could sleep anywhere at any time.

I longed for that gift. I tried to turn over on my air mattress but got tangled up in the mosquito net. Why was it, I wondered, that the hours just before dawn were always the longest? I had spent most of the night scratching — almost frantically at times. Dr. Dodds had warned me to douse my legs liberally with insect repellent before getting out in the high grass the day before. Now I was beginning to believe the made-in-USA repellent served to attract the Amazon chiggers. Unable to sleep, I turned on my flashlight and started counting. I stopped at one hundred thirty-one bites, all located between ankle and knee on my right leg alone. Unbelievable. I didn't have the heart to look at the left leg, which was even worse. I glanced at my watch. Another thirty minutes until sunrise. I wondered if I could keep my sanity that long. Pilots could pray for sandbars in the river if they wanted; I prayed for relief from the horrible itching as I listened to the soft patter of rain on the overhead panels of the big plane. It sounded as if we might be trapped in the jungle for still another day.

Except for the bites, I had enjoyed these four days in the jungle of southern Peru. Leaving Yarinacocha early Monday morning, we had expected to spend one night with a tribe and return the following afternoon. Now, on Friday, I was waiting for the sun to rise, and we were still four hundred miles from home. Bad weather had forced us down twice, and we still had a trip to make over to the Brazilian border. It looked like we *might* get back to home base by Saturday — if the rain stopped.

I remembered a childhood adage as I drifted back to sleep. "If it rains before seven, it will stop before eleven." I hope so,

I thought. And maybe I can borrow some fingernail polish from Evelyn Elder and suffocate these little beggars on my legs and ankles before I scratch my skin off.

The first day out had been good. George Woodward was flying left seat, with Ralph as copilot. Bart was flight engineer, and Larry Dodds and I were going along for the ride. As we started our approach for the Camisea River, I took a seat in one of the big Plexiglas "bubbles" near the tail. As we landed on the river, a huge gush of spray covered the bubble — pretty spectacular from my vantage point. George kept the plane on the step with three-quarter power in order to negotiate a sharp turn in the river where the current could sweep us into the bank. Then the power was off, and I saw the big wheels letting down out of the side of the plane. They produced the drag necessary to bring us to a stop before we plowed our nose into the steep mud bank ahead.

Bart was up on the nose, and Dr. Dodds had scrambled up on the wing to cast a line to Jerry Hamill, SIL teacher who had replaced Harold Davis among the Machiguengas. We quickly unloaded all supplies from the plane and within the hour we were off again, this time headed for an isolated military outpost in the Andes—Mazamari.

Our plan was to load more than eight hundred gallons of gasoline into the wing tanks of the Catalina and then return to Camisea where the gas would be unloaded and left for JAARS planes flying in southern Peru. The base commander supplied soldiers to roll the heavy drums out to the airstrip where we pumped the gas up to the wing tanks overhead. By the time we had finished our sweaty, back-breaking job of pumping and then loading the empty barrels in the back of the Cat, it was dark. We spent the night in a tiny cabin beside a roaring river that cascaded down out of the Andes.

It was raining the next morning, so after spending about an hour in a Bible study and prayer time, we checked the plane and then wandered around the mountain post.

The clouds were still on the mountains the second morning, and Bart entertained some of the troops with a demonstration of his remote-control model airplane. Even the base commander, a handsome Peruvian major, came out on the airstrip and "oohed and aahed" as Bart put the little gasoline-powered plane through a series of loops, stalls, and strafing runs on the troops.

By noon we could see some blue holes at the end of the long valley. George and Ralph felt the weather would probably be clear over the jungle, so we packed up to take off. Waving good-bye to our soldier friends, I climbed the ladder into the bubble and pulled the hatch shut behind me. Fighting my way over the empty gasoline drums to the cockpit area, I hung on to a bulkhead as we bounced off the runway and into the thin mountain air. An hour later, we were throwing spray on the Camisea River as once again we nosed into the mudbank.

Jerry was waiting for us, along with about a hundred Indians. After tying securely to the bank, we started the filthy sweaty task of rolling the empty barrels up the slippery cliff. Then, using a small gasoline-powered pump, we emptied the excess gasoline out of the wing and by way of a long hose up the bank, refilled the barrels. Anyone who thinks being a jungle pilot, or a jungle mechanic, or a jungle doctor, or a jungle writer, is all glamor should have been with us that hot, sticky afternoon in the Amazon basin.

Trapped once again by darkness (federal law in Peru prohibited all night flying over the jungle), we made plans to bunk down in the Catalina before leaving the next morning for Esperanza on the Rio Purus near the Brazilian border. There we would pick up a number of Indian passengers and finally return to Yarinacocha — four days late.

Just at dusk, Jerry, Dr. Dodds (with his black medical bag), and I walked through the village to visit a sick Indian girl. Down a deep ravine, we crossed a roaring stream on a tiny, slippery log and then fought our way through a maze of banana trees and up a steep hill to a small Indian house.

It was almost dark when we entered. Bits of yucca, banana peelings, and scraps of bones littered the floor which, like the walls, was made of some kind of flattened reeds and stalks. Dozens of pear-shaped gourds filled the corners and space under the eaves. The gourds contained an assortment of things — water, beads, needles, corn, and a nest of birds, obviously being fattened for the pot. Bows and arrows were stuck among the rafters; an array of palm-fiber baskets was suspended from the roof, which held a mirror, a spoon, carved bone needles, and other family "valuables." A bunch of black wild-turkey feathers for a future fire-fan hung in a corner. Another colored bunch of feathers for arrows was stuck in the palm-thatched roof. In a circular frame suspended in the corner of the room, fish and salt were kept out of reach of the dogs. A mosquito net, change of clothes, and a tattered blanket were dumped untidily on the sleeping platform.

As I stood in the door, waiting for my eyes to accustom themselves to the dimness, I became aware of several crouching children, huddled closely in the dim light, solemnly surveying us from against the far wall. In the middle of the floor, lying on a straw mat, was a young girl who looked about sixteen, but was perhaps older than that. Indians do not seem to show their age. Her father, who had met us at the door, had slipped back outside.

Dr. Dodds knelt beside the girl, pulled her cotton blouse away from her stomach, and placed his stethoscope against her bare flesh. Her face remained expressionless. He thumped his fingers on her ribs and chest, then mashed hard against the stomach area. She winced, but made no sound.

He probed again with his fingers. "¿Duele?" (Hurt?)

"Si," she said, her face expressionless.

"¿Aqui?" (Here?) He poked in a different place.

"Muy!" she said through gritted teeth.

Larry turned to Jerry Hamill and handed him a small bottle of pills. "Tell her father to give her two of these every morning and two every evening until they are gone."

Jerry shook his head. "Machiguengas have no concept of numbers. The girl can count, but the father is liable to give her ten in the morning and two at night. All he knows is singular and plural — and plural is any number from two to a million."

Dr. Dodds scratched his head. "Well, tell him to give her one every morning and one every evening."

Jerry smiled. "Okay, he can handle that."

Then, beckoning to Jerry and me to join him, Dr. Dodds knelt beside the girl again. Reaching out, he gently put his hands on her body.

"In the name of the Lord Jesus Christ, I command every evil spirit in this place to go."

Then, praying softly, he said. "Lord, I ask You to heal my little sister in the name of Your Son, Jesus. Amen!"

The young girl looked up and smiled. She had not been able to understand the words of the prayer, but she understood the gesture of love. And, if I was not mistaken, she had felt the touch of God as well. I doubted seriously whether she would even need the antibiotics now.

By noon the next day, my legs still itching and my eyes drooping from lack of sleep, we were off the river and winging our way on a long eastward crossover toward the Brazilian border. Jerry Hamill was with us on this leg, returning home to his wife Eunice and his four children. After a three-hour flight, George landed the big plane on the soggy grass runway at Esperanza.

We got out and stretched our legs. I walked over to the edge of the jungle clearing and inspected the six or seven part-frame, part-thatched houses. Thirty minutes later, I heard the drone of a JAARS Helio and watched as Eddie Lind put his little plane down in a graceful landing. Five Indians got out. Eddie waved and took off again. He'd return early in the morning with five more from another village. All ten would fly back with us to Yarinacocha. They were candidates to work in a language school which would start the next week and run for thirty days. Most of them were carrying everything they owned with them, strapped to their backs in mesh bags or stuffed into skin pouches which they carried over their shoulders. One woman had a tiny black monkey clinging tightly to the hair on the back of her head — much like a hat. The Indians disappeared into the jungle for the night, leaving the air mattresses and seat cushions in the plane for their white brothers to sleep on.

That evening, five of us — Ralph, Bart, Jerry, Dr. Dodds, and I — decided to go swimming in the Rio Purus.

"Leave your clothes up here on the bank," Bart said, "then follow us down the cliff."

The river was swollen and running a dull red in color. But oppressive heat, swarming gnats, and the itch of the chigger-bites on my legs made even that rushing stream of liquid mud look enticing. I finished stripping to the skin and had just started down the slippery mud bank when I had a distinct impression I was being watched. Turning, I saw about twenty-five deadpan Indian women and children staring at me from the brink of the cliff. It was too late now; I was already exposed. I waved and slid down the thirty-foot embankment to the red mud below.

The mud at the bottom of the cliff was a gooey ankle-deep bog. Each step made a giant suction sound as I pulled one foot out and moved it forward, letting it slowly sink in again. I finally reached the place where my friends were already cavorting and found, to my surprise, that despite its color, the water seemed clean and pure. Dr. Dodds told me I could probably drink it with no ill effects.

Ralph had a bar of soap which he passed around. When Bart dropped it, we all made a splashing lunge for it as it disappeared under the red water. I heard laughing and looked up. I had forgotten all about our audience. They were doubled over in mirth, pointing and howling in delight at all those white bottoms sticking out of the red water as we grappled for the soap.

We waded back through the mud, clambered up the dirt bank, grasping at tufts of grass and roots, and finally got to the top where we had left our clothes. The women were still there, their faces once again expressionless. They watched solemnly as we put our muddy feet into our pants legs and headed back toward the air strip, shoes and socks in hand.

The sun was sinking, and the jungle breeze felt good as it blew through my hair. The cool water and the caked mud had eased the itching on my legs. I could smile again.

As night fell over the Amazon jungle, I climbed up on the tail assembly of the big Catalina to finish drying and to feast my eyes on the sunset. A thousand miles from the nearest factory smokestack, I could see into forever. The western sky, silhouetting the tall jungle trees — palms, mahoganies, teaks, and trees which defied name or description — was bathed in streaks of red, purple, mauve, orange, and yellow. It stretched from horizon to horizon in indescribable splendor.

As the night sounds began to filter in from the jungle, Jerry Hamill joined me on the Cat. We sat and talked, our feet dangling off the leading edge of the elevator.

"Several years ago," he said, "a group of geodetic surveyors officially designated Esperanza as the most remote location in South America. They described it as 'the uttermost part of the jungle.' And here we are — with the Word of God."

I thought of the words of the Psalmist, who quoted the promise of God: "Ask of me, and I shall give thee the heathen for thine inheritance, and the uttermost parts of the earth for thy possession" (Ps. 2:8).

A quiver of excitement ran down my spine. Tomorrow I would return to Yarinacocha. The next day I'd be in Lima, and then back to the States. Tonight, however, I was seated in the uttermost part of the earth. Prophecy, spoken three thousand years before, was literally coming true. And I was here with the men God was using to bring it to pass.

169

Chapter 14

Ask and Ye Shall Receive

Ye have seen what I did unto the Egyptians, and how I
bare you on eagles' wings, and brought you unto myself.

Exodus 19:4

Shortly after the Billy Graham Crusade closed in Charlotte,
North Carolina in 1958, Lawrence Routh, Greensboro, North
Carolina businessman, paid a visit to Ed Darling with the Graham
party. For some time Routh had been trying to locate facilities in
Greensboro for a JAARS training center. Unsuccessful, he asked
Darling to contact Henderson Belk, a wealthy Charlotte businessman who had helped in the Graham crusade in Charlotte. Routh
hoped that Belk, who along with his brothers owned a large chain
of department stores, might help JAARS locate a training center
in the Charlotte area. It was a long shot, but Routh had learned
from Uncle Cam that you never receive unless you ask.

Belk caught the vision. He arranged for JAARS to use a big,
vacant warehouse at an old Army ammunition depot, and got
permission for them to use Charlotte's Carpenter Airport for training purposes.

As soon as it looked like Charlotte would become the training center JAARS so badly needed, three families moved up from Peru to get things started. They were pilots Larry Montgomery and Merrill Piper and their wives, and mechanic Les Bancroft and his family. They were joined by Bill Nyman from another department of the Wycliffe organization. Vernon Patterson, a friend of Uncle Cam's, volunteered to introduce them to the Christian community in Charlotte.

Patterson arranged some luncheon meetings at the Charlotte-town Mall and sent letters to a select group of people, inviting them as guests. A short time later, a prayer rally was held at the old warehouse. About a hundred and twenty-five interested people showed up, and Merrill Piper put on a demonstration with the Helio Courier, landing on the dirt road in front of the warehouse. The city of Charlotte was becoming interested.

During the next two years, a number of Wycliffe missionaries on their way to the field migrated to Charlotte looking for temporary housing. Belk allowed them to use an old home, where his father had been raised, as a group house. Here the missionaries lived, had offices, and held prayer meetings before going on to the foreign fields.

By 1960, when it was obvious the Lord had chosen the Charlotte area as a center for this kind of ministry, Patterson once again contacted Henderson Belk.

"What JAARS really needs is a place where they can have their own airfield, where their missionaries can come and stay for a short period of training, and where those engaged in the work can live with their families in a Christian colony." It was another instance of asking in order to receive.

Belk donated two hundred fifty-six acres of land south of Charlotte near the little town of Waxhaw. Montgomery, Piper, and Bancroft flew out in the Helio and landed in a hayfield. There the three of them knelt and claimed the gift of land for God's outreach to the tribes.

Uncle Cam made the new JAARS Center his stateside home. A radio station, communicating with all the foreign fields, and a radio lab to build and repair equipment were established. A printing office was built, along with a headquarters building. Before long, an entire community had been formed, and the JAARS Board, with Lawrence Routh as president, asked Harold Goodall — director of the work in Peru — to return to the States as Executive Director for JAARS

While all this was going on, a young pilot from Pennsylvania, Bernie May, was growing up with the JAARS program in Peru. Only God knew that Bernie was being groomed for the day when he would assume the helm of the entire JAARS program as Executive Director.

Training for such a position is always painful—and long. A former U.S. president once remarked, "When God wants to grow a squash, He takes only two months. But when He grows an oak tree, He takes forty years." Bernie May was no squash.

Having met the JAARS requirements — a commercial pilot's license, an A & P (airframe and powerplant) license, training at both the Summer Institute of Linguistics at Norman, Oklahoma, and the Jungle Camp in Mexico, and having secured promises from friends and churches that they would support him financially, Bernie and Nancy arrived in Peru in 1956. It was while flying the Aeronca that Bernie became vividly aware of the provision of God which was his for the asking.

The float Aeronca was slow—eighty to ninety miles an hour at the most. Once the pilot left his river runway and started his slow crossover, there was always the nagging feeling that he should have stayed back home in Pennsylvania. One hot April morning, Bernie took off in an Aeronca with two girl translators for a remote jungle location. He was at three thousand feet over the Ucayali basin and was just starting to relax when things went wrong.

Suddenly, the control wheel began to shudder in his hands. It was the same kind of shimmy he had experienced driving an old

Ford back in Pennsylvania—the kind that comes when the front wheels start waving at each other. Of course, an Aeronca didn't have front wheels, just floats. But the vibration was identical, and it was getting worse. The control wheel almost shook out of his hand.

All at once, the plane gave a giant shudder—and stalled. The nose dropped over, and the plane plummeted toward the river below in an almost vertical dive—the engine racing at full RPMs.

The two girls screamed, and Bernie pulled back on the controls as hard as he could. Nothing. It was as if his elevator had fallen off. He was heading straight down. At two thousand feet, the plane suddenly pulled out of the dive and back into level flight. There was no indication as to what had caused the problem.

For the next two minutes, Bernie frantically checked every dial on the instrument panel. Everything was normal. He wiggled the control surfaces. The plane responded perfectly. He turned to the girls and gave a crooked smile.

"Lots of things happen in the jungle that don't happen in Pennsylvania," he said halfheartedly.

He put the plane in a climb and started back to his previous altitude. He was at twenty-four hundred feet when the front floats started waving at each other again. The buffeting grew worse, until the instrument panel almost shook loose. Bernie did everything he knew to do—he hung on. Then it happened again. The airspeed indicator started to unwind, and suddenly the nose went over. The plane was once again in a screaming, terrifying, vertical dive toward the wide jungle river below.

At twelve hundred feet, with Bernie tugging desperately at the controls, the plane pulled out of the dive and flew level again. By this time, the girls were in near panic. It was their first time to fly with the young pilot, and they weren't too sure he wasn't doing all this on purpose. Bernie reached for the mike. He didn't know what was going on either, but he knew he would feel a lot more secure if the people back at Yarinacocha were sharing his fright.

Before he could punch the button on the mike, the vibration started for the third time, moving from the tail toward the wings, and suddenly the airspeed dropped off, and the plane nosed over in another steep dive. All Bernie could see through the windshield was the river rushing up to meet him. Even though he had the wheel all the way back to his stomach, the plane continued its vertical dive toward the water. He prayed. It wasn't a long prayer, filled with thees and thous. It was a simple, "Help, Lord!" And that was all he needed to ask.

Just feet off the water, the plane responded to the controls. With a mighty roar, it pulled out of the dive back into level flight. But three times was enough. There was no more room for another thousand-foot power dive. Bernie chopped the throttle and splashed his floats on the broad surface of the Ucayali.

The Aeronca taxied to the bank, and Bernie tied it to a small tree. The two girls, still trembling from their harrowing descent, climbed out and rested on the shore. Bernie remembered reading an Air Force survival book that suggested the first thing a downed pilot should do was smoke a cigarette to relax. Being a nonsmoker, Bernie carried bananas. So while the plane rocked gently on the Ucayali, Bernie sat on the bank eating a banana and thanking God for answering prayers—even short ones.

Finishing his banana, he started a bolt-by-bolt inspection of the tail section. He was sure the trouble was a broken hinge or loose elevator, but he found nothing wrong there.

Starting at the prop and working back, in minutes he spotted the trouble. The wing fabric on top of the cabin area had peeled loose where it was attached to the windshield. In level flight, the suction that formed on top of the wing had pulled the fabric upward four or five inches. This deflected the air from the tail of the plane, preventing the elevator from responding to the controls, and causing the plane to stall. As the plane nosed over in its vertical dive, the suction on the wing decreased, allowing the fabric to snap back into place. With the air once again flowing over the elevator, the plane had returned to level flight. Then the process started all over again.

Bernie patched the fabric with a roll of tape, and then made some small incisions with his knife so if it pulled loose again, it would tear rather than block the flow of air over the tail. Two hours later, they were safely back at the base. As one of the older pilots asked Bernie that night, "How will you ever know God takes care of you unless you find yourself in a position where you can't take care of yourself?"

It was a good lesson—but one Bernie fervently hoped he had learned well enough so it would not have to be repeated.

Bernie and Nancy returned to the States on furlough after four years in Peru. He used the time to complete work on his instrument rating and get his multi-engine ticket. Back in Peru, he built up twin-engine time on the Catalina. He was, without being aware of it, being groomed for the DC-3 which God knew was about to fall into JAARS' hands.

Thus it was during his second furlough that Bernie spoke to the Sunday school of the First Presbyterian Church in Pittsburgh and suddenly JAARS owned a DC-3. Bernie obtained his ATR (Aircraft Transport Rating) and eventually became the captain on the DC-3 in Ecuador. However, before sending Bernie back to South America, God had still another seed that needed to be planted in Pennsylvania.

The money had been raised to purchase the DC-3, and Bernie took the big plane to Reading, near his home, for an annual inspection. A number of men from Bernie's home church, the Marcus Hook Baptist Church, volunteered to polish the plane. They worked in shifts, half a dozen of them coming out to the big hangar in the morning to paint and polish while another group worked from dusk until almost midnight.

One afternoon, about four o'clock, the president of a local construction company landed his personal Helio Courier at the Reading airport. Walking through the hangar on his way to his car, he saw the crew of men crawling all over the big DC-3, working, laughing, and occasionally saying, "Praise the Lord!" Since most hangars aren't filled with spiritual expletives—especially at four o'clock in the afternoon—he turned aside to see this great wonder.

The men used the opportunity to tell the pilot all about the Wycliffe Bible Translators, JAARS, the DC-3, and their hometown jungle pilot, Bernie May. A committed Christian, the man was impressed. He was even more impressed when he learned JAARS was using Helios in the jungles, for he personally owned the first Helio Courier ever made—Helio number one.

Six years later, Bernie was home on another fulough—this time from Ecuador. He had just completed an around-the-world trip for JAARS, during which time he had visited fifteen Wycliffe bases. It was obvious JAARS needed more planes. Especially Helios. It was a matter of asking again. Bernie, Nancy, and the three boys were back in Pennsylvania when a phone call came through from the construction company president.

Bernie knew nothing of the encounter in the Reading hangar six years before. But he immediately recognized the call as an answer to his prayer.

"If you'll stop by my place, I have an airplane I'd like to donate to JAARS," the man said. "It's a Helio Courier, serial number one."

When he handed Bernie the keys to his airplane, which was in excellent condition, Bernie asked if he didn't want a tax receipt. After all, JAARS was a nonprofit corporation.

"No," he said seriously, "when I promised God I would give my plane away, I didn't tie any strings to it. I just want JAARS to have the airplane."

Ten minutes later, Bernie was on his way with Helio number one which today is still in use in the JAARS training program.

Working with JAARS, Bernie found that God's miracles were

not limited to the airways. They also occurred on the ground. A vivid example was the miracle of the runway at Waxhaw.

For several years, the JAARS pilots had flown their planes off the bouncy dirt strip which was marked on the Charlotte sectional chart as "Townsend Field." The AOPA Airport Directory listed it unceremoniously, and added a cryptic comment: "Runway 4-22/3,000 dirt. Obstructions: trees both ends. Caution: reported slippery when wet, unmarked ditches on both sides." If JAARS had tried to scare people away intentionally, they couldn't have done a better job.

Despite the need for a new runway at the JAARS Center, there were other needs with higher priorities—planes, pilots, and airstrips on the mission fields. However, at times, things were almost critical at Townsend Field. During a rainy spell, the field often had to be shut down, sometimes for several weeks at a time. Training programs had to be postponed. Highly skilled pilots and mechanics often had to spend valuable time working on the runway. Yet it would cost almost a hundred thousand dollars to have it paved. Only God could provide funds like that.

One December afternoon, just before Christmas, Bernie was standing beside the muddy strip. The planes had not been able to get off the ground for three days, and the training program was temporarily stopped. A group of teenage boys who lived on the Center, missionary kids, including Bernie's oldest son, Bern, sauntered past.

One of the boys looking at the messy runway said, "Uncle Bern, it's too bad this runway isn't paved."

Bernie knew prayer worked in the jungles. Why not here? "Do you boys believe in miracles?" he asked.

They looked at each other and then looked at him. Was this some kind of a joke?

"I mean it. Would you boys like to see a miracle with your own eyes? God knows how important this runway is to our work. Why don't we stand right here and ask Him to pave it? Let's ask Him to pave the whole three thousand feet. Let's ask Him to pave that taxiway in front of the hangar, too."

The boys started to edge away. It seemed they had stirred up a fanatic. Bernie was serious, however. Bowing his head, he led them in prayer.

"Lord, You know our situation. You know what we are trying to do. You know we have more pilot candidates coming than ever before. You know how hard the training is, how tight the schedule. Lord, we want to reach all the tribes in the world with Your Holy Word. I ask You to pave this runway for us. In the name of Jesus. Amen."

Bernie opened his eyes. The boys were staring in dismay. They had never heard anyone pray like that before. And, as Bernie later reflected, neither had he. But the prayer had been prayed, and he believed God would answer it.

"Now I want you boys to get on your knees and thank Him for paving the runway," Bernie said, as they continued to look at him incredulously.

"But it isn't paved, dad," young Bern spoke up, hoping to salvage some respect from his friends. "How can we thank God for a paved runway when it's still mud and holes?"

"Just thank Him anyway. Thank Him because He said if we ask we would receive."

"Yes, sir," the boys said, edging away. "It's been good talking to you, Uncle Bern. Yes, sir, we're sure glad we stopped to talk to you." And they were gone.

A month later, Harold Goodall, who was at that time the director of operations, suggested Bernie might want to call Harold Shirley of the Dickerson Construction Company in nearby Monroe, North Carolina. Dickerson had a big asphalt paving business, and maybe they could help.

The appointment was set up for four-thirty Wednesday afternoon. However, when Bernie arrived at the office, the secretary shook her head. "He's been tied up in an important meeting since eleven," she explained. "I don't see any chance for you to see him. Unless you just want to sit here and wait."

"Well, I think God's business is pretty important, too," Bernie said. "I can pray here just as well as somewhere else."

The secretary gave him a strange look, but nodded toward a chair in the waiting room.

At six-thirty, Harold Shirley came out of his office. Bernie was still waiting.

"I can give you five minutes," Shirley told him.

"That's all I need," Bernie grinned. "I just want to know what I can do to get your help on paving our runway." Bernie pulled out the runway plans and spread them on Shirley's desk.

"How much money do you have?" Shirley asked.

"Forty-eight hundred dollars," Bernie answered.

Shirley grunted something that sounded like, "That's not very much," and started calculating. His engineering crew, still in the office, got involved as the men began figuring costs and estimating materials.

"Tell you what," Shirley said. "I'll go out there and have a look at it. I want to see what's going on anyway."

After walking over the runway with Bernie the next morning, he asked, "Now when do you need this done?"

"Ah . . . well . . . we are starting a training program in a couple of months."

"Okay, we'll take care of it," Shirley said and headed back toward his car.

On a rainy Wednesday morning, several weeks later, Bernie got a call from Shirley's secretary. "The equipment will be out there Friday. However, they can't work if the runway is wet."

"Don't worry," Bernie almost shouted over the phone. "We know the Man who controls the weather. You just get the equipment out here."

There was more asking—and more praising—and the rain stopped Thursday at noon.

179

Shirley had contacted some of his competitors, and they had agreed to help. Equipment from four different construction companies began to show up. One company sent a bulldozer. Another a road grader. Then came the gravel, the big rollers, and the asphalt machines. Humble Oil and American Oil had donated seven carloads of asphalt. Gulf Oil donated the diesel fuel to run the equipment. The Dickerson crew did the work.

As a bonus, Harold Shirley paved the taxiway and the big apron in front of the hangar. He also volunteered to come back later and pave the dirt streets at the Center.

The entire project was finished in a week. The day the equipment rumbled out of the JAARS Center and back to the highway construction jobs, it started raining again.

Harold Shirley was too busy to talk about price. "Nobody would bid on a job like this for less than a hundred thousand dollars," he told Bernie. "Let's just say it was a gift from the Lord and let it go at that."

After Shirley had gone, Bernie walked out to the runway to stand and look—and give thanks to God. He turned when he heard the sound of feet on the gravel behind him. It was one of the boys who had been in that original runway prayer group. His hands were deep in his pockets, his knit cap pulled down over his ears against the biting wind.

"Uncle Bern, I didn't believe very much, but I prayed anyway," the boy said solemnly. "You know, God really does answer prayer, doesn't He?"

Uncle Cam's discovery, passed along to Bernie May, had been passed to still another generation—"Ask and ye shall receive."

The miracles, which the men of JAARS took as a sign of God's blessing on their mission, cropped up all over the place. For several years, JAARS had been using a three-place helicopter in New Guinea in places where the terrain was too rugged for landing strips. More choppers were needed, not only in New Guinea, but in the rugged mountain areas of the Philippines. In the past, three things had prevented JAARS from considering additional helicopters: cost, maintenance, and lack of trained pilots. The Vietnam war had taken care of the last two objections. For the first time, a number of military-trained helicopter pilots and mechanics were interested in JAARS. Yet there didn't seem to be any way to get around the cost factor. A helicopter, even a used one, would cost fifty thousand dollars. And JAARS was spending every cent they had just to keep their fleet of forty fixed-wing planes flying. Unless God performed a miracle, helicopters were an impossible dream.

Yet dreaming the impossible dream had become a way of life with Bernie May. The very fact there was a need, and the fact the helicopter could fill that need, was all the raw material he needed to begin praying. After all, the Lord could provide a sandbar in the river, a DC-3 in the air, and asphalt on the ground—why not helicopters, too?

Soon after Bernie started praying for helicopters, he received a letter from Jim Burroughs, a helicopter mechanic in Bakersfield, California, asking how he could help provide a helicopter for JAARS. "Three couples in our church have been getting together at our house one night a week," he said. "We're wondering if we could help overhaul a surplus military helicopter for JAARS."

Bernie and Bob Griffin headed to California.

Bob Griffin, a jovial forty-nine-year-old pilot who had logged more than five thousand hours as a missionary aviator—both in South America and the Philippines — had recently moved to JAARS Center to help coordinate the growing ministry in the States. Like Bernie, he was something of a fanatic when it came to prayer. He believed in asking and receiving and was convinced Burroughs' letter was part of the receiving.

Visiting in Burroughs' home, Bernie said, "I've been praying for six ex-military helicopters. If the Lord gives them to us, would you and your wife be willing to quit your job, move to Waxhaw, overhaul them, and teach our mechanics at the same time?"

"Would we!" Burroughs exclaimed. "That's what we've been praying for all the time. You know," he went on, "they keep all those surplus military helicopters at Davis-Monthan Air Force Base in Arizona. Why don't you stop by there on your way home?"

The next day, Bernie and Bob rode through the huge military depot near Phoenix. Stretched out across the desert, as far as they could see, were surplus military planes. Their military escort drove them past half a mile of helicopters, nose to tail.

"Uh . . . we're looking for Bell helicopters," Griffin said. "All these are Hillers."

The escort shook his head. "Sorry, but we don't have anything but these Hiller H23s," he said.

"But we wanted Bells," Bob said dejectedly. "I guess we'll have to keep on looking."

The following week, Bernie was in Washington, D.C., asking that he might receive. "You've got to put feet to your prayers," he told me. "Sometimes, God expects you to stand and wait, just like Moses did at the Red Sea. That's faith. Other times, God wants you to wade in and run the risk of drowning, like Joshua did at the Jordan River. That's faith, too. With the helicopters, we just waded in, asked the right government sources the right questions, and within two months, seven (God's idea, we asked for six) military surplus helicopters were on their way to Waxhaw—as gifts."

There was only one thing wrong. They weren't Bell helicopters. They were all Hiller H23s.

Jim Burroughs quit his job in Bakersfield, moved his family to Waxhaw, and went to work putting the helicopters together. When the first machine was complete, the FAA inspector came out to the base to license it. After seeing the helicopter was in perfect condition, he certified it and then turned to Jim Baptista.

"You guys are really lucky," he said.

Jim shook his head. "It's not luck. It's the Lord."

"Well, whatever it is, you should be thankful you have Hillers and not Bell helicopters. The Florida State Police bought some excess Bell 47s and can't get them licensed. They can't even be overhauled at the factory."

"Thank you, Lord," Jim said quietly. "Thank You very much."

Jim Baptista wasn't the only man thanking God for the helicopters. Several months later, Bernie May received a letter from Neil Anderson, translator to the Polopa people in New Guinea. He wrote:

"My wife and I are translating the Bible for the twenty-five hundred Polopa people. We are located in the center of sixteen hundred square miles of very rugged rain-forest jungle. The terrain is very sharply broken limestone, with calcite ridges running generally east and west. The village where we live is located on top of one of these sharp ridges, accessible only by native trail. We began living among the Polopa people thirteen months ago, realizing that we would be thoroughly dependent upon JAARS' only helicopter to bring supplies and help us in case of an emergency. Otherwise, it is a three-day hike over a trail heavily infested with lichens and over knife-sharp calcite rocks, festooned with a moss camouflage. It doesn't take much imagination to guess what a helicopter means to us. It brings us mail from loved ones and fresh food every six weeks. It gives us an opportunity to talk to another white person—the pilot—once every six weeks. I can truthfully say, 'Praise the Lord for the helicopters.' "

Later, in a surplus depot in Pennsylvania, Jim Baptista spotted sixteen metal engine containers used by the military to ship new engines. Since JAARS had been having trouble with their old wooden crates, Jim asked the officer in charge if he could have the metal ones.

"Take all sixteen," the man said.

Looking closer, Jim discovered each container had a spare Hiller engine inside.

"Ask and ye shall receive."

Chapter 15

The Land of Promise

For years, Cameron Townsend had dreamed of and prayed for the time when one of the natives would leave the jungle, receive proper training, and then return to his people. Nard Pugyao was that dream come true.

An Isneg tribesman from the Philippines, Nard had become a disciple of WBT translator Dick Roe in the rugged mountain region of northern Luzon. Roe, a tall, easygoing bachelor, had taken Nard in tow, privately trained him, and with help from Uncle Cam, financed his way to the States for further education. The twenty-three-year-old brown-skinned tribesman who spoke ten dialects had easily passed his A & P mechanics course at Le-Tourneau College in Longview, Texas, and had been tutored for his private pilot's license at JAARS Center at Waxhaw. Now Nard was prepared to leave for flight school at Moody Bible Institute in Chicago. His ultimate goal was to return to the Philippines as a JAARS pilot.

When I talked to him in the hangar at the Waxhaw Center, he said his greatest day would be the one when he fired up a JAARS Helio at the SIL base at Bagabag in the Philippines and flew Dick Roe out to his Isneg village.

Nard's description of his native islands spurred me in my desire to visit them. As a child, I was enamored by tales of the Philippines. My mind had been full of pictures of the ruggedly beautiful land, a land of rice terraces like green steps to the sky, of people who lived in houses on stilts, of beautiful brown-skinned girls with sparkling black eyes, of agile men and boys scaling tall coconut palms, of a land where every child played a ukelele and every face wore a happy smile. I admired the great courage of the Filipinos who fought beside us at Bataan and Corregidor. Although more than a million of them were slaughtered by the Japanese, they continued to fight in the jungles and mountains until General MacArthur fulfilled his promise to return.

The Philippines are a galaxy of seven thousand islands strung out north and south for almost twelve hundred miles between the Pacific Ocean and the South China Sea. New islands appear from time to time as volcanoes thrust their smoking cones above the sea. Because of the terrain of the land and the character of many of the natives (headhunters still exist less than two hundred miles from Manila), the Philippines provided SIL with its most formidable challenge.

When Dick Pittman, later to become SIL's Area Director for Asia and the Pacific, made his first exploratory trip to the Philippines, he met Simon Gato, of the Ivatan people on Batan Island, who begged him, "Send someone to help us." Pittman returned to the Wycliffe recruits gathered at the University of North Dakota and presented the challenge. Morris and Shirley Cottle volunteered to go and eventually found their way to the rocky village of Mahatao on Batan where they lived in a strong stone house built to withstand the devastating typhoons. Since that time, scores of Wycliffe personnel had come to the Philippines and were scattered throughout the island archipelago, living in lonely mountain villages or in primitive nomadic settlements where they learned the aboriginal languages.

Six years after the Cottles began their pioneer work on the tiny island off the coast of Luzon, the first Helio Courier ever to be flown in the South Pacific arrived. It was a gift of the Christian community in Seattle, and was transported by the U.S. Navy. The crate in which the aircraft was shipped became the JAARS radio shack in Manila.

Less than a year later, the plane was badly damaged in a crash on a tiny landing strip in a remote location in the mountains. It had to be disassembled and floated on a raft down a raging mountain stream to level ground where it was finally repaired. Meanwhile, another Helio was shipped to the islands. The planes were titled to the national government and used under an agreement with the Department of Defense. It was an act of goodwill, strengthening that already established through Cottle, Pittman, and others.

In 1957, when Pittman met with President Magsaysay, the president asked Pittman to promise to take special care of the pygmy Negritos of Zambales, his home province where he led guerrillas in World War II. Although Magsaysay died shortly afterward, Pittman never forgot the request.

On August 18, 1961, translators Charlotte Houch and Harriett Minot called in on their little radio from the pygmy Negrito village where they were on location. A little two-year-old boy was desperately sick. Although the USA had just given the Philippines eighteen new supersonic fighter jets, the planes were powerless to help. Although Clark Air Force Base on the eastern flank of Zambales and Subic Bay Naval Base on the west had some of the world's most powerful radios, they could not help either. It was up to Bob Griffin to take the Helio *The Spirit of Pontiac* which had just that morning been delivered to the government of the Philippines, fly out to the tiny airstrip, pick up the sick boy, and fly him to the Manila Sanatarium that evening. A skilled surgeon operated the next day, and very shortly the boy was returned—well and happy—to his home in the hills. Neither the Negritos nor the people of the Philippines ever forgot how JAARS fulfilled their honored president's request—even after he was dead.

I found Manila to be a cacophony of sound and color. Jeepneys—World War II jeeps turned into agile jitney buses, ablaze with circus-wagon paint, arched tops, rakish fenders, oversized bodies glittering with chrome, reflectors, and an array of hood ornaments—filled the streets. In a hopping, skipping gallopade they danced to the hysterical melody of a thousand horns. Some were emblazoned with religious signs —"Jesus Is My Lord," while others bore more earthy slogans such as "Love Hunter," and "You're My Baby."

On my way from the airport to SIL's beautiful group house on the outskirts of the city, I crowded into a jeepney with twelve other people. We raced through the streets of Manila, a city of almost three million, in a raucous frenzy. I could hardly hear over the sounds of blowing horns, squealing tires and brakes, and loud music which blared from the open door of every shop.

"How can you stand it?" I shouted at the driver.

He flashed a huge grin. "I love it!" he shouted back—and turned his radio up louder. I had previously decided Lima had the worst traffic in the world. It didn't take me long to change my mind after riding through the streets of Manila in a jeepney.

A JAARS board meeting was in progress behind the walls that surrounded the quiet group house in the suburbs. I was impressed with the deep faith of these expert technicians. The meeting opened with prayer, but it wasn't the usual quick, formal, powerless invocation. This prayer lasted for more than an hour, and everyone around the table entered in.

Then pilot Joe France reported on a new airstrip recently opened near the northern SIL base of Bagabag. The field was located in Luzon's *bundok,* or mountain country. I recognized the term which had become famous as "boondocks"—military slang for "just about as far away from civilization as a person can get." Pilots agreed that no other place in the world afforded more difficult flying conditions than the rugged mountains of Luzon.

Two days later, dressed in a fancy *barong tagalog* shirt, I left the teeming capital city and flew via Philippine Air Lines (PAL) down the archipelago almost six hundred miles to the southern island of Mindanao. We landed on the airstrip at Cagayan de Oro on the Mindanao Sea where JAARS pilot Ken Kruzan was waiting for me. I quickly transferred to the Helio for our last hop over the mountains to Nasuli in the central part of the island. Dark clouds had gathered, and sudden lightning slapped the hills. When we touched down on the grass strip at Nasuli, it was raining hard.

I had dinner that night with Gordon and Thelma Svelmoe, who had just completed translating the entire New Testament in the Mansaka language. After attending a prayer meeting in their house with about thirty others from the Nasuli base crowded into their living room, I walked across the open plaza to the home of translators Carl and Lauretta DuBois where I was staying. It was almost midnight. I stood in the open field and looked upward, feasting my eyes on the billion stars that twinkled in the clear Pacific sky. To the south was the Southern Cross. To the north, the Big Dipper. Although we were only eight degrees from the equator, the weather was cool, and the air so clear I could see to the edge of eternity. A half moon was just setting in the western sky over the South China Sea, silhouetting a giant bay tree that surely stood two hundred feet tall. To the north, a magnificent volcano, its jagged cone still white with ash, reared its peak into the dark sky. Banana trees, coconut trees, avocados, payayas, and citrus circled the base. Cascades of bougainvillea and white orchids covered the fronts of many of the houses, leaving no doubt why the Filipinos called Mindanao "the land of promise." Somehow, I hoped our western

civilization—hamburger stands, concrete streets, and beer cans—
would never find its way to this primeval garden of Eden where
God still spoke in whispers.

Not wanting to wake my hosts, I tiptoed to my ground-floor
bedroom under the main part of the DuBois house. The base generator had gone off at nine-thirty, leaving us without lights and
water until dawn. I lit the kerosene lamp and surveyed my sur-
roundings—a strange mixture of poverty and wealth. All the walls
were paneled with mahogany cut from the lauan tree. The floor
was inlaid mahogany tile and the door solid teakwood with beautiful cast bronze doorknobs. The ceiling, however, was some kind
of frayed woven rattan from which hung a naked light bulb. The
screenless windows opened to the cool night air, and a million
night sounds lulled me to sleep.

It was at Nasuli that the full impact of the "R" in JAARS hit
me. The radio was actually the missionaries' lifeline in the isolated, remote villages. I spent most of the day with George Ehara,
radio technologist, and Edith Murdoch, JAARS radio operator.
Edith was just starting her morning "sked" with the translators
in the remote *barrios*. She had a long list of things to be relayed
to those living in the *bundoks*. Questions and answers came back
and forth from translators to base: questions concerning what
kind of fertilizer to use on cabbages, what the doctor would sug-
gest concerning a skin rash, and when the plane would be coming
to bring supplies. A native language helper, who was homesick
and wanted to return to his tribe, was allowed to talk with his own
people on the radio. Satisfied, he then agreed to stay on at Nasuli
until his job was finished.

Edith told me that every JAARS flight was monitored by radio
from before take-off until after touch-down. Unlike the South
American flights, JAARS flights in the Philippines were mostly
under an hour in duration. However, they covered mountain-
jungle regions which were impossible to walk through.

When Bob Griffin learned I planned to fly out to visit Shirley

Abbott the next day, he told me how the radio had recently saved her life.

Shirley called in on the regular afternoon radio sked and asked to speak to the doctor. Shirley didn't live far from Nasuli — twenty-one minutes by air. But it was a week if you walked, trekking over a rugged mountain range with peaks that towered beyond eight thousand feet.

Dr. Lincoln Nelson had installed a two-way radio at his ABWE (Association of Baptists for World Evangelism) clinic which was only nineteen kilometers from Nasuli. He tried to be on the radio each afternoon when the translators called in from their tribal locations.

Soon Shirley was describing a series of medical symptoms — pain in the abdominal area, fever. Bob was listening in on the conversation from the hangar. He realized he would probably be called on for a medical evacuation.

Finally, Dr. Nelson said, "Shirley, who's the patient?"

There was "dead air" for fifteen seconds, and then Shirley's meek voice came back on. "Me," she answered.

"Well, you've got a severe case of appendicitis, and we've got to get you out of there fast."

Bob came on the radio. "Shirley, what's your weather out there? It's overcast here, but over toward the mountains it looks really grim."

"It's just the same here, Bob," she said with a quiver in her voice.

Bob shook his head. It was late in the afternoon. He knew the mountain passes were socked in with thunderstorms. One miscalculation and he could be trapped by darkness, because in the tropics, when the sun goes down, the lights go out. Immediately.

There was nothing to do but wait until the next day.

"I'll call you at six in the morning," Bob said, "and we'll see how the weather is."

At six o'clock the next morning, the weather at Nasuli was

perfect, but Shirley's weak voice said, "It's fogged-in here, Bob. Right down on the ground."

Bob visualized what it was like out in the Ata of Davao. Shirley's valley, bracketed by craggy mountains, was probably filled with clouds like a saucer filled with cream. It would be impossible to get in. They'd just have to wait.

"I'll call you back in thirty minutes," Bob said, knowing the chances of getting in before noon were very slim. He bowed his head in prayer, remembering that the entire base was also praying.

Finally, by seven o'clock, two radio contacts later, Shirley said, "Bob, I can see some blue holes in the sky."

It was a slim chance, but Bob crawled in the Helio Courier and took off.

"Lord," he prayed, "give me the kind of weather that will allow me to get through."

He crossed the mountains, and to his dismay, below him lay a river of fog. Only the high peaks pushed through. He was able to identify Shirley's valley, but there were no holes. He knew that down below Shirley was looking up, no doubt hearing the sound of his engine. Bob prayed again.

After ten minutes of circling, he finally called Shirley on the radio — air to ground. "How much ceiling do you have down there?"

Her voice, pinched with pain, came through his speaker telling him she had about two hundred feet. She could tell by looking at the sides of the mountains where the fog began.

"Okay, hold on," Bob said. "I'm going up the valley, see if I can find a hole and come up underneath."

It was a remarkable bit of flying skill. Ten miles up the valley, Bob found a tiny hole. Putting the Helio over on its wingtip, he spiraled down and came out at the far end of the narrow valley, squeezed in between the fog and the river, with the steep mountains on each side almost scraping his wingtips. Then at forty miles an hour, in a flying procedure impossible in any plane except a Helio Courier, Bob threaded his way down the valley to Shirley's airstrip. He had four seconds for final approach. Chopping the power, he was on the ground.

Shirley was in so much pain that she was unable to get out of her house. Bob carried her out to the plane and made her comfortable in the back seat. They thanked the Lord, together, and asked for His protection as they flew out.

Throttle at full, Bob pulled the plane off the ground, up through the ugly, gray fog, and out on top.

Picking up the mike, Bob called the clinic. "I'll be there in twelve minutes," he said.

Dr. Nelson met them at the little airstrip just behind the clinic. The operating room was ready, and attendants carried Shirley right to the operating table. Two hours later, the appendix was out, and she was resting comfortably.

Later that day, Bob returned to the clinic to talk to Dr. Nelson.

"Bob," he said, "if you had been two hours later, it would have been too late. We would have buried a missionary."

Radio and airplane — they were the only links that girls like Shirley Abbott had with civilization while they were living with the Indians.

It was almost noon the next day before the weather cleared enough at Nasuli for Ken Kruzan and me to take off in the Helio on our trip out to Shirley's location. The landing strip, which Shirley and her partner, Pat Hartung, had paid for out of their own support, was in the center of the village — surrounded by a circle of small houses on stilts.

As we approached, I saw a naked little boy running as fast as he could to spread the word the plane was coming. A collection of leaf-covered shacks flashed by on either side of the runway, and then Ken braked us to a stop right in the middle of the village.

Immediately, we were surrounded by what seemed to be the entire village population. I counted eleven women in ragged shirts, nine men — some of them in trousers and three in nothing

embrace each other in affection. But [...]
flected on the faces of these beautiful, [...]
of God.

As I climbed into the plane to fly out over [...]
back to civilization — Manila, Hong Kong — a [...]
edged up to me and handed me a small blue flower. H[...]
stained with tobacco juice, and he could not speak m[...]
but the broad smile on his face said more th[...]
the human vocabulary. It was the lan[...]
let, so bereft of material things, [...]
battle over the darkness of Sat[...]
women was bearing tasty, nou[...]
joy, and peace.

The Philippines — and M[...]
the land of promise.

more than a loincloth tucked in lik[...]
a score of children — nearly all of [...]
cept for seven hogs, four chickens, and [...]
Without exception, everyone except t[...]
ugly wad of tobacco stuck on their front te[...]
ciate the charm of this practice, but here as i[...]
all over the world, it was a social amenity—a[...]
the excuse to spit — everywhere.

While Pat prepared dinner, Shirley took us on a quick t[...]
the village. The grass was a glossy green with colorful explosion[...]
poinsettias, hibiscus, plumed banana plants, and coconut palm[...]
As in most native villages, everything was wet and muddy, and [...]
the flying and creeping insects were everywhere.

All houses were on stilts for protection against roving animals
and the river which occasionally flooded with no warning at all.
Most were just one room and were entered by climbing up a
notched log. Two weeks ago, Shirley told us, an angry husband
from another tribe — who suspected one of the Ata tribesmen
was courting his wife's suitor. Not knowing which hut the man lived in,
killing his wife — had entered the burrio at night intent on
he went from house to house jabbing his sharp spear through the
split-bamboo floors. He seriously wounded three people before
running off through the forest, satisfied, although he had failed
to spear the right man.

Shirley pointed out a vacant house at the end of the runway.
The family who built it had died there of cholera. In spite of
Shirley's warnings, another family had moved in. Within a few
days, they, too, were dead from the lingering cholera germ. Now
the house was vacant.

"It needs to be burned," Shirley said sadly, "but they hate to
destroy anything, so there it sits, still infected with the deadly
disease."

I shuddered, kept my distance, and spent a long time washing
my hands before we sat down to eat.

at looke...
was a long prayer. Altho...
chiefs. I was grateful...
guage, I was praying fervently. Altho...
"Lord, make me thankful for that which I am...

The prayer over, I took my cue from the chief beside...
idea was to grab a handful of rice from the banana leaf, dip...
into the bowl of boiled things, collect as much as you could...
your fingers, and then put it all in your mouth. Rice grains fell...
through my inept fingers, continuing on through the flooring, to...
the delight of the chickens below. I was pleased and amazed to...
find the Lord had answered my prayer. The meal was delicious.

The only thing I missed was salt. I resolved if I ever returned,
I would bring several bags as gifts to these who were treating me
with such cordiality and love.

After dinner, we stood under the wing of the plane talking. No
matter at whom I looked, any sex, any age, I got a smile in return.
"They are pleased. Very few people love them," Shirley
said. "I've told them you are here because you love them." No

There was a striking lack of "things" in the barrio. No shoes,
no towels, no refrigerators, no guns, no toys, no toothbrushes —
none of the trappings of civilization. But there in that possession-
less village I saw evidence of things that seemed to have eluded
many in the thriving cities of the world. I saw a flower garden
planted where once the witch doctor had danced his incantations.
I saw children sharing with one another and men unafraid to

Chapter 16

New Guinea—Prelude to a Miracle

Thy mercy, O Lord, is in the heavens; and thy faithfulness reacheth unto the clouds.

Psalm 36:5

The sun was just rising over the China Straits as our Qantas
jet banked steeply away from the towering mountains and
screeched to a halt on the runway at Port Moresby, New Guinea.
We had flown all night from Hong Kong, crossing the equator in
the wee hours of the morning on our way to this huge island off
the northern coast of Australia.

Towering halfway to the sky, New Guinea was the home of a
culture buried deep in the past. On one end were boiling mud
pools, geysers, creeks of yellow sulphur, and pools of boiling water.
On the other were the towering mountains, volcanoes, and jagged
limestone pinnacles which protruded through the mountain jungles like giant inverted icicles. In the remote areas, tribes still

practiced headhunting and cannibalism, but in many areas, the white man's presence had been felt for years. Now, inexorably, the effects of western politics and institutional religion were changing the colorful life-styles of these primitive people, and the result, more often than not, was confusion and frustration — accompanied by fear.

It was April, which was fall below the equator; however, this close to Latitude Zero, seasons were replaced by "dry" and "wet" times, governed by the monsoons in the summer and tradewinds in the winter. April, which came between the windy seasons, fell into that period called the *doldrums*. This meant it was hot without wind. The rest of the time, it was hot with wind.

The airport was swarming with black aborigines, most of them dressed in white shorts and various kinds of shirts, some outfitted with white knee-stockings and shoes, most barefooted. All seemed intent on their own business, which was shuffling from one place to the other or simply leaning on the fence watching the plane disgorge its passengers into the hot, sticky early morning. It didn't take me long to find out that in Port Moresby, no one was in a hurry. When I commented on this to the Australian customs official who was poking through my bag and examining my passport, he grinned and nodded.

"I understand a man got in a hurry two years ago," he said with a heavy Aussie twang. "But when he got to where he was going, he found he was early."

Even though it was only seven o'clock, I was already perspiring heavily, and my traveling companion, Al West, editor of *Logos Journal,* was hunting for something to drink. We ruled out the water fountain, since we didn't have any anti-malarial tablets, and settled on going into the dirty restroom at the end of the open, concrete-block terminal building, to splash a little tepid water on our faces. It helped some.

I agreed to watch our cameras and bags while Al checked with the ticket counter of Trans Australian Airways (TAA) to inquire about a flight to Lae, on the other side of the island. From there, we hoped to make contact with a JAARS plane to fly us inland to the Wycliffe base at Ukarumpa.

The agent was black, and like most of the others in the airport, barefooted. I was intrigued by the tattoo scars on his face and could trace the faint outline through his white shirt of other scars on his back and shoulders. Even today, some New Guinea boys undergo a grueling initiation into manhood when their "mother's blood," which is deemed inferior, is cast out to allow them to form virile blood of their own. After the elders of the tribe incise the youth's skin with scores of small cuts, the wounds are rubbed with ash and oil to raise permanent welts.

My information on this rite had come firsthand from a black traveling companion on the plane from Hong Kong. His face was similarly scarred — though he talked with a clipped Oxford accent and was dressed in a conservative business suit. Raised in the Parambei tribe on the Sepik River, he was taught to read by the Wycliffe translators, educated in Australia, and had recently returned from England with a master's degree from Oxford. He was now part of the newly formed government which was helping set up independence in Papua, a territory of New Guinea.

Although grateful for the ministry of Wycliffe, he was bitter toward other "missionaries" who tried, in his words, "to stamp out traditional ceremonies while urging the people to hide their nakedness with ill-fitting European clothes.

"Wycliffe translators are different," he said warmly when he discovered I was interested in their ministry. "They come only to teach us how to read, and to translate the Bible into our languages. Their goal is not to destroy our culture, but to preserve it and leave behind the Word of God."

With a twinkle, he added, "If God had wanted us to be Europeans, He would have said so in the Bible. Wycliffe has learned the secret of not trying to convert us into Frenchmen, Germans, or"—here he paused and raised one hand in a mock sign of praise

—"Americans. If the Word of God is as powerful as the missionaries say it is, it will change our people without Westerners having to come and tell us to put on clothes."

I grunted and nodded my head. Deep inside, I was shouting "Amen!" I came to the conclusion that the new independent government of Papua, New Guinea, was going to be in good hands if this fellow was representative of others in the parliament.

Al had finished his conversation with the ticket agent at TAA. Hurrying back across the rough concrete floor of the terminal, he mopped his brow with his handkerchief and said, "We've got to hurry. There's a plane leaving for Lae right now."

We grabbed our bags and rushed through the side door. Sure enough, the deHaviland Otter was sitting on the apron — but its big engines were silent. Despite the fact that it was time for takeoff, the loading area was empty. I had forgotten the customs agent's remark about being in a hurry.

We plopped our bags down and took a seat on a dust-covered bench. Half an hour later, we were on board the Otter, an amazing airplane for mountain and jungle flying. We got a good view as we climbed out over the 14,000-foot-high Mount Victoria. The territory's size and its ruggedness had caused the road-builders to stop forty or fifty miles out from the main towns. From that point on, transportation was by canoe, trekking, or air. I could see where the airplanes of JAARS were an absolute necessity in this area of the world. In good trekking conditions, it would take twenty men one hour's hard walking to carry the same amount of cargo that one small, single-engine airplane could transport over the same distance in one minute. Following that through, it was easy to compute that three months of flying would save something like twenty-five years of trekking — not to mention the safety factor. New Guinea abounded with dangers for those on foot. That did not mean, of course, that flying in New Guinea was not dangerous. The rapidly changing weather coupled with the extremely rugged terrain had caused aviation experts to dub it —

along with the Philippines — one of the worst flying countries in the world.

I glanced at the map in my lap, plotting our course as we crossed the island. The names brought back memories of a generation ago when some of the fiercest battles of the war were fought around these shores. The Solomon Sea, New Britain, Rabaul, Bougainville and the Bismarck Sea — all still echoed the sounds of shot and bomb.

Our plane came in high over the Huon Gulf. I heard the whine of the flaps going down. Moments later, we were touching down at Lae.

Again the heat, this time accompanied by a new and different threat. Picking up our bags, I was suddenly aware the building was shaking. Things rattled, and the floor seemed to sway like an open boat on the ocean. I looked around, but no one else seemed to be afraid, all going about their normal shuffle while holding onto the sides of the building to keep from falling. Moments later, it was over, and I realized we had been through a *guria* — a tricky tremor caused by the volcanoes. I looked at Al. We both decided we'd be safer outside than in and started through the door toward the street. Outside, a pretty young woman was struggling with an oversized suitcase, heading toward the curb. I nudged Al. "See that girl? She looks like a Wycliffe gal. Let's find out."

I was right. An American, she was returning from Hong Kong after spending a few days checking with some linguistic experts. She offered to let us ride in the Wycliffe van which had come to meet her, taking her to the local group house where she would stay a few days before flying up to Ukarumpa. There, at least, we would have shade from the blistering heat and could find something to drink that didn't look like it was filled with amoebae.

Lae, a langourous natural greenhouse of a town — with a climate to match—was eighty-three air miles from the Wycliffe base at Ukarumpa. Waiting for the JAARS plane to pick us up, we had a chance to wash our hands and faces (for the nineteenth time) and catch up on some much-needed sleep. I dozed on a bamboo couch directly in front of a whirring electric fan, which at least kept the hot air stirring so I would cook a bit slower — while Al disappeared, hunting for something that looked like an American bathroom. Like myself, he was having trouble adjusting to the South Pacific custom of going in the great outdoors.

There are more than twenty thousand islands in the South Pacific, and the 150 million people who live on them speak more than twelve hundred different languages — most of which have never been written down. Papua New Guinea, is the largest of these. The western half of the island, Irian-Jaya, was under Indonesian rule, while the eastern half was now independent from its former position as an Australian territory. However, on the island alone, there are something like seven hundred different language groups scattered all the way from the treacherous New Guinea highlands to the almost inaccessible and still uncharted Papuan lowlands.

Wycliffe Bible Translators began their work in New Guinea in 1956. In early 1973, they entered their one hundredth language. Six hundred New Guinea languages remained!

Ken Wiggers, a tall, muscular pilot qualified in both helicopters and fixed-wing aircraft, flew down from Ukarumpa in a pot-bellied Cessna 206 to meet us at the Lae airport. The Cessna was standard equipment in New Guinea where the landing strips were either long enough to accommodate a conventional plane — or so rugged and remote that only a helicopter could get in. For this reason, New Guinea was the first JAARS base to utilize helicopters, which were able to fly into the high mountain areas and land in tiny clearings.

On this particular flight, Al and I helped Ken load the big cargo pod under the fuselage with frozen meat, several sacks of dried beans, sheet metal to be used in a building project, and some new radio equipment given by a generous supporter in the States.

Three others from the group house were also going up to the base, making a full load.

After a preflight check, we took off in the sweltering heat at Lae and circled out over the Huon Gulf before setting a heading toward the pleasant atmosphere of the mile-high base at Ukarumpa, forty minutes away. Climbing on up to seven thousand feet so he would have enough clearance to land on the highland runway at Ukarumpa, Ken trimmed out the Cessna and turned to me.

"Maybe you'd like to hear about a miracle."

Then over the steady roar of the big engine in front of us, he told me the story of the Piper Aztec, the other twin which used to be stationed in New Guinea. He called it the "finger-of-God story."

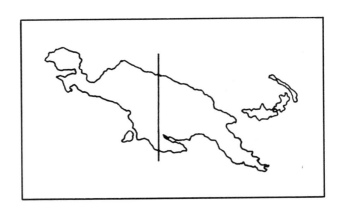

EAST NEW GUINEA

Sepik

Ukarumpa •

Lae

Port Moresby

Watch those ruts. Luzon, Philippines.

Author (left) and Ken Wiggers in New Guinea. (*Prelude To A Miracle*)

Ralph Borthwick at the controls of the Cat

Dr. Darlene Bee, New Guinea.

Welcome, pilots, to Corequaje - Colombia. *(Bloom Where You Are Planted)*

Each one teach one.

Radio operator Edith Murdoch at Nasuli, Philippines, talks to translators in remote areas with their tribes on the southern island of Mindanao.
(Land Of Promise)

Shirley Abbott and friend on allocation in the Philippines. *(Land Of Promise)*

Uncle Cam Townsend and friends.

Sendoff for a JAARS plane as it leaves an Indian village in Peru.

Clear off the pigs and goats, we're coming in. Mindanao, Philippines
(Land Of Promise)

Logos Journal Editor Al West and pilot Ken Kruzan in Philippines.

Watch that bump! Lomalinda, Colombia.

Chapter 17

The Finger of God

Our outlook through this peephole at the vast mysteries
of the universe only confirms our belief in the certainty
of its Creator.

Wernher Von Braun

Close by the base at Ukarumpa is the Aiyura airstrip where
pilot Doug Hunt was finishing his final walk-around inspection
of the twin-engine Piper Aztec. The registration letters painted
on the tail were, appropriately, SIL. Chief Aviation Mechanic
Jim Entz, a stocky American with a waxed handlebar moustache,
slapped Doug on the shoulder.

"She's all ready to go," he said. "We'll be praying for you as
you climb out."

Bible translators Glenn and Dotty Graham were buckling their
four small children into the back seats of the plane. It was not
yet eight o'clock, but they had been up for hours, preparing for
the flight which would take them back to their tiny thatched
home in the Amanab village. Even at 180 miles per hour, it would
still take two and a half hours of flying time to reach their base,
plus a stopover at the coastal city of Wewak to refuel.

Doug, a New Zealander with a balding head and constant
grin, had thirteen years flying experience, most of it in New

Guinea where he formerly flew with Missionary Aviation Fellowship (MAF). Doug's family doctor had advised him against becoming a pilot because of an early attack of spinal meningitis which had left him with spinal problems. But after he and his wife, Glennis, heard Marj Saint, young widow of pilot Nate Saint who was martyred by the Auca Indians in Ecuador, give her testimony while visiting New Zealand, Doug never doubted that he would live his life — give his life, if necessary — as a jungle pilot. When he and Glennis and their four children moved to Ukarumpa, they were never more certain they were directly in the center of God's will.

Because of his experience, Doug was appointed chief pilot of the JAARS group in New Guinea. He had a pocketful of exciting stories about his flying experiences. At one time, he stopped a tribal war in Irian by buzzing the battleground four feet off the ground — several times. In 1963, he took a badly injured pilot from Djajapura to Port Moresby across the Papua New Guinea, mainland at night in a Cessna 185 — a feat which is still considered impossible by flying experts.

Pulling up his knee stockings and polishing his dark glasses on the pocket of his shirt, he finished his examination of the airplane and smiled at Jim.

"Every time I take off, I praise God these poor folks don't have to walk. God willing, I'll have them on the ground at Amanab before noon. If they had to go by ground, it would take them three months."

"Amen!" Glenn Graham said as he pulled the door shut. "Pray for us, Jim, we're counting on it."

Entz grinned and waved his hand. A plane never took off from Aiyura that the mechanics, radio personnel, and other pilots did not pray. Little did they know how vital their prayers would be to return the Aztec safely to the ground. Not at Amanab, but back at Aiyura.

The flight westward through the Madang District to Wewak

was uneventful. The four small Graham children quickly fell asleep in the back seats. Thankful that the rising sun was at his back so he wouldn't have to fly into the early morning glare, Doug pointed out the Sepik River to Glenn and Dotty. Meandering through the swamps where headhunting tribes battled in decades past, the seven-hundred-mile river coiled like a gigantic brown serpent across the green plains, bordered on each side by towering mountains. Swamps, floods, and mosquitoes — and the hothouse climate — had held settlement along the Sepik to a scattering of villages.

Doug cranked the trim wheel to begin his letdown for Wewak. Circling the town, he lowered his landing gear and touched down gently—a perfect three-point landing. Flying time from Aiyura had been one hour and thirty minutes.

While the children stretched their legs, Doug had the plane refueled, topping the tanks and checking the oil. Stepping off the runway, he checked the weather for the inland leg of their flight. The sky was clear. Coming out of the tiny office building, he stopped to chat with a black-skinned Boiken tribesman who was squatting in the shade of a coconut palm. Doug never missed a chance to speak to these people he loved so well. The man spat a red jet of betel-nut juice through his lips before he answered Doug's question. The juice splattered on Doug's white knee-stockings.

"*Sori, tru, masta,*" he apologized quickly in pidgin English.

Doug grinned, waved off the apology, and continued his conversation with the man. Close by, another tribesman was rolling a cigarette from twist tobacco and newspaper. Doug spoke to him also, then made his way back to the plane. They still had another hour of flying time ahead, and he wanted to get over the six-thousand-foot mountains before the clouds started to build up. Clouds above and mountains below — it was the story of dangerous flying in New Guinea.

Like all pilots, Doug had a healthy respect for bad weather —

especially since the monsoon season was just beginning. He was eager to get started toward Amanab while the sky was still cloudless.

Making sure all the children were safely strapped in, Doug made a final recheck of the plane, noticing especially to see that his two new Boiken friends had not followed him out on the apron and were standing near the props.

Shouting "Clear!" he hit the starters, and the powerful engines coughed and roared to life. Moments later, the plane lifted off the runway, over the Catholic mission hangar, and turned out over the sea to head back inland.

As they were settling down in the cockpit, Doug had a feeling that something was wrong. The airplane didn't seem to be climbing as fast as it should. Suddenly his radio came to life, and the voice of the tower operator at Wewak crackled through his overhead speaker.

"Sierra India Lima, your nose wheel has not retracted."

Checking his instrument panel, Doug noticed that he did not have an orange light to show that all three wheels were up and locked. Looking down in the little mirror on the cowling of the left engine, he could see that the nose wheel was indeed in a "down" position.

Still climbing, Doug reached down and pushed the landing gear handle into a down position. He could hear the two main wheels under the wings going down. They "click-clicked" into position, but his instrument panel showed only two green lights. The nose wheel light was not on. Something was wrong.

He tried again. The same thing. Two green lights came on, but not the third. Circling the field, Doug spotted another airplane coming down the coast. He called him on the radio.

"Would you mind coming alongside and taking a look at this landing gear?" he asked.

The other plane, a MAF plane coming in to land at Wewak, pulled alongside the Aztec. Just at that moment, Doug pulled the gear up to retract it once again. This time he heard a loud, metallic "CRACK!" In the little cowling mirror, he could see that the nose wheel, which prior to this had appeared rigid, was now swinging limply back and forth.

The mission pilot in the smaller plane radioed over. "The main wheels are going up okay, but the nose wheel looks like a lame duck. It's swinging in midair."

Doug knew it was impossible for his heavily loaded Aztec to land on the two main wheels alone. Besides that, he had just filled his tanks with highly explosive gasoline.

Doug grinned at Glenn Graham who was sitting beside him. "You pray." The Grahams did pray. Not for safety, because they knew they were safe in the hands of God regardless of what happened. They prayed, rather, for the Holy Spirit to touch Doug with the gift of wisdom. Even as this prayer was going on, Doug was climbing for more altitude. He reached for the mike, switching the radio to the emergency channel at Aiyura.

Moments later, Doug was talking with Jim Entz, more than two hundred miles away.

"What do you think, Jim?" he asked.

Because he knew where every nut and bolt on the plane was, Jim assumed the problem was caused by a broken link in the nose gear.

"Well, first of all, you've got plenty of time," he said. "With that full load of fuel, you need to do a couple of hours flying just to burn it off. If you land with no nose wheel, there's going to be damage to the aircraft. My advice is to head home."

Doug had confidence in his mechanic friend and headed for Aiyura.

Dotty Graham opened a box of sandwiches — lunch they had intended to eat on the ground at Amanab. Doug had a thermos of hot coffee which Glennis had fixed that morning. Everyone had a bite to eat as the plane droned through the morning sky, the nose wheel still swaying in the breeze.

Doug gave the Grahams instructions on emergency procedures, explaining what could be expected if the plane flipped over on landing. He pointed out the emergency exits and asked them to repeat the escape instructions back to him. Even the smallest Graham children, preschoolers, were made to pay attention. What they understood at that time could save their lives later on.

There was an air of calmness and peace in the cockpit as the plane climbed over the mountains and continued eastward.

Deep inside, Doug believed the Lord would repair that dangling nose wheel in midair. He was ready to die, if this was God's time, but he had a deep inner feeling that God still had work for him to do. Somehow, this problem was going to be resolved to the glory of God.

The assurance of the touch of God is usually an intangible thing. A man knows because he knows—in the deep places of his soul. Using the best of his knowledge and training, Doug was trusting God to take care of the circumstances.

As soon as Jim Entz got the first call concerning trouble on the Aztec, he had called Skip Firchow, the acting Director. Immediately, Skip's secretary started telephoning key women on the base. They, in turn, took the Ukarumpa phone directory, divided it up, and called every family on the base — asking them to begin praying. While the Aztec was winging its way homeward from Wewak, a great cry was going up to God from the home base.

The men at the sawmill stopped their work while Lex Collier and Ben Frieson called them together in prayer. Blacks and whites pulled off their gloves and reached out to join hands over the dirty, rugged logs.

In the radio lab, the technicians took off their goggles, laid down their soldering irons, and gathered around Ben Clary and Dave Colvin. They had a special stake in this, for like Doug Hunt, they were JAARS men.

The word was passed to the translators who were working with their informants in the little cubicles at the linguistic center.

Laying down their books and tape recorders, white translators joined hands with black tribesmen — all of whom had flown in the airplanes and knew the danger — and asked God to spare the Aztec and its occupants.

In the printing plant, where the big presses were rolling publishing Bibles and grammar texts in the tribal languages, Don Gates called the men and women, many of them black New Guinea natives learning a trade, to come together and pray.

And in the hangar at Aiyura, Jim Baptista, Jim Entz, and the other pilots and mechanics gathered in the little office next to the hangar and knelt before God.

"Spare our friends," was the cry from all over the base. "Lord, grant them mercy."

At home, Glennis Hunt called little Dale, their preschooler, to her side. Kneeling beside a chair in the living room, she asked God to protect her husband and his precious cargo — the Graham family.

Minutes later, the Aztec came out over the base. Everywhere people came from their houses, straining their eyes upward. As the plane circled low over the base, all could see the dangling nose wheel, flapping back and forth. They could also see that Doug was putting the plane through a series of radical maneuvers, trying to shake the wheel forward so it would lock in place.

Coming high over the field, he slowed the plane to about one hundred miles per hour, pulled it up into a full stall, and then let the nose drop over sharply. He hoped the resulting loss in airspeed would relieve the aerodynamic pressure against the gear so the momentum of the gear, as the airplane snapped forward in its stall, would cause the wheel to swing forward and lock in place. It did not work. He tried again. The plane looked like a porpoise, rollicking up and down in the air, but the gear continued to dangle. The force of the wind against the wheel was too much.

Doug turned the plane back out over the jungle and came in low over the runway so Jim Entz and the others at the hangar could get a close look at the wheels.

Jim was on the radio. "It's just like you said, Doug. The main gear is down and locked into place, but the nose wheel is still hanging loose. Hold steady. The fire truck and ambulance are on the way."

Up at the schoolhouse, the teachers had been called together to pray. The headmaster felt it wise not to tell the children of the problem and possible disaster. However, as Dick Harder, a soft-spoken teacher, returned to his fifth and sixth grade classroom, the children were all up at the windows.

"Mr. Harder, the ambulance and the fire engine just went speeding by, heading for the airstrip."

Just at that time, the Aztec made another pass over the base. The children sensed something was wrong.

Dick stood at the window with the children, watching the plane circle back out over the jungle. Then he quickly explained the emergency.

"Children, I believe he is going to attempt to land. Let's all go to our desks and pray."

The children scampered back to their seats and, with their heads on their desks, bowed before God in prayer.

At that moment, Doug was on approach to the airstrip. Once again he slowed the plane down, and for a final time repeated the maneuver he had tried three times earlier. He pulled the nose of the plane up until the aircraft began to shudder. Then, with the stall warning blaring, he let the nose drop over. He heard a click — and saw all three green lights flash on. Three green!

Pushing the throttles forward, he gave the plane full power and roared in low and fast over the runway. He wanted to see if the wind was going to push the nose wheel back to its dangling position. On the ground, the other pilots and mechanics were out in front of the hangar. All eyes were on the nose wheel. It *seemed* to be locked into place. But was it?

Pulling up in a steep, graceful turn, Doug once more circled the field. He gave final emergency briefing to the Grahams on how to get out of the plane in case it crashed and burst into flames. Then, lowering his flaps, he came in and gently touched his main wheels on the runway. He held the plane back on the two wheels as long as possible and then allowed the nose wheel to settle. There was a screech as the tire bit into the runway — but the wheel held. They were safe.

Later, the Aztec was wheeled inside the hangar where it was jacked off the ground. Jim discovered a broken link in the gear, which allowed the wheel to dangle freely, unable to retract or lock into place. While the plane was in its jacked-up position, the mechanics retracted the gear and tried time and time again to lower it so the nose wheel would lock into place. However, even without the force of a hundred-mile-an-hour wind blowing on it, it still refused to swing forward and lock. The only way Jim could get it to lock in place was to place his hand against it and, by exerting great pressure, force it so the elbow locked down over center.

Straightening up, Jim shook his head. There was only one way that nose wheel could have locked down. God simply took His finger and pressed it forward until it snapped into place.

At the praise service the following Sunday night, Doug said he was thankful that the God they served was still a God of miracles.

The service closed with someone reading from Philippians where Paul said, "So now also Christ shall be magnified in my body, whether it be life, or by death. For to me to live is Christ, and to die is gain" (Phil.1:20-21) .

Doug Hunt didn't know it at the time, but five months from that night, those words would take on profound meaning—an eternal meaning — to those he would leave behind.

Chapter 18

A Time to Die—

If you are able to read
and if you have a copy of
the Word of God in your language
that Word will flood your soul with Light.
You do not need anyone to
shed light on the Word for you.
Granted there are mysteries
in its pages too great for a mind,
any mind of man to grasp —
the mystery of
the creator of
this vast universe—
we mere creatures must stand on tiptoe
and on each other's shoulders
to catch a glimpse of His wonder.
But the light of the good news shines in our hearts
when we expose ourselves to the printed page.
We live in darkness not because we are buried
under the mountain of an alien tongue
but because we never take down the shutters from

the windows of our minds and hearts
to let the magnificent Sun of the Sacred Scriptures
flood our souls with the unspeakable, undimmable light.
You can turn down a lantern
and you can turn off a light
but you can't regulate or turn off the light of the Sun.
In our efforts to find light to dispel darkness
let us not forget that we have in our hands the light
which will not only dispel darkness
but will also dispel every lesser light.

Dr. Darlene Bee
(Found in her belongings soon
after her death, April 7, 1972.)

When Jim Dean, a Canadian, and Des Oatridge from New Zealand settled at Ukarumpa in 1956, the only way to the highland tract of land was by jeep. Driving an unpaved and dusty road into the hills, their throats parched and nostrils clogged with dust, fording rivers and pulling the jeep behind them, they laid claim to the five hundred acres leased by SIL from the New Guinea government. At that time, they had no idea that less than two decades later this would be Wycliffe's largest and most modern base, home of six hundred people who would be tightly knit together as a Christian family.

Those first houses were made of rough timber cut straight from the bush and covered with Kunai grass, a broad-bladed grass which grows in huge patches across the New Guinea highlands. Water was carried from the river in buckets until Alex Vincent, an Australian, decided he could make a water race from a higher point so running water would flow through the community. Shortly afterward, the first translators were coming in, building their own houses at the base, and then trekking out to their tribal assignments. Jim moved on to help open Wycliffe's work in India, Nepal, and Indonesia, while Des remained behind with his wife,

Jenny, and two babies to work with the Binumarien language group.

Among the first of the pioneer translators to arrive was Dr. Darlene LaVerne Bee, a beautiful, brilliant young scholar with a PhD in linguistics from the University of Indiana. Turning her back on marriage as a way of life, she chose to devote herself to taking the Bible to those who had no written language. Her choice of a tribe — the Usarufa people in the Eastern Highlands District with a population of less than eight hundred and fifty souls. Across the years, she and her partner, Vida Chenoweth, completed the translation of Genesis and Mark, interrupted by Bee's trips back and forth to Auckland where she was the Principal of the New Zealand SIL. They had begun working on the Gospel of John when God intervened in her plans.

Three years after Bee, as she was affectionately called, started to work among the Usarufas, Jim Baptista flew a leased Cessna 170 onto the airstrip at Aiyura, about half a mile from the rapidly expanding base at Ukarumpa. Jim was soon joined by Ken Wiggers, and the two of them did all the flying and all the maintenance. Little did either of them know that ten years later the JAARS program would have expanded to include helicopters, twin-engine airplanes, a fleet of sturdy Cessnas, a complete mechanical shop, and a first-class radio lab.

In 1972, the year before I visited New Guinea, there had begun a deep move of the Holy Spirit which affected most of the people at Ukarumpa. That spring, the administration invited the Reverend Graham Pulkingham, rector of the Church of the Redeemer (Episcopal) of Houston, Texas, and a leader in the worldwide charismatic move, to come to New Guinea for a Bible conference.

Father Pulkingham arrived the Wednesday after Easter. The theme of his messages was "The Power of Love through the Christian Community." No message could have been more appropriate for a group of people who had only recently been drawn together in love, praying for chief pilot, Doug Hunt. Then, just the week before Easter, the base had come together again—this time around Clara Wagner whose husband, Ed, retired from the States to live at Ukarumpa as an electrician, had died of a heart attack. Everyone was in agreement that Graham Pulkingham had arrived in God's timing. His sensitivity, his authority in the Word, his tenderness in ministering the Baptism in the Holy Spirit, his desire to bring evangelicals and charismatics into unity through love spoke deeply to the "family" that had formed at Ukarumpa.

No one, though, in their wildest imaginations, dreamed of the far greater reason God had brought Graham Pulkingham to Ukarumpa at just that time.

Friday, April 7, dawned as another heavy work day for the JAARS personnel. The Cessnas, flown by Paul Carlson, Vic Dickey, and John Mabry, were flying up and down the coast taking translators in and out of their bases. The helicopter, piloted by Roger Dodson, had been dispatched on an emergency mission to a remote section high in the rugged mountains to pick up a pregnant New Guinea woman who needed medical attention. Stu Nelson was scheduled to fly the Aztec on a cross-country flight to Port Moresby, then back to Lae to pick up some passengers, returning home in time to get to the meeting that night.

Doug Hunt was just finishing up two weeks' vacation during which he had remodeled a house he had bought at Ukarumpa. He and Glennis had spent a full, meaningful time together. In Glennis' words, "It was beautiful in every way. We were in perfect, happy harmony, spiritually, physically, and as a family."

Friday was Doug's last day off from work, and though he had made his house livable and moved his family in, there were still a few things to do. But Doug felt that Stu Nelson, who had been piloting the Aztec for two weeks, needed a break. As chief pilot, Doug preferred to do essential weekend flying himself rather than assign it to others. Since he was scheduled for Saturday and Sunday flights, he decided to go ahead and fly Friday as well. Thus, even though he still had one day left on his vacation, he bumped Stu and chose to make the flight himself.

On Wednesday the Aztec had been pulled into the hangar for a routine 100-hour inspection, which included minor engine repair. Friday morning, the plane was checked out and ready to go. During the engine run-up, there seemed to be a slight amount of vapor coming from under the right engine cowl. This is not uncommon on a freshly washed-down engine, however, because of the solvent lying in the exhaust system joints. Nevertheless, the two mechanics who had worked on the engine commented on it, so when the engine was shut down, they both made a close inspection for fuel or oil leaks. JAARS had twenty-five years of flying experience in eight countries without ever having had a fatal crash. It was an enviable record, unmatched by any flying outfit in the world. The mechanics knew the responsibility that rested on them. All perfectionists, they took every precaution. They found nothing amiss, and nodded to Doug that the plane was ready to go.

Only the day before, the JAARS administration had decided to sell the Aztec and buy a much-needed larger twin—a Cessna 402. But until the new plane arrived, the Aztec would stay in service. And on this bright, sunny morning, five days after Easter, Doug Hunt would be at the controls.

Glennis stood in the yard of her new home and watched the Aztec take off for Port Moresby. It had been such a happy two weeks she and Doug had spent together that she was even pleased he was taking this unscheduled flight—which isn't always the way of a pilot's wife. But she knew how much he loved flying, and how dedicated he was to the mission to which God had called him. Following the plane with her eyes as it climbed into the clear, sunny sky and disappeared over the mountains, she thought, "If Doug should go, this would be a grand day for it . . . a day when we are so much together in every aspect of our lives."

In Port Moresby, Doug had a hard time getting the right engine started. When it finally coughed into life, it ran rough and belched black smoke from the exhaust. For a long time, Doug sat at the controls, adjusting the throttle and mixture control until it finally smoothed up. He knew the Aztec engines were difficult to adjust to proper mixture, and the rich black smoke was nothing new or unusual. Doug gave the concerned mechanic who was standing by a thumbs-up sign, flashed a grin, and taxied out to take off on the second leg of his flight, this time back across the island to Lae. He had expected to pick up four passengers in Port Moresby for the flight to Lae and on to Ukarumpa. For some reason, they had not shown up at the airport, so he loaded the plane with cargo instead. He knew there were six people waiting at Lae who expected to find transportation on another JAARS plane. Now, however, he would have room to take them all. He radioed ahead, giving his ETA so the waiting passengers could be ready for the short ride from Lae to Aiyura.

Waiting at the airport was Dr. Darlene Bee, who had flown in from New Zealand. She had tried, several times, to get an earlier commercial booking into Lae. Had she been successful, she could have been aboard the Cessna 206 which left earlier. When she heard the Aztec was on the way from Port Moresby, she turned down an offer to ride overland in a car to Ukarumpa. Now she found herself in the little SIL building near the terminal, waiting for the arrival of Doug Hunt in the Aztec.

Standing with her were Oren and Francine Claassen. Oren, a young anthropologist, had come to New Guinea fom Kansas where he met Francine Dirk, a vivacious, fun-loving girl from Philadelphia. They had been married at Ukarumpa in 1966 and moved to live with the Rawa people of the Madang District. After waiting five years for a baby, Francine had given birth to a child only weeks before. But it was stillborn. Francine and Oren had made a quick trip to Lae for her final check with the doctor. They were now waiting to catch the Aztec to return to Ukarumpa—and to pick up their lives among the people they had learned to love, the Rawas.

Outside on the concrete apron, watching the Aztec land, were Nore and Beb, two New Guinea men working with the SIL program, helping the translators. Nore and Beb would also be passengers on the Aztec.

The final seat would be occupied by Kathleen McNeil, buyer for the SIL members in Lae. When supplies were needed at Ukarumpa, a radio message would be sent to Kath in Lae. Perhaps it would be a spool of blue thread, or a carton of soybean milk for a finicky baby, or maybe a box of tenpenny nails for someone who was building an addition on his house. Whatever it was, Kath could be counted on to pick it out and send it up to Ukarumpa on the plane.

Kath had left a dress-shop management in Auckland, New Zealand, in 1967 to come as a short-term associate in New Guinea. Despite her nearly sixty-one years, she was full of vitality and zest for life. The year before, she had volunteered to go with Penny Kooyers to the Washkuk tribe in the Sepik River area to teach the women how to sew. Now Kath had finished her work in Lae, having trained a replacement, and was returning to Ukarumpa to seek the Lord's next purpose for her life. Like Bee, she too had turned down the offer to ride overland to the base.

As the Aztec circled out over the Huon Gulf preparing to land, Kath turned to Penny who had come to see her off.

"My work is finished in Lae now. We'll just wait and see what the Lord has ahead for me. . . . You know, Penny, I might never see you again. I might go just as quickly as Ed Wagner did."

Penny smiled at her old friend. She had no premonition that those words were prophetic.

It had been a long day for Doug, and he was eager to get home. Glennis and the children had never seemed more precious to him.

Lynda, of course, was at the university in New Zealand, while Garry was an apprentice mechanic in New Guinea. Then there was his "second" family—Jannette, who was in primary school, and little Dale, not quite big enough to go to school yet. Glennis would have a good supper waiting for him, and then they would all go, as a family, to the service to hear Graham Pulkingham.

After unloading the heavy cargo he had brought up from Port Moresby, Doug folded the back seats into position and made sure everyone was buckled in tight. Once again he made his customary walk-around inspection of the plane, then climbed aboard and started the engines. They caught perfectly, and he carefully checked the instruments to make sure the oil pressure, oil temperature, manifold pressure, and engine RPMs were normal. Everything checked out.

"Lae tower, this is Sierra India Lima. Ready for takeoff."

"Roger, Sierra India Lima. Cleared for takeoff runway three two."

Doug pushed the throttle handles forward, and the heavily loaded plane roared down the runway. The wind was calm. Visibility was twenty-five miles. Behind him was the sea. Before him, the setting sun.

"Lae tower, Sierra India Lima. Reporting takeoff at seventeen twenty seven (5:27 P.M.)."

"Roger, Sierra India Lima. Reported traffic is one of your chaps. Cessna Sierra India Bravo is inbound from Aiyura at three thousand. You should spot him near Nadzab. Over and out."

Doug knew his good friend, Paul Carlson, would be flying the Cessna carrying several passengers on their way into town. He'd pick up the cargo Doug had left behind and return to Aiyura before dark.

Doug kept full power on the heavy plane as he climbed up to his assigned altitude of sixty-five hundred feet. He looked over at Francine in the seat beside him and smiled. She was one of his favorite people, always laughing and calling everyone "George."

Doug set his trim tabs for level flight, leaned out the mixture control, reduced power on the engines, and set the props for cruise. To his left and falling behind was Nadzab, the old abandoned World War II base with its seven thousand-foot runway. Somewhere below him to the left was Paul Carlson in the Cessna. He was difficult to spot because of the glare of the setting sun.

Suddenly he saw a brilliant flash out the right window. Francine saw it at the same time.

"Doug! We're on fire!"

After flying more than a thousand hours in the Aztec preparing for such an emergency, Doug reacted almost automatically, instantaneously. He cut the power, pulling the throttles all the way back. His hand flew to the mixture control, next to the fuel selector and cross feed. Now feather the prop. Full flaps. Gear down. Anything to increase drag. He had to get the plane on the ground which was six thousand feet below him. Nose over in a radical attitude. Heavy right rudder. Trying to reduce pressure on the starboard wing. He was turning back toward the abandoned military airfield. His voice was calm and steady as he reached for the mike.

"Lae tower, Sierra India Lima. This is mayday, mayday, mayday. I have a fire in my starboard engine and am now feathering the engine. Stand by." Lae tower recorded the call at 5:34 P.M.— exactly seven minutes after takeoff.

Paul Carlson heard Doug's "mayday" call. He and his three passengers strained their eyes to see if they could spot the Aztec, which they knew was somewhere behind them and to the left. They all saw him at the same time, orange and white flames streaming from the starboard engine, with a long trail of inky black smoke which followed the plane as it spiraled downward.

Inside the cockpit, there was no panic. Everyone, including the two New Guinea men in the back seats, had faced death many times before. It was simply a matter of waiting to see if they could make it to the ground before the engine exploded. The gasoline to the engine was shut off, but the turbo oil in a tank in the back was now feeding the flames. Doug's only hope was to get the plane on the ground before the fire reached the gas tanks—or the wing burned off.

Holding the plane in a tight, descending spiral, Doug pressed the button on his mike again.

"Sierra India Lima. Mayday. I am landing at Nadzab. The right engine is completely on fire. A lot of flame—out the back—could Sierra India Bravo return to Nadzab immediately please?" A minute and twenty-one seconds had elapsed since he made his first mayday call.

The Aztec had completed a 360° turn and was lining up to try to land at the airstrip. They had lost an incredible six thousand feet in two minutes. Doug leveled off about one hundred feet above the flat, grassy terrain. If they didn't have time to make a final turn onto the blacktop, he'd just have to try to force it on the ground in the bush.

Suddenly there was a brilliant flash of fire, and the right wing bent upward. The spar, melted and twisted like warm cheese, gave way, and the right wing and engine broke loose from the plane. The plane rolled violently to the right, jerking the wheel out of Doug's hands. For an instant, the seven in the plane saw the beautiful red and gold New Guinea sunset flash through their windows as the plane turned upside down.

The next instant, they were looking into the face of Jesus.

The Aztec—and its occupants—had flown into the glory.

Glennis Hunt was right. It was a grand day for Doug to go to meet his Father.

Ken Wiggers was waiting by the radio in the hangar, expecting Doug's call giving him his estimated time of arrival at Aiyura. Instead, he heard Paul Carlson's broken voice come through the speaker, telling him what had just happened.

"It doesn't look good," Paul said. "I'm landing at Nadzab and will report back as soon as possible."

Paul Carlson, his eyes brimming with tears, circled the wreckage. The area was strewn with bits of twisted metal. Little fires were smoldering here and there where the burning fuel had sprayed the grass. Everything was quiet.

As he touched down, Paul saw that another eyewitness plane, a Cessna on a charter flight, had already landed. He taxied as close to the accident as possible. Then he and the others in the plane jumped out and began running through the high grass and bushes toward the crash site, about a mile away.

Pieces of wreckage were scattered for about five hundred yards along the swath cut from tall grass and saplings. The rest of the fuselage was lying upside down with the remaining wing torn off. The area was scattered with debris—bundles of clothing and personal belongings of the passengers. Seven badly broken bodies were lying amidst the wreckage. All had perished instantly.

Fifteen minutes later, officials from the Department of Civil Aviation (DCA) were on the spot, putting out the scattered fires. The sun had already sunk below the crest of the New Guinea mountains, and the saddened officials worked under the glare of floodlights for about six hours, removing the bodies from the wreckage. Posting a guard at the site, they made plans to return early the next morning to try to determine the cause of the crash.

Before leaving for the night, one of the officials walked back over to the twisted hulk of what had once been the Aztec. Looking dejectedly at the broken fuselage, he remarked, "There lies one of the best maintained planes in the territory." It was the finest compliment that could be paid to the professional ability of the JAARS pilots and mechanics.

Back at Ukarumpa, Ken had received the report from DCA that there were no survivors. He dropped his head in prayer. Glennis would have to be told first, then he would have to make an announcement at the service which was just getting started in the auditorium. It was the hardest thing he had ever been called on to do.

While Pat Wiggers and some of the others ministered to Glennis and the children, Ken walked toward the auditorium. Inside, he could hear the sounds of joyful singing, and his long legs just did not want to climb those last few steps up to the building. But as the news of Jesus' death eventually became the "good news" of the world, so Ken believed that, somehow, even this news would be used for the glory of God.

Over and over, a verse of Scripture kept running through his mind, a verse he had learned as a small boy in Sunday school. "And we know that all things work together for good to them that love God, to them who are the called according to his purpose" (Rom. 8:28).

That's who they were, Ken thought. *The Called.* Not only Doug, Bee, Kath, Oren, Francine, Nore and Beb—but all who are following the will of God are The Called.

Pushing open the door, Ken made his way across the side of the auditorium and whispered to someone on the platform. Moments later, he was before the microphone. The packed room sat in awesome silence as he choked out his report.

As Ken finished, Graham stepped forward, reaching out in pastoral love and understanding to gather the sheep at Ukarumpa around the Chief Shepherd. It was a moment of tender love, divine sensitivity. "For thy sake we are killed all the day long." It was the words of Romans 8. "We are accounted as sheep for the slaughter. However, in all these things we are more than conquerors through him that loves us . . . "

There was peace at Ukarumpa that night. Comfort. The Holy Spirit was there. Grief? Yes, but there was an overriding impression, almost an aura, that this was not a mistake. It was not a tragedy. Somehow, someway, this was part of God's great purpose.

Following the prayer at the auditorium, Ken left the building. The meeting would continue, but he had things to do. The first was to go by and see Glennis. But as he turned down the path toward the Hunts' new home, a figure burst out of the shadows.

It was one of the mechanics, the one who had been responsible for the 100-hour check on the Aztec. He grabbed Ken by the shirt and hung on, weeping. "I was sitting there in that meeting, wracking my brain trying to remember. Now I know. It was my fault. The whole thing was my fault."

Ken let him weep it out, then listened to him talk.

"Yesterday afternoon," the highly skilled young mechanic said, "Jim Entz had assigned me and Paul Carlson to work on the starboard engine while you and Jim worked on the left one. We were putting the engine back together, and Paul was having some problems reinstalling the magnetos. I was down underneath the engine and had just finished hooking up the fuel line when Paul asked if I could give him a hand with the mags. I tightened the B-nut on the fuel line with my fingers and came out from under the engine to help Paul. I intended to give the nut one extra twist with the wrench when I came back, but since the fuel line was hooked up, and not hanging loose, I don't think I checked the nut."

He paused, took a deep gulp of air and continued. "I was a litttle late getting to the hangar this morning. Jim had looked at my sheet, saw everything was signed off, and asked Stu Nelson to put the cowls back on. I was startled, for a moment, for I have made a practice of making a final inspection of everything I do. But with the cowls in place, this was impossible, so I passed it off as okay. I forgot all about that nut until tonight." He collapsed against Ken's chest in tears.

By this time, Ken had gotten the picture. The lack of a final twist of the wrench on the fuel line meant a fine spray of gasoline could have escaped. The mist would have gone unnoticed in the final check-out, but after several hours of flying, it could have built up a condensation around the hot engine and then . . . WHOOSH! Fire!

A subsequent inspection of the engine by the DCA proved the mechanic's theory was correct. When they disassembled the engine, they found the nut on the fuel line was only finger-tight, one-third of a turn loose from where it should have been torqued up. The lack of one-third of a turn with a wrench on a tiny nut had cost the lives of seven people.

Ken reached out and put his arm around the shaking shoulders of the mechanic. "It takes a big man to face up to a thing like this," he said, his own voice choking. "You could have kept your mouth shut, and no one would have ever known the difference. But through your honesty, I am able to see Jesus even more clearly."

Ken was not the only one able to see Christ through the mechanic's honesty. A full report was filed with the DCA, and several weeks later, after a top-level investigation, a letter, signed by the regional director of the Department of Civil Aviation, was received. Addressed to the mechanic, it said in part:

> I have carefully examined all the circumstances relating to this incident and have noted your excellent previous record as a licensed aircraft maintenance engineer and the regard in which you are held by your employers and fellow members of the aviation industry. I have also noted the commendable way in which you voluntarily brought the matter of the line to our attention and the frankness of your statement to investigating officers of this department.
>
> As a result, I am satisfied that your failure to fully tighten the fuel line was not due to any gross negligence or lack of technical competence on your part but rather, your attention was distracted at a critical moment, when you briefly left the job to give guidance to another aircraft maintenance engineer.
>
> I am sure that the feeling of doubt and remorse that you have suffered will have impressed on you, more than anything else could, the dangers of letting your attention be diverted, even momentarily, from the job in hand. I do not, therefore propose to take any action against your aircraft maintenance license.

The following week, the mechanic called on Glennis Hunt and

made his confession before the entire family. He wanted the children to know, in particular, that their father was in no way to blame for what had happened.

It was soul-shattering for a perfectionist like this skilled mechanic to acknowledge he had made a fatal error, but somehow love and forgiveness reached out to him through Glennis and the others. And the man who could have become the eighth fatality of the crash of the Aztec was salvaged from a life of guilt-ridden despair to continue as a top-rate mechanic with JAARS. When the new Cessna twin, the replacement for the Aztec, landed at Lae after being ferried across the Pacific Ocean by Bernie May and Ken Wiggers, the same mechanic was asked by his associates to lead the prayer of dedication.

Graham Pulkingham's theme, "The Power of Love through Christian Community," was never more appropriate. The apostle Peter was right. "Love covers a multitude of sins" (I Pet. 4:8 RSV).

Of all the things that were written during those days, the words that Glennis Hunt wrote on a little card she sent her friends said it best.

> Dear Lord,
> thanks for a daddy,
> thanks for a husband,
> thank You for a friend.
>> thank You for his strength,
>> his tenderness,
>> his time, his vitality,
>> his compassion,
>> his discipline . . .
> his love for You
> his love for us.
>> No ifs, no buts, no whys
>> just thank You, Lord.
>>> Glennis, Linda and Garry
>>> Janette and Dale

Chapter 19

And a Time to Live

One of the last entries in Darlene Bee's notebook, a book of devotional thoughts, was "Longing for His presence."

This was the desire of all those who packed the auditorium at Ukarumpa on Sunday morning after Easter. Father Pulkingham called it a "graduation service." And so it was.

A group of Usarufa men came from their village to mourn the loss of their translator, Darlene Bee. The congregation sang Doug Hunt's favorite hymn, "If Jesus Goes with Me I'll Go . . . Anywhere." Des Oatridge, who had helped settle Ukarumpa back in 1956, led in prayer, thanking God for particular things in the lives of each of the seven who had died. Director Skip Firchow read from Job, Doug's favorite book of the Bible. "I know that my redeemer liveth, and that he shall stand at the latter day upon the earth: And though worms . . . destroy this body, yet in my flesh shall I see God." (Job 19:26) . Dennis and Nancy Cochrane, translators, sang the song that had been sung at Oren and Francine's wedding, "The King of Love My Shepherd Is." Then the man whom God had obviously selected as His spokesman, Graham Pulkingham, came and ministered words of challenge, striking at the very heart of the Christian's purpose for existing. "God is not glorified because we go off and do something for Him. He is glorified when we give our bodies to be the habitation of His Spirit."

The auditorium was jammed. People were standing around the walls. Pilots, mechanics, radio technicians, linguists, young people —all were hanging on every word.

"The world will tolerate you coming out here to do something they don't understand," Father Pulkingham said gently. "As long as you can produce something that is useful to the rest of mankind, the world will put up with your bizarre behavior. But if you told the world you had come out here simply to be the living demonstration of Jesus Christ together, the world would turn upon you and rend you—for in their eyes that is a foolish thing to do."

He closed his message talking about that one extra quality which set apart as special people the seven who died. It was not their technical ability, nor even their dedication unto death. It was love. Then he challenged the missionaries to emulate that quality.

"If I see a hungry person and offer him a seed, it does not give him much nourishment. But if I give him an apple, he has not only the seed, but the apple to eat. So as you carry the seed of the Spirit into the world, make sure you have it encased in the fruit of the Spirit—which is love. Then men will find nourishment as well as life."

Very early the next morning, all the cars on the base, twenty-five of them, began the rugged, four-hour trip down the mountains to Lae for the mass funeral service. The planes made shuttles back and forth, carrying those who could not squeeze into the cars. Hundreds came from Lae and the outlying communities to attend the 2:00 P.M. service at the United Church. The pastor spoke briefly and then Beverly Entz, Jim's wife, sang meaningfully, "Each Step I Take."

Thirty-six pallbearers, including five Usarufas, carried the caskets to the waiting police trucks. The entire Wycliffe family was deeply moved as the trucks rolled by one after another . . . after another . . . after another . . .

At the Malahang Plantation Cemetery, the caskets were tenderly placed beside the mounds of freshly dug dirt. The Wycliffe family gathered around for the committal service with the joyful thought, "Not here . . . risen!"

As the bodies were lowered into the graves, the group of saddened believers, their hearts torn with pain, turned their faces upward toward the blue sky, spotted with fleecy white clouds, and broke into spontaneous song:

> When we've been there ten thousand years,
> Bright shining as the sun,
> We've no less days to sing God's praise
> Than when we first begun.

Yet, even with this note of victory, there remained so many unanswered questions in my mind.

I asked these questions of Ken Wiggers as we stood in the hangar at Aiyura. Al and I were preparing to fly back to Port Moresby where we would spend the night before catching a jet to Australia and finally home to the States. Ken leaned against the wing of the sleek Cessna 402-B, the replacement for the Aztec, and chewed his lower lip. He answered slowly, deliberately.

"As technicians, we strive for perfection. We take pride in the fact that JAARS is the finest, one of the most professional flying groups in the entire world. Now you ask how we should react when we find God's sovereignty has overruled our striving for careful workmanship.

"For years, JAARS has lived with the motto: 'We do our best and the Lord does the rest.' From the human standpoint, an error was made which caused people to die. The Lord has laid down natural laws for us to live by. If these laws are broken, we suffer. But deep inside, I also know that in spite of our errors, in spite of our best-laid plans, God's final purposes are always achieved. All I can say is, those who died were *chosen.*"

He handed me a scrap of paper. "Read this when you have a chance," he said. "Perhaps it will give you some insight into what I am talking about."

My plane was ready to go. I slipped the paper into my shirt pocket and crawled into the back seat of the Cessna. Our flight plan called for us to fly directly over Nadzab. As I watched the abandoned airport pass by under my window, I found it hard to keep from crying.

Late that afternoon in Port Moresby, standing at the edge of the Coral Sea, the rugged mountains and dense jungle behind me, I looked out over the water toward Australia. The ocean was leaden, barely reflecting the heavy mottled overcast. Brittle shards of sunlight began to burst through the swollen bellies of clouds, storm-tattered remnants driven west by the monsoon winds. Bands of striated sunlight stalked like brassy shafts, illuminating the olive-tinted water, fracturing it like bits of broken green-glass bottles, then tarnishing it in deep gold.

I reached in my pocket and unfolded the paper Ken had given me. It was a sheet out of Darlene Bee's notebook. Shortly before her death in the Aztec, she had brushed aside her fears and written down her feelings of hope.

A Time to Die

Perhaps the moment after ecstasy;
    after feeling the full, fierce force of life;
    after knowing love, and while love is still warm . . .
Perhaps that is the time for dying;
    before everything and one has turned sour;
    before life is a burden,
    before the thrill of waking to a new day is gone;
    before we long for death . . .

To die while
   bursting with life,
   brimming with vitality,
   longing to live ...
Perhaps this is the time to die—and live.

So they died. And so they live.

Sixteen years before, five men had given their lives in the jungles of Ecuador that their killers might come to know God through Jesus Christ. That was a true sacrifice—the innocent dying for the guilty.

It was the testimony of the widow of one of these men, Marj Saint, that inspired Doug Hunt to lay down his nets and follow the Master as a jungle pilot—loving not his life unto death. That, too, was true sacrifice. Presenting his body totally to the Lord.

Halfway around the world from Ecuador, I had just flown over the soil of another land stained by the blood of those whom God had chosen. Once again, the call went forth across the land: "Whom shall I send, and who will go for us?"

In the stillness of the jungle evening, with only the sound of the sea lapping against the foreign shore, I waited to hear who would answer, "Here am I; send me!"

Oh God, and shall my heart be cold when men go out to die for Thee?

Those interested in the ministry of the Jungle Aviation and Radio Service or the Wycliffe Bible Translators should write:

JAARS
Box 248
Waxhaw, NC 28173
     or
Wycliffe Bible Translators
Huntington Beach, CA 92648

Appendix: Ferry Flight

Just before Jim Price died, in late 1973, he gave me a copy of his day-by-day diary of his first ferry flight to Peru. It was made in an Aeronca sedan with Ollie Bryant. I share it here, almost as he wrote it, back in 1949.

March 26:
We took off at 7:25 from El Monte, California, in the usual smog overcast and headed for Indio. We went low through Beaumont Pass but still found the air rough. The little Aeronca was a sturdy plane, however, and behaved itself in a commendable manner. Lunch and gas at Indio and off again. After more rough air and dead-reckoning navigation, we stopped for gas at Tucson at 5:15 and by 7:45 we were in El Paso for the night. We found the service here excellent even though everything was full of sand from a recent windstorm.

March 27:

At 8:25 we started our long haul over dry, desolate Texas. We stopped at Del Rio for fuel and lunch at a small field at the edge of town where the approach was over the local cemetery. After setting our time back, we headed for Brownsville. This part of the trip down the Rio Grande valley was more interesting, and we were on the ground at 4:35. As it was Sunday, we did not attempt to clear customs. So after a good night's rest and a shower, we were all set to clear Monday morning, only to find a number of discrepancies in our papers requiring phone calls and wires to L.A. and Washington, D.C. It seems we were flying Aeronca 15AC 296 and our export license read we were exporting 15AC269—which we could not produce. We put our troubles in the hands of an export broker and went back into town to spend the day and try again on March 29.

An early phone call to our broker on Tuesday informed us that we may just as well relax as the papers had not arrived from L.A. So we sat it out another day waiting for clear skies and clear papers.

March 30:

The papers that did come through did not give our broker power to act for us. So we waited again. Meanwhile a Stinson from Missionary Aviation Fellowship (MAF) came in with Grady Parrot and Don Kennedy. We spent some time comparing notes until our broker finally decided to take a chance. He got our papers through, even though they were not just right, and we were set to go.

March 31:

After a humid, restless night, we arose to a good overcast and took off a day after the MAF Stinson and headed down the coast to Tampico. We spent most of the air time flying along the beach at altitudes ranging from three hundred to a hundred feet, due to poor visibility and overcast. After two hours and forty minutes, we landed at a small field at the edge of town. The surface was bumpy, and we waited two hours for gas service.

There was an old Stinson trimotor and a Spartan biplane on the field as well as the remains of an Aeronca Sedan which had come in low and picked up some wires and a house. We were off at 2:30 for Veracruz and followed the coast again, as the area is either wooded or hilly or both, and further south, the hills come down to the sea. The beach is not always open for emergency use, but much oftener than the back country. The landing strips shown on the charts were often not to be seen and either were overgrown or never were existent.

We went around once at Veracruz waiting for a Christian and Missionary Alliance DC-3 to take off, and then set down on five thousand feet of fine-surfaced runway. With a taxi to town, we stayed at the Hotel Victoria which was on the *embarcadero* (waterfront). We had a suite of rooms for $5.00 (U.S.). The meals of red snapper and steak for $1.60 were good as well as reasonable. We spent the evening sitting in the plaza listening to the civic band and marimbas play as the traditional youthful promenaders strolled around and smiled and appraised each other. At the early hour of ten o'clock, we hit the sack so as to be out by seven o'clock mañana.

April 1:

Seven o'clock and time for breakfast after a shower and packing. We took on a hundred liters of eighty-octane gas, checked the weather, and leaped off. About an hour out on course, the visibility got poor, and as our route led over some mountains, we altered course when we came to the railroad and flew the iron beam on across the Tehuantepec peninsula.

We averaged only sixty mph ground speed because of the headwind which was making the palms below all one-sided. The terrain was rugged hills and much jungle cover until the divide was crossed; then the area became dry brush country.

The old Aeronca did not want to land at Ixtepec because of the stiff headwind. But with ten thousand feet of surfaced runway, we had all day to coax her down. After efficient and rapid service, we were back in the air with only thirty-five minutes on the ground.

We headed down the coast for Tapachula, a city we were told to avoid if possible. We found it to be an interesting and well-to-do town with the Gran Hotel International as fine as any on the trip. We spent the evening with the new Pan Am mechanic who had been in town only two days and spoke less Spanish than we. As at Veracruz, the evening promenade was in full swing until a drizzle at 9:30 dampened their spirits and headed a good number into the local bars to drink and play dominoes. We hit the sack, hoping for a day with smoother air tomorrow.

April 2:

Off the ground in a drizzle of rain by 10:05, and we had rain of varying intensity the full length of Guatemala and on to El Salvador where the ceiling lifted and we made San Salvador in the sun. This part of the trip was over much jungle at first but became dry brush country in El Salvador. From San Salvador on south, the country was dry and mountainous with many volcanic peaks to serve as navigation checkpoints. The lake at San Salvador was clear and blue, but that at Managua, our next stop, looked very muddy. The trip up the valley from Corinto to Managua was over some good-looking farmland although somewhat dry. Again it was the Gran Hotel, and as at most of the tropical hotels, the dining room opened onto the patio, though this time the patio contained a fine swimming pool which we made use of before saying "Buenos noches."

April 3:

Sunday, and we roused out the officials at 6:30 even though we had to pay double fees for clearance. Upon running up the engine, we found the right mag was very rough and missing. We replaced the plugs, and it seemed to clear up the trouble. We took off for David, Panama, a long hop but necessary as we had no permit to land in Costa Rica and they had just started another round of threats and gun play over some political argument. It would be over in a day or two, but we did not care to wait. We passed many volcanic peaks between Managua and Puntarenas, taking some pictures into the cone of one strong with sulfur fumes.

From the long sandy point of Puntarenas south, we flew over miles of banana plantations and along the coast as the visibility was poor from the smoke in the air. This is caused by the practice of burning off the grassland to kill the insects and supposedly to improve the grass. When we did turn inland, we hit rain squalls and mountains. After four hours and ten minutes, we set down at David with three gallons of gas still in our tanks. Praise the Lord we didn't run into headwinds, or we'd be out there yet.

We received good service and had our cameras sealed and then cleared for the Canal Zone control area. The flight to Albrook Field was routine except for the very poor visibility due to smoke. We followed the coast to the point, then headed out into the bay and picked up Tobago Island, and then headed for the field. After clearing on the Army side, we parked on the PAA side and cleared customs.

We had some problems since few light planes land here and procedure was not familiar. In fact, the fees of six dollars per calendar day made it twelve dollars for overnight, and the three dollars military landing permit made it sort of high. While our pilot, or ship's master, as Ollie was listed, secured our room at the Hotel Tivoli, I, copilot, mechanic, etc., checked the mags with the aid of a Braniff Airways mechanic. We found very little if any clearance on the points in the right mag and consequently they were much pitted and burned. We filed and gapped both sets of points, and things sounded better. After wandering around Panama City, we shooed the cockroaches into the dark corners and hit the sack.

April 4:

By 7:00 we were eating breakfast in the PAA crew lunchroom and then, after making the rounds of weather, fees, flight plan, and briefing, were off by 9:30. We headed across the peninsula where we followed the Caribbean coast to Turbo, Colombia, our first stop in South America and one not soon forgotten.

After gas and a chat with a German rancher and a Swedish businessman from Medellin, we took off into what was supposed to be broken overcast. After twenty-five minutes of flying at eight thousand feet, we got into instrument stuff. With mountains on ahead and all around up to thirteen thousand, we did a 180 and headed back on our reciprocal. We picked up the coastline of the Gulf of Darién and then once again Turbo. We resigned ourselves to staying, and so in the evening accepted an invitation from some of the local boys to go fishing. They told us to bring a flashlight and a machete. Strange fishing gear, to say the least. But during the evening, the fellows hit four catfish and two sawfish with their machetes and gave us the sawbills. We decided we no longer cared to swim in the Gulf of Darién. If the sawbills didn't get you, the fishermen might. We slept good and were awakened in the night by rains such as are found only in the tropics.

April 5:

After seeing the leaden sky and getting weather from Medellin we got ready for the day at Turbo. However, after breakfast, the overcast had holes showing blue sky and a reported ceiling unlimited at Medellin. So we bade so long to our fishermen friends and once again tackled this north-western branch of the Andes mountains in the land of the great liberator, Simon Bolivar. Did I say tackle? That's all, brother. We took off and went out over the gulf and climbed eight thousand feet. Then took our heading in a steady climb. We were over two layers of overcast with occasional holes which coincided enough to give our checks down. At the correct time-distance out, we had a large hole and took our check and our new heading but were only at ten thousand feet and not near the tops of the buildups on the mountains ahead. At eleven thousand, the plane lost all desire to go higher. We were above the tops of the mountains in the pass, but it would mean instrument flying to get through. We headed in, taking advantage of every slot in the huge cumulus clouds. Then the slot closed and we were on instruments. It was frightening, knowing that on each side of us towered the mighty Andes and with the pass not accurately charted, there was always the danger of a peak sticking up in front of us also.

We bore on for three minutes on compass, altimeter, and ball and bank as our only instruments. Then the altimeter started to unwind. At eleven thousand feet we made a 180 (we hoped) and headed out of the pass on the reciprocal of our course in. After eight minutes of hairy flying, we broke out over an overcast with high, mean-looking cumulus build-ups all around. Feeling much older and much wiser, we held our course, having lost our second round with old man weather in the Andes.

After twenty minutes, we recognized some lakes on the

Atrato River—at least we hoped they were lakes on the Atrato. We were west of our incoming leg, so from the lakes we plotted a new heading for Turbo. Shortly, we sighted the village of Rio Sucio, and the overcast closed in again, so we decided to let down, as we were over jungle according to charts. We let down to forty-five hundred feet, still on instruments, only to break out of one layer to find ourselves still sandwiched between clouds. We let down another three thousand feet more and came out over the jungle in a driving rain. Still holding our heading, we ploughed along, looking for the shoreline of the Gulf of Darién.

Our time showed we should see the shore soon. Ah, a light line ahead, but it turned out to be only the sun breaking through onto the steaming jungle. Then off to our left, a definite shoreline appeared. How could it be over there? That meant mountains to the right, and we could see none through the rain. The shore turned out to be a lake which gave us a check, and we soon sighted the shore of the gulf and headed across to the point and hit the strip at Turbo three hours and fifteen minutes after leaving—weary but much wiser.

The rain let up, so we took a couple of magazines and went to the beach to relax, but not to swim. After supper, we went fishing again, and the boys brought in a fifteen-pound catfish —flashlights and machete style, that is.

April 6:
This morning the visibility was unlimited, but there was an unbroken overcast at two thousand feet. We planned for another day at Turbo, even though the funds were getting low, and we were far from our journey's end. I investigated a cage and found it held a young capybara, an interesting large rodent which reaches eighty pounds and is good eating. I went down to the south end of the point, and Ollie arrived shortly with some crabs for bait to do a little fishing U.S. style.

Then overhead, an old Navy SNJ broke through the overcast, made a pass at the strip, and let down his gear. No more fishing. We hotfooted it to the plane to meet Captain Richard W. Mallon of the U.S. Air Force flying for the Inter-American Survey. We had a coke, pumped him for information, and then borrowed his chart of the area to the north which went around this branch of the Andes.

An L-5 came in with two more U.S. personnel, and we chatted and fueled up. The L-5 offered to lead the way as far as Montereia. We had just piled in and were ready to take off when the MAF Stinson with Don and Grady touched down at the strip. A regular American day at Turbo. We exchanged a few words, and then feeling guilty for leaving them behind, took off following the L-5 for Montereia.

The L-5 tore on ahead and was soon out of sight. Then the weather thickened, and I mean, *thickened*. Rain, rain, RAIN!! Lightning, more rain, thunder, rain! We bore on, first with ground contact, then instruments, then we broke out of the overcast to see more dark areas ahead. At first we tried to go around them, but it put us too far off course, and there was no sign of the L-5. After too long, we found the river and Montereia where we took our new heading. The L-5 had disappeared.

After some more thundershowers and instrument time, we picked up our checkpoint on the lower Cauca River after going by it on the left then turning back to investigate. We headed for Amalfi Field on the Porco River but never found it. The river canyons all looked the same in size and ruggedness. It was getting late, and we admitted to each other that we were lost with the maze of river canyons below. We picked the largest and headed down. We did not have sufficient gas nor time to go to the coast to the north and then around to Turbo, but hoped for flat land in the low country. After we had done some sweating and praying and waiting, an airstrip showed up right down there along with a town and some river dredges. We had made Pato, an American-Canadian gold mining camp.

We sat down and were taken to the "hill," given a house, shown to the mess hall, and introduced around the club. We latched on to three fellows from California, one of whom turned out to be an old college buddy of mine. Small world. After a good meal, we shot some pool, some breeze, and then hit the sack.

April 7:

We waited until 11:30 for some gas which never came, and as the overcast had reached its clearest, we took off for Medellin with about fifteen gallons of fuel on deck. With a good tail wind, we made the hop in one hour and fifteen minutes, which was just about all the gas we had left. We found Captain Mallon and his SNJ waiting for us. We all went to town and, after borrowing coats, had lunch. (It seems you must wear a coat to meals even though you do not have a pair of shoes or a shirt.)

Back in Captain Mallon's room in the hotel, we began searching for the source of a high squeak. We determined it was not coming from a small parrot who was perched on an overhead lamp. Finally, in the springs of a chair, we discovered a monkey — a small fellow about the size of a squirrel.

Back at the airport, we found the MAF Stinson in from Turbo via Pato. After fueling, we all headed up the valley for Cali. We rendezvoused at the Cali airport and agreed we had just flown over the most beautiful valley we had yet seen to one of the most beautiful cities in South America. With a river through the center of town which was planted like a park, with paved streets which were well-lighted at night, one would think he was back in the U.S.A. We spent a comfortable night, thanking God that the water supply was the purest in all South America.

April 8:

The next morning was overcast, so we strolled around town and took some pictures. About noon, we went to the field and took off — the Stinson for Dos Rios, and we for Tumaco. After leaving the ground, we saw a storm coming up the valley. The pass was no go. It was closed, so we headed back for Cali, knowing the Stinson was doing the same. The rain beat us. I've never flown in rougher air. The rain was displacing the air and causing a very turbulent wind front. We made three passes at the field before we could see the runway far enough away to get lined up with it. Then, just as the stall-warning indicator sounded, we were picked up like a leaf and set down two hundred feet to the left, in grass taller than the tops of the wings. We rolled a short distance in this dense forest of grass and stopped. We could see nothing. Grass was higher than the plane, and the wind was howling and rain pouring down. We sat out the worst of the storm and then took a compass heading and prop-mowed our way out onto the runway. Bad weather. *Tiempo muy malo!*

April 9:

The next day was overcast again, so we mailed letters, and Don, who had also returned in the MAF Stinson, went with me to the local market for a pina and some bananas. About 2:00 P.M. we got off again, both planes headed for Dos Rios this time. The weather was good, with visibility unlimited, but a high overcast at five thousand feet. Our oil pressure began to drop, so we sat down at Popayán but could find nothing wrong, so took off again in the rain for Dos Rios. There we talked the operator out of fifteen gallons of gas, and after taking a few photos, bade a last farewell to the

MAF boys and headed up the valley for another try at the Cordillera Occidental.

We held our breath, climbed to nine thousand feet, and came out of the overcast on top. There were no mountain peaks sticking through, so we took a heading of 270° out toward the Pacificona. Through the breaks in the clouds, we could see we were over jungle, which meant we had finally (praise the Lord!) cleared the mountains. We let down through the layers. Spread out before us was the sight of our lives. What a jungle! Nothing but trees — trees and water. Rivers, lakes, and trees. We cruised on, and soon recognized the shore outline and landed on the point at Tumaco. We were rowed across the bay to town in a "canoa" to find a lot of new construction, as half the town had burned a year before. The hotel, as such, was fair, but we argued over the exchange rate the next morning. We had not slept well because of the dogs running the halls and fighting in the kitchen over leftovers.

April 10:

Another dugout trip, and we were on our way to Ecuador. We had some more of the usual bad weather. Rain reduced our visibility so we could see only one direction — down. And then only if we were no higher than three hundred feet. As we were over jungle at times, we dared not go lower because of occasional tall trees. Because of the low altitude, we failed to turn when the coast turned, so went up the bank of a river and finally decided we were headed in the wrong direction. We took a new compass heading and got back to the shoreline which we held to faithfully all the way to Esmeraldas.

No gas! We were told we had to have a letter from Avianca to authorize us to buy gas. They had to radio Quito, then Lima. We waited for two hours; then a fellow just happened to remember he had some eighty octane we could have for fifty cents a gallon. It was obvious bribery, but we bought it just the same, rather than face the hassle. Off in a rainstorm again.

Then at 3:52, five miles below Punta Pedernales flying at two thousand feet on Palm Sunday, I hit the wheel. Ollie jumped and made a grab for it, then gave me a questioning look until I explained we had just hit the equator. Down the coast a ways, we got brave and headed inland for Guayaquil, only to lose all interest when the ceiling dropped to zero about the place the mountains got higher. We went back to the coast and set down at Manta. Service on the spot. Want gas? Now? Okay. Just like the U.S.A.

We took a taxi which came out to the field because we had buzzed the town. These taxis are built on a truck with three wide seats in the front and then a stake bed on behind for cargo. The taxi may be full of passengers, then loaded with livestock, a load of sand, or crates of chickens. The Hotel Europa was neat and clean and right on the beach. We had a wonderful swim in the Pacific and watched the local fishermen launch their loaded dugouts through the surf. Their fishing boats were locally built and were cutter-rigged with a short mast and long boom as they carried no ballast. The dugouts were loaded athwart the gunwales and used to set the nets. Fish were plentiful, but the people were listless, so the supply never met the demand. Rubber, coffee, coconuts, and panama hats were the chief export. We spent the evening chatting with a Czech who had spent nine years in Quito. Finally, we turned in.

April 11:

We left about ten o'clock after the morning overcast had burned off and made good time to Playa, then headed across the Gulf of Guayaquil and on down the coast to Talara, our first stop in Peru. A letter in Talara for gas on credit was a help, as we had spent the last of the funds allotted for the trip in Manta. We took on thirty-three gallons and two five gallon GI cans for the long haul from Chiclayo to Lima as there was no gas at Trujillo. From Talara, which is a dry, hot, oil field, we flew on to Chiclayo over the deserts of northern Peru. Dry, arid, sandy wastes. No towns. No water. No *nada*. At Chiclayo, we received word to remain overnight, as Larry Montgomery was coming in the morning with the Duck. We were cool for the first time since leaving El Paso, Texas. Gasoline had dropped from sixty cents U.S. in Manta to ten cents U.S. Of course, no one was trying to cheat us here.

April 12:

Larry and Don Burns, one of the early Wycliffe translators, arrived about noon, and we went to town for lunch, then visited the Nazarene school at Monsefu which is about a thirty-minutes taxi ride to the south. In the evening, we visited a missionary in Chiclayo who is a radio ham, and we contacted the Canal Zone and Lima.

April 13:

Larry accepted a ride over the Chachapoyas and return on one of Faucett's airliners to see the route and the weather. Stinko! We stayed another night.

April 14:

Planes from the U.S.A., Mexico, Venezuela, and Ecuador were at the field for some sort of air conference. Uncle Cam phoned from Lima, welcoming us to Peru, and after we got the weather, we left Larry behind and took off for the jungle. We'd see Lima some other time.

246

We headed due north to Olmos and then up the river valley into the mountains once more. The clouds were broken cumulus, and we kept under and around them, flying contact with the river as the gorge got deeper and the peaks higher. We had some rough air, and after much twisting and climbing, we sighted the Marañón River, and after buzzing the cattle off the strip, we set down at Bella Vista. The gas shed revealed the remains of an old Sikorsky single-engine biplane amphibian as well as much of our gas missing. We went to the village and got lunch for fifteen cents U.S., and then fueled up and swung our jungle hammocks from the wing hooks and tie-down rings and turned in. The area is malarial, so we used our nets religiously.

Camping on the Marañón. It was hard to believe. At long last, we were on the headwaters of one of the tributaries of the Amazon. On the fringes of the greatest river basin in the world. A beautiful night, full moon through broken clouds. It was good to be there.

April 15:

We took off about ten and followed the Rio Urubamba up the valley from the Marañón to the steep, deep, narrow, and rugged headwater gorges to an airstrip at Chachapoyas and landed at seventy-six hundred feet in the rain. As always, some people came out to meet us, and we went in to town and were shown around the village by one of the local residents. It was a very quaint and typical Andean village, well off the tourist route, although it was served by Faucett Air Lines. As it was Good Friday, we were observers of the annual religious procession around the town plaza. The area bishop led the group, followed by an image of Christ on a casket, then the band and finally the ornate gold-clothed image of Mary. After the procession was over, and the people had dispersed, we headed back to *el campo*. All those doings, and we had left our cameras in the plane. We scrounged around for food for supper and then hung our hammocks under the wings and turned in.

April 16:

We had a cold night and awoke to a cold drizzle overcast. About 11:30 a Faucett C-47 broke through the *tiempo malo* and the captain told us we could make it to Yurimaguas at 12,500 feet — but we would have about twenty minutes of instrument time. No thanks. We had all the instrument flying we wanted in a small plane in the mountains. We decided to sit it out. We hiked into town with some of the local girls, and for once, took our cameras. After lunch we said howdy, or rather its bowing and scraping equivalent, to the prefect, and again toured the town. A visit to a home where two women were working at native looms, and then to the cemetery just as a box was being carried through the gate. We followed and witnessed the routine burial of a local servant girl. She was taken out of the box and laid in the hole and covered with dirt. No friends. No service. *Nada.* She was just a servant girl.

We could find no eggs, but bought some bread, and a truck took us back to the field. The prefect came out to see the plane, and again there was more bowing and scraping. Another evening, but we had the use of the radio room and equipment with which to listen to the Wycliffe Broadcast Network and then to HCJB in Quito.

April 17:

Easter Sunday! Our Lord has risen. Hallelujah! A cold drizzle and heavy overcast kept us on the ground. Even so, Faucett brought their C-47 in after ten minutes of circling looking for a hole in the clouds. They had radioed for us to leave yesterday, but we didn't receive the message. So, we sat out a cold, drizzly Easter Sunday high in the Andes. It was good to know Jesus was alive on a day like that.

April 18:

The sky was overcast but only thinly, so about ten o'clock we took off and headed for the pass and had a swell trip to Yurimaguas. We hit some overcast and some rain but cleared all ridges at 11,500 feet. Suddenly there was the Amazon basin spread out to the east as far as the eye could see. Miles of green, broken by an occasional river with groups of huts or villages dotting a riverbank now and then. It was for those out there, in those huts and villages, those living in darkness, that the plane was delivered. We landed and were met by Harold and Juanita Goodall.

April 19:

We took off as soon as the jungle mist would permit and headed straight for Pucallpa. We had some rain squalls but hit the Ucayali River and set down just two hours and two hundred miles out of Yurimaguas. Our journey had come to an end. We had delivered the Aeronca Sedan 5,300 miles having flown in all kinds of weather and over all types of terrain, landed on all sorts of fields in the U.S. and seven foreign nations, and crossed the Andes three times. In all, the little crate gave a good account of herself. Looking back at some of the scrapes, we can be very thankful we had arrived, and we praised God for His care.